STRATEGIC DILEMMAS
AND THE
EVOLUTION OF GERMAN FOREIGN POLICY SINCE UNIFICATION

STRATEGIC DILEMMAS
AND THE
EVOLUTION OF GERMAN FOREIGN POLICY SINCE UNIFICATION

JEFFREY S. LANTIS

Westport, Connecticut
London

Library of Congress Cataloging-in-Publication Data

Lantis, Jeffrey S., 1966–
   Strategic dilemmas and the evolution of German foreign policy since unification/
   Jeffrey S. Lantis.
      p. cm.
   Includes bibliographical references and index.
   ISBN 0–275–97751–X (alk. paper)
   1. Germany—Foreign relations—1990– 2. International relations. 3. National
   security—Germany. 4. Peacekeeping forces—Germany. 5. Security,
   International. 6. Germany—Military policy. 1. Title.
   DD290.3 .L36 2002
   327.43—dc21   2002022469

British Library Cataloguing in Publication Data is available.

Library of Congress Catalog Card Number: 2002022469
ISBN: 0–275–97751–X

First published in 2002

Praeger Publishers, 88 Post Road West, Westport, CT 06881
An imprint of Greenwood Publishing Group, Inc.
www.praeger.com

Printed in the United States of America

The paper used in this book complies with the
Permanent Paper Standard issued by the National
Information Standards Organization (Z39.48–1984).

10 9 8 7 6 5 4 3 2 1

For Holly

Contents

Figures

Preface and Acknowledgments

The world has witnessed a dramatic evolution in German foreign policy in the decade since unification. This change can be best understood as a function of the combination of both international and domestic circumstances. Germany has been invited, encouraged, and even challenged to redefine its foreign policy posture in response to strategic dilemmas and opportunities around the world in the post-Cold War era. The Persian Gulf War, European Monetary Union, civil strife in the Horn of Africa, genocide in Bosnia, the Kosovo crisis, and the war on terrorism are just some of the challenges that have demanded German responses. At the same time, Germany has undergone domestic political, economic, and social transformations.

This book tells the story of continuity and change in German foreign policy in the decade since unification. Research questions to be examined include: How has German foreign policy evolved in response to moral imperatives for the use of force in the post-Cold War era? Why have the rate and scope of German foreign policy change varied in response to different types of strategic dilemmas? How have domestic political actors, conditions, and historical lessons influenced the development of new foreign policy orientations? What are the theoretical implications of these changes for foreign policy analysis, security studies, and international relations?

This book presents a model of external–internal linkages derived from two important areas of scholarship on the role of international crises as catalysts for foreign policy change, and the importance of domestic political conditions that ultimately determine the scope and pace of such change. The thesis of this study is that German foreign policy restructuring in the 1990s was primarily a function of shifts in elite attitudes, party politics, and public opinion in the domestic environment relative to external, foreign policy challenges. The book presents five original case studies of foreign policy development in the Federal Republic of Germany in response to strategic dilemmas, including the Persian Gulf War, the humanitarian crisis in Somalia, the disintegration of the former Yugoslavia, the war in Bosnia, and the Kosovo crisis. Each case study places German political debates in social and historical context and explores the interplay between external strategic dilemmas and the interpretation of new realities through these debates.

The book draws three primary conclusions. First, cases document ways in which domestic political conditions have significantly affected the scope and pace of German foreign policy responses to crises in the past decade. In some situations, domestic coalitions were difficult to construct, causing a deceleration in the rate of foreign policy change. However, some international crises actually accelerated domestic coalition building and prompted decisive foreign policy behavior. Second, a structured, focused comparison of the case studies provides strong evidence of the importance of elite consensus and party politics in the evolution of German foreign policy. Leaders have played key roles in reinterpretations of historical lessons for contemporary German policy. Third, the book examines the rise of a new consensus on the political left about foreign policy responsibilities and moral imperatives for action in the post-Cold War era. This helps to explain the normalization of German foreign policy in the past decade, the political victory of the Social Democrats and Greens in the 1998 federal elections, and active German involvement in Kosovo and the new war on terrorism.

I am grateful for the support that I have received for this project from colleagues near and far. At The College of Wooster, members of the Department of Political Science and the International Relations Program have offered their encouragement and advice on this project over the past few years, and I benefited from the assistance of several excellent student researchers. I gratefully acknowledge research support provided by the Henry Luce III Fund for Distinguished Scholarship, Faculty Development Grants, and the research sabbatical program at The College of Wooster. I have received professional support for this project from colleagues in the International Studies Association and the Conference Group on German Politics. Juliet Kaarbo, Robin Dorff, Steve Saideman, Brigitte Schulz, Ralph Carter, Randall Newnham, and Arthur Gunlicks have reviewed and commented on this project in various forms over the years. In addition, I received valuable advice from Michael Snarr, Ryan Beasley, David Bearce, and others.

I would also like to express my gratitude to the many scholars and policy makers in the Federal Republic of Germany who took an interest in this project and supported my work. Karl Kaiser, Franz-Josef Meiers, Heike Zanzig, and their colleagues at the Deutsche Gesellschaft für Auswärtige Politik in Bonn generously provided research support. Wolfgang Rüb and Herbert Kossmann offered valuable research assistance and access to the archival collection at the Bundesregierung Presse- und Informationsamt in Bonn. Archivists at the Auswärtiges Amt, Friedrich Ebert Stiftung, and the Konrad Adenauer Stiftung also provided assistance for this project.

Thanks are also due to my editor at the Greenwood Publishing Group, James Sabin, who has provided guidance in the refinement of this manuscript, and to the production staff who saw the project through to conclusion.

Finally, I owe a debt to my wife, Holly, and to my extended family in Germany, for their inspiration during the past fifteen years. They have supported (and endured) my exploration of German and European politics, including a series of research trips and countless hours of archival work and writing.

The final version of the book—and responsibility for its contents—of course remain my own.

1

The Evolution of German Foreign Policy

It is in our interest to preserve peace whereas, without exception, our continental neighbors harbor desires, secret or officially known, which can only be realized through war. We must formulate our policy accordingly; that is to say, we have to prevent or contain war, we must avoid our hand being forced in the European game of cards, and we must not allow ourselves to be pushed by either impatience, favors at the expense of the country, vanity, or friendly provocation from a wait-and-see attitude to one of action too early. . . . We should strive to reduce the irritations which have been aroused by our becoming a real great power by making honest and peace-loving use of our influence to convince the world that a German hegemony in Europe is more helpful, impartial, and innocuous to the freedom of others than either a French, Russian, or British one.

—Otto von Bismarck, 1898[1]

Germans should not be the first to stick their necks out. One will not be overlooked even if one remains a bit more in the background.

—Helmut Kohl, 1992[2]

Dramatic changes in world politics have produced a series of new and difficult foreign policy challenges for countries such as the Federal Republic of Germany. Unified in 1990, Germany emerged as a fully sovereign state with a unique opportunity to develop a distinct, post-Cold War identity that would guide its behavior into the new millennium. This change would not be easy, however, and Germans have been engaged in an intense debate over the scope and pace of foreign policy restructuring ever since.

This book describes the continuity and change in German foreign policy in the decade since unification. Case studies of foreign policy decision making on challenges like the Persian Gulf War, the humanitarian crisis in Somalia, and the Kosovo War explore the interplay between external strategic dilemmas and the interpretation of new realities through domestic political debate. These cases illustrate the rise of a new consensus on the political left for engagement in global affairs, reinterpretations of historical lessons for contemporary German policy, and the constitutional challenges of global activism in the post-Cold War era. This survey of recent developments also enhances our understanding of German responses to new challenges such as the 'war on terrorism.'

A GRAND STRATEGIC OPPORTUNITY

The foundation for contemporary German foreign policy was established during the Cold War, when the Federal Republic (as West Germany) pursued one of the most consistent foreign affairs profiles of any democracy from 1949 to 1990. Along the way, Foreign Minister Hans-Dietrich Genscher developed the distinct *Verantwortungspolitik*, or "foreign policy of responsibility," focusing on the themes of restraint, humanitarianism, and multilateral cooperation. Germany quickly prospered through integration with the European Community (EC), cooperation with the North Atlantic Treaty Organization (NATO), and later, membership in the United Nations (UN).[3] At the same time, restrictions on an assertive German military posture became deeply rooted in the public psyche, in foreign policy tradition, and in the *Grundgesetz*, or Basic Law.[4] Oxford historian Timothy Garton Ash has argued that the Federal Republic "excelled at the patient, discreet pursuit of national goals through multilateral institutions and negotiations" during this period.[5]

The German commitment to restraint and multilateralism paid off in the late 1980s, as Cold War tensions began to fade and new openings emerged between East and West. In November 1989, the East German Communist regime led by Erich Honecker collapsed, and Berliners danced atop the Wall, which had become the most hated symbol of the Cold War. Less than one year later, on October 3, 1990, Chancellor Helmut Kohl, Foreign Minister Hans-Dietrich Genscher, and former Chancellor Willy Brandt stood at the Brandenburg Gate and celebrated the unification of Germany.

Unity and the end of the Cold War represented a grand strategic opportunity for Germans to reflect on their country's past, present, and future. In reality, Germany had achieved many of the objectives of its Cold War foreign policy programs, and the country was in a position it had never before enjoyed. Accordingly, some experts predicted that Germany would soon "normalize" its foreign policy by taking on a more assertive foreign profile that focused on strategic interests, and was backed by the threat of the use of force.[6] Neorealists argued that modern European states like Germany would begin pursuing a natural path towards military dominance.[7] Others cited Germany's economic position as leader of the European Union (EU) and predicted that the government would be more willing to flex its economic muscles inside and outside the EU in the future. Meanwhile, German scholars suggested that post-Cold War behavior should be "commensurate with political and economic weight, as well as the expectations of allies," and that Germany would gradually take on a greater role in world politics.[8]

Government leaders were more cautious in this transition, however, and they assured the world (and their own citizens) that the new Federal Republic of Germany would behave much like the old. Foreign Minister Genscher pledged to maintain the commitment to foreign policy traditions, values, and calculability that had brought the Federal Republic such success in the past. He argued that "German foreign policy based on responsibility rather than power has remained unaffected by unification. It is only through the continued adherence to these basic principles that a European Germany can secure the kind of influence in the future that it had acquired in the years up to 1989."[9] In 1992, the new Foreign Minister, Klaus Kinkel, proclaimed that:

Germany owes its unity and present status in the world to the trust we have built up with our consistent policy of conciliation and readiness for compromise. This trust is our greatest asset. We must not carelessly jeopardize it by committing ourselves to adventures which could reawaken dangerous misunderstandings among our friends and neighbors. Germany's policy will remain consistent and calculable. Our reluctance to use military force has been, and will continue to be, part of this calculability.[10]

Leaders of the new Social Democrat–Green coalition government, elected in September 1998, expressed a similar commitment to foreign policy continuity. Green Party Foreign Minister Joschka Fischer said that given its special history, "the most important change for German foreign policy with the new government is no change. Continuity is the main focus of our policy, because other ways will not produce the desired results."[11]

Nevertheless, the Federal Republic was no longer the same political entity after the fall of the Berlin Wall, and the world began to undergo incredible political transformations in the years that followed. Put simply, Germany entered new geopolitical territory with the end of the Cold War. The international parameters that had guided German foreign policy for forty years suddenly fell away. There were no strategic threats to Germany for truly the first time in its history. Enemies of the past had become partners in projects such as the promotion of international security and European integration. As leaders struggled to respond to new challenges in the post-Cold War era, they faced some surprising opportunities to revisit the assumptions and norms that had driven German foreign policy for half a century.

STRATEGIC DILEMMAS: FROM KUWAIT TO KOSOVO, AND BEYOND

The crisis in the Persian Gulf that began in August 1990 with the Iraqi invasion of Kuwait became the first serious strategic dilemma for Germany in the post-Cold War era. In fact, the crisis drew German leaders into a constitutional debate about their country's proper role in the new international order even before official unification. From the outset, Germany's leaders steadfastly refused to commit forces to Operations Desert Shield or Desert Storm based on the Cold War domestic political consensus that the Basic Law prohibited any use of force outside the NATO arena. The dramatic success of Operation Desert Storm prompted a reconsideration of the question, however, and cabinet leaders decided to send *Bundeswehr* soldiers to Turkey, Iraq, and Iran to assist Kurdish refugees in April 1991.[12]

Humanitarian crises around the world also prompted legal, political, and moral debates in Germany about new foreign policy responsibilities. Civil war and starvation in Somalia eventually led to the deployment of 1,700 German troops for humanitarian relief operations as part of UNO-SOM II and Operation Restore Hope. The German government not only deployed 450 members of the *Bundeswehr* to Cambodia for medical support of the UN Transitional Authority mission (UNTAC), but also sent medical relief and military officers for the UN Observer Mission in the former Soviet republic of Georgia (UNOMIG).[13] In 1996, Defense Minister Volker Rühe called for an expansion of participation in future humanitarian operations and outlined a plan to train 54,000 German troops for multilateral peacekeeping duties.[14]

Conflicts in the former Yugoslavia presented the Federal Republic with arguably the most serious strategic dilemmas of the post-Cold War era. A series of wars for independence in the Balkans led to soul searching and political debates in Germany about proper foreign policy responses in the

1990s.[15] After three years of relative inaction in Bosnia, German pilots were allowed to fly support missions for NATO air strikes against Serb artillery in 1995, and 4,000 *Bundeswehr* soldiers were deployed to Croatia and Bosnia for NATO peace enforcement operations in 1996.[16] Success fostered support for greater foreign policy activism, and German pilots conducted air strikes throughout the NATO's 78-day war against Yugoslavia over Kosovo. Green Party Foreign Minister Joschka Fischer became personally involved in directing the air strikes, mediating alliance disputes, and in maintaining unity within the coalition government during the war. The general public reacted calmly to the Kosovo War at first, leading one critic to conclude in 1999, "the last victim of the fall of the Wall was German pacifism."[17]

Events in 2001 prompted a new wave in the evolution of German foreign policy. In the wake of the September 11, 2001, terrorist attacks on the United States, Chancellor Gerhard Schröder pledged strong support for the United States and the war on terrorism. Dozens of German soldiers were deployed in NATO AWACS (Airborne Warning and Control System) planes to the United States for combat air patrols over major metropolitan areas. In addition, on November 6, 2001, Chancellor Gerhard Schröder pledged the support of 3,900 Bundeswehr soldiers for the war against the Taliban in Afghanistan. Noting that the war on terrorism would extend beyond the use of military force, the German government also froze hundreds of bank accounts worth an estimated $4 million that it believed to be linked to terrorist networks and increased its support for humanitarian relief operations in Afghanistan by nearly $25 million. Schröder stated that the German government "is convinced that we will support the international fight against terror with these measures and we will fulfill our responsibilities."[18]

THEORETICAL FOUNDATIONS

This study of the evolution of German foreign policy responses to challenges and opportunities in the post-Cold War era is influenced by major theories of foreign policy analysis. The model of external–internal linkages presented in this book is derived from two important areas of scholarship: the role of international crises as catalysts for foreign policy change; and the importance of domestic political conditions and constraints that ultimately determine the scope and pace of foreign policy restructuring.

Primat der Außenpolitik? International Catalysts for Restructuring

In this study, *strategic dilemmas* are defined as regional or international crises that demand a response from great powers and may prompt a realignment in foreign policy. Military invasions, civil wars, genocide, and humanitarian crises that receive extensive media coverage challenge the status quo (international law, international institutions, and regional or global order). These challenges are *strategic* in that they relate directly to a country's foreign and security policy orientations, and they are *dilemmas* in that they demand state attention and often prompt domestic political deliberations on a proper response. In the case of Germany, strategic dilemmas have presented constitutional challenges and produced realignments in foreign policy behavior.

Foreign policy analysts have recognized the importance of strategic dilemmas as catalysts for restructuring.[19] Jerel Rosati argued that international crises can act as immediate causes of change, "reflecting the underlying relationship and contradictions which exist between the sources of continuity and change emanating from the interaction of the state, society, and the environment."[20] Charles Hermann's model of restructuring emphasizes the importance of "external shocks," which he defined as dramatic international events that have great visibility and can account for the majority of foreign policy change.[21] Robert Putnam's work on two-level games also suggests that strategic dilemmas can create pressures and incentives for leaders to act through channels including alliance commitments, summits, and economic ties.[22]

Domestic Constraints

Strategic dilemmas may serve as catalysts for foreign policy restructuring, but any conceptual framework seeking to account for dramatic changes in state foreign policy orientations must also understand those forces that inhibit major changes.[23] A second dimension of this study involves the determination of the key domestic political factors that have the greatest impact on foreign policy restructuring.

Once again, a foundation for examining the complex relationship between external and internal conditions can be established by using theories of foreign policy decision making.[24] In a seminal work on this subject, James Rosenau argued:

[O]ur understanding of politics can be deepened and broadened by treating political phenomena as forms of human adaptation . . . the political organism is always experiencing both continuities and change, and thus is always in motion, slipping behind, moving ahead, holding fast, or otherwise adjusting and changing in response to internal developments and external circumstances. To analyze how the adjustments are made, the changes sustained, and the continuities preserved is to engage in the study of political adaptation.[25]

More recently, Rosati contended that in spite of external pressures, governments actually tend to resist foreign policy change. He said that the "patterns of stratification that exist in the structures and beliefs through-out society and the state tend to favor the status quo and continuity over the political forces in support of change."[26] Thomas Volgy and John Schwarz's model of "webs of restraint" suggests that factors including bureaucratic politics, governmental institutions, resources, and regional and global conditions can limit change. Ultimately, they argued, domestic barriers to change often become "webs which enmesh and restrict leaders' abilities to effectuate fundamental changes in the direction of their foreign policies."[27]

Wolfram Hanrieder was one of the first scholars to explore the impact of external–internal linkages on German foreign policy. Hanrieder collaborated with Rosenau in the 1960s to consider the dynamics of these linkages and their resultant effect on state foreign policy behavior.[28] Hanrieder argued that analysts must examine the linkages between the "internal predispositions" of the country (including value systems and political culture) and conditions in the external environment in order to reach a comprehensive understanding of foreign policy. He said that foreign policy restructuring ultimately hinges on *compatibility*, "the degrees of feasibility of various foreign policy goals, given the strictures and opportunities of the international system," and *consensus*, the amount of domestic political agreement regarding the ends and means of foreign policy change.[29]

For this study, German foreign policy change will be examined as the product of leaders' efforts to respond to international crises by building three levels of coalitions for policy redirection: among elites, in political parties, and with the public. First, a chief of government must build support among his or her cadre of *party elites*—a surprisingly small number of leaders who can sharply influence foreign policy decisions in parliamentary democracies—in order to effect change. Putnam has concisely defined the political elite as "those who in any society rank toward the top of the (presumably closely intercorrelated) dimensions of interest, involvement, and influence in politics."[30] This elite authority has the power to allocate government resources.

The attitudes of these key decision makers often define foreign policy goals and direction, and it is important to identify the perceptual lens through which elites view foreign and security policy choices. Rosenau has suggested that the connection between the adaptive behavior of a society and the consequences of that behavior "exists primarily in the minds of foreign policy decision makers," who strive to minimize costs and maximize opportunities based on their images of the world around them.[31] Thus, the perceptions of elites often set the parameters for foreign policy choices.[32] In the case of Germany, John Duffield has suggested that political elites possess a "distinctive, widely shared, and rather elaborate set of beliefs and values" in relation to foreign policy, and historical memory remains an important perceptual lens through which these leaders view foreign policy challenges and opportunities.[33]

Second, *party politics* can significantly constrain foreign policy restructuring. Political parties in parliamentary democracies greatly influence leaders' abilities to construct domestic coalitions for the implementation of policies, and they can influence change throughout all echelons of the party organization.[34]

Recent scholarship on domestic coalition building lays the foundation for this level of inquiry. Joe Hagan has argued that building coalitions for change often becomes a central preoccupation for leaders in democratic systems. Coalition building is so important in foreign policy development, he argued, that issues are often viewed less on their substantive merit than for their perceived effect on political balances in the government.[35] Helen Milner added that foreign policy is affected less by fears of other countries' relative gains or losses than it is "by the domestic distributional consequences of cooperative endeavors."[36] Consideration of the coalition building dynamic is particularly relevant for those parliamentary democracies based on proportional representation, where power is often shared among major and minor parties, and where there is a special role for the parliament as arbiter of government power.[37] The relationship between the major party in government and those parties needed to assure a majority in control of parliament (junior parties) represents the foundation of government stability in these systems.[38]

Public support is a third force that can affect the scope and nature of foreign policy restructuring. Generally, public opinion and attitudes may influence foreign policy by setting broad parameters in debates about change. The theory that public opinion can constrain state foreign policy behavior was originally derived from the works of Germans including Immanuel Kant and Clausewitz. A post-World War II, socially scientific interpretation of the role of national feeling in the foreign policy process centered on the significance of *political culture*, which Pye and Verba defined as "the system of empirical beliefs, expressed symbols, and the values which affect the situation in which political action takes place."[39] They contended that for individual leaders, "political culture provides the guidelines, controlling guidelines for effective political behavior; and for the collectivity, it gives a systematic structure of values" that give coherence to foreign policy.[40] While the existence, definition, and role of political culture has been debated in international relations scholarship for decades, several contemporary studies have linked political culture to the transformation in German foreign policy.[41] For example, Thomas Risse-Kappen argued that political culture can affect the choices of top decision makers "by changing policy goals or how those goals are prioritized, by narrowing the range of options and/or means to implement goals, or by winning symbolic concessions in the sense of changed rhetoric rather than policy reforms."[42] Thomas Berger contended that "political military culture," a subset of the larger political culture that focuses on security issues and the use of force in international affairs, can be linked directly to Germany's behavior in the past 50 years.[43]

For this study, I contend that the three domestic political conditions described previously in this chapter—elite consensus, coalitions of party organizations, and public support—may be necessary for foreign policy restructuring, but none are sufficient alone. Conversely, timely and dramatic foreign policy restructuring in response to strategic dilemmas and opportunities may be constrained by government division, party differences, and public opposition. A more focused, in-depth look at German foreign policy change is a story of extreme (and sometimes desperate) efforts by some politicians to build consensus for more decisive foreign policy action, dramatic shifts in party stances on policy development, and the ebb and flow of public support for foreign policy change.

Methodology

This study employs the comparative case studies method to explore the significance of domestic political constraints on German foreign policy restructuring in the 1990s. The method of structured, focused comparison of cases, working from a set list of theoretically relevant, general questions, was originally developed by Arend Lijphart (1971) and Alexander George (1979). Specifically, a decision process-tracing technique is employed to assess the importance of domestic political conditions with regard to foreign policy restructuring.[44] This approach is consistent with George's call for "conditional generalizations . . . that identify the causal process or causal mechanism which explains how an antecedent condition/variable is linked to variance in the outcome variable."[45] Ultimately, the methodology allows for a mixture of richness and rigor in a comprehensive study of political behavior.[46]

Five original, multistage case studies of the foreign policy restructuring process in the Federal Republic of Germany are presented in subsequent chapters. In some ways, Germany represents a prototypical parliamentary democracy based on a modified proportional representation electoral system. Political power is derived from universal suffrage, interest group support, and party organizations, and is manifest through representation in a bicameral legislature. In other ways, however, Germany has been a special player on the world stage. Divided by the victorious allies after World War II, the Federal Republic of Germany and the German Democratic Republic were highly dependent on support from the United States and the Soviet Union, respectively. United in 1990, German leaders suddenly faced an incredible array of domestic and international challenges.[47] For the social scientist, Germany's efforts to overcome structural obstacles represent an interesting opportunity to explore the dynamics of foreign policy restructuring.

Case studies include the German foreign policy response to the Persian Gulf crisis (1990–1991); the decision to participate in the UN peacekeeping operation in Somalia (1993); decisions to recognize the independence of Croatia and Slovenia and to participate in monitoring operations in the Balkans (1991–1994); diplomatic and military initiatives to deal with the war in Bosnia (1992–1996); and German responses to the crisis in Kosovo (1998–1999). Each case study examines the interplay between strategic dilemmas and the ways in which German policy makers interpret and debate new foreign policy initiatives. Data for these cases are drawn from analyses of government documents and parliamentary debates, extensive interviews with participants, public opinion surveys, and secondary sources.[48] Ultimately, these case studies represent what George terms "heuristic case studies," which provide an opportunity to learn more about the complexity of foreign policy restructuring.[49]

CONCLUSION

The case studies developed for this book explore the decision-making processes related to dramatic episodes in the Federal Republic of Germany's recent history, and they illustrate the evolution of both the international system and domestic conditions in the post-Cold War era. This book takes the reader from the German government's uncertainty about how to respond to the Gulf crisis in the aftermath of unification to a more assertive foreign policy profile established during the Balkan wars for independence. The Kosovo case study highlights both continuity and change in foreign policy development under the new Social Democrat–Green Party governing coalition. The book concludes with an analysis of the utility of this model of restructuring for interpretation of change in the post-Cold War era, and projections for the future of German foreign policy.

NOTES

1. Otto von Bismarck, *Gedanken und Erinnerungen*, originally published 1898; complete edition of three volumes published 1929 (Stuttgart: I. G. Cottasche Buchhandlung Nachfolger, 1989), p. 543.

2. Statement from interview first printed in *Handelsblatt*, 7 February 1992, translated in *Foreign Broadcast Information Service—Western Europe*, no. 92-027, 10 February 1992, p. 13.

3. Helga Haftendorn argued that *Einbindungspolitik* was in fact a much more "cost efficient variant to a strategy based on narrowly defined national interests."

See Helga Haftendorn, "Gulliver in der Mitte Europas: Internationale Verflechtung und nationale Handlungsmöglichkeiten," in Karl Kaiser and Hanns W. Maull, eds., *Deutschlands neue Außenpolitik. Band 1: Grundlagen* (München: Oldenbourg, 1994); for more information on the history of German foreign policy ties through multilateralism, see Christian Hacke, "Die Entscheidung für politische Westbindung nach 1945," in Rainer Zitelmann, Karlheinz Weißmann, and Michael Großheim, eds., *Westbindung: Chancen und Risiken für Deutschland* (Frankfurt: Verlag Ullstein, 1993), pp. 129-172; on the history of Cold War German foreign policy evolution, see Thomas Banchoff, *The German Problem Transformed: Institutions, Politics, and Foreign Policy, 1945-1995* (Ann Arbor, MI: University of Michigan Press, 1999).

4. See Thomas U. Berger, *Cultures of Antimilitarism: National Security in Germany and Japan* (Baltimore, MD: Johns Hopkins University Press, 1998).

5. Timothy Garton Ash, "Germany's Choice," *Foreign Affairs*, vol. 43, July–August 1994, p. 71.

6. See select chapters from *Deutschlands neue Außenpolitik, Band 1: Grundlagen*, Karl Kaiser and Hanns. W. Maull, eds. (München: R. Oldenbourg Verlag, 1995), including: Christian Tomuschat, "Die Internationale Staatenwelt an der Schwelle des Dritten Jahrtausends," pp. 15–37; Michael Stürmer, "Deutsche Interessen," pp. 39–61; Norbert Kloten, "Die Bundesrepublik als Weltwirtschaftsmacht," pp. 63–80; Hans-Peter Schwarz, "Das Deutsche Dilemma," pp. 81–97; Ludger Kühnhardt, "Weltgrundlagen der Deutschen Aussenpolitik," pp. 99–127; Helga Haftendorn, "Gulliver in der Mitte Europas: Internationale Verflechtung und Nationale Handlungsmöglichkeiten," pp. 129–152; see also Michael Brenner, Wolfgang F. Schlör, and Phil Williams, *German and American Foreign and Security Policies: Strategic Convergence or Divergence?*, Interne Studie, no. 98 (Sankt Augustin, Germany: Konrad Adenauer Stiftung, December 1994).

7. Kenneth N. Waltz, "The Emerging Structure of International Politics," *International Security*, vol. 18, no. 2, Fall 1993, pp. 66–67; see also Christopher Layne, "The Unipolar Illusion: Why New Great Powers will Rise," *International Security*, vol. 17, no. 2, Spring 1993, pp. 5–51.

8. Author's interview with Franz-Josef Meiers, Bonn, 4 June 1996, p. 4.

9. Hans-Dietrich Genscher, *Erinnerungen* (Berlin: Siedler Verlag, 1995), p. 62.

10. Klaus Kinkel, "Peacekeeping Missions: Germany Can Now Play Its Part," *NATO Review*, vol. 5, no. 3, October 1994, p. 7.

11. Joschka Fischer, Transcript of Press Conference with Madeline Albright at the U. S. Department of State, Televised on C-SPAN, 8:00 p.m., 3 November 1998.

12. "Umfragen zum Krieg," *Die Zeit*, 25 January 1991, p. 16; "The Mood in January," *Süddeutsche Zeitung*, 29 January 1991, p. 10; for an analysis of these trends in German public opinion, see David B. Walker, "Germany Searches for a New Role in World Affairs," *Current History*, vol. 34, November 1991, pp. 368–373.

13. For more information on German troop deployments, see Jochen Thies, "Germany: Europe's Reluctant Great Power," *The World Today*, vol. 51, no. 10, October 1995, pp. 186–190.

14. For an excellent overview of the restructuring of the German armed forces in the post-Cold War era, see Thomas-Durell Young, *Trends in German Defense Policy: The Defense Policy Guidelines and the Centralization of Operational Control* (Carlisle, PA: Strategic Studies Institute of the U.S. Army War College, 14

June 1994); see also Wolfgang F. Schlör, "German Security Policy: An Examination of the Trends in German Security Policy in a New European and Global Context," *Adelphi Paper,* no. 277 (London: International Institute of Strategic Studies, June 1993).

15. For a description of the constitutionality debate, see also Karl-Heinz Börner, "The Future of German Operations Outside NATO," *Parameters,* vol. 26, no. 1, Spring 1996, pp. 62–72.

16. Confidential interview, Mershon Center, The Ohio State University, Columbus, Ohio, 1 June 1995.

17. Stephan Speicher, *Berliner Zeitung,* 25 March 1999, p. 6.

18. Steven Erlanger, "Germany Ready to Send Force of 3,900; Not Clear If They Would Be Combat Soldiers," *New York Times,* 7 November 2001, p. B4; see also "German Troops to Join 'Terror War,'" CNN Worldnews, 6 November 2001, http://cnn.worldnews.com.

19. In another early study, James Rosenau argued that foreign policy is essentially a mechanism for the state to adapt to changes in its environment and that governments hoping to survive have to balance the internal tensions and the external demands to which they are subjected; James N. Rosenau, *The Study of Political Adaptation: Essays on the Analysis of World Politics* (New York: Nichols Publishing, 1981), p. 42.

20. Jerel Rosati, "Cycles in Foreign Policy Restructuring: The Politics of Continuity and Change in U.S. Foreign Policy," in Jerel Rosati, Joe D. Hagan, and Martin W. Sampson, eds., *Foreign Policy Restructuring* (Columbia, SC: University of South Carolina Press, 1994), p. 233.

21. Charles F. Hermann, "Changing Course: When Governments Choose to Redirect Foreign Policy," *International Studies Quarterly,* vol. 34, no.1, 1990, p. 14.

22. See Robert D. Putnam, "Diplomacy and Domestic Politics: The Logic of Two-Level Games," *International Organization,* vol. 42, no. 3, Summer 1988, pp. 427–460; see also Andrew Moravcsik, "Introduction: Integrating International and Domestic Theories of International Bargaining," chapter 1 in Peter B. Evans, Harold K. Jacobson, and Robert D. Putnam, eds., *Double-edged Diplomacy: International Bargaining and Domestic Politics* (Berkeley, CA: University of California Press, 1993), pp. 3–42.

23. James Caporaso commented on this predictive defect in realism by noting that systemic theories have a tendency to "underpredict outcomes . . . meaning that the theoretical information is insufficient to generate specific predictions about foreign policy behavior"; Caporaso, "Across the Great Divide: Integrating Comparative and International Politics," *International Studies Quarterly,* vol. 41, no. 4, 1997, pp. 566–567.

24. On the relationship between external and internal pressures, see John G. Ikenberry, Davic Lumsdaine, and Lisa Anderson, "Polity Forum: The Intertwining of Domestic Politics and International Relations," *Polity,* vol. 29, 1996, pp. 293–310; Jeffrey W. Legro and Andrew Moravcsik, "Is Anybody Still a Realist?" *International Security,* vol. 24, no. 2, Fall 1999, pp. 5–55; Susan Peterson, *Crisis Bargaining and the State: The Domestic Politics of International Conflict* (Ann Arbor, MI: University of Michigan Press, 1996); Thomas Risse-Kappen, *Cooperation Among Democracies* (Princeton, NJ: Princeton University Press, 1995).

25. Rosenau, 1981, pp. 1–2.

26. Rosati, 1994, p. 225.

27. Thomas J. Volgy and John E. Schwarz, "Foreign Policy Restructuring and the Myriad Webs of Restraint," in Jerel Rosati, Joe D. Hagan, and Martin W. Sampson, eds., *Foreign Policy Restructuring*, 1994, p. 27.

28. See Wolfram F. Hanrieder, "Actor Objectives and International Systems," *Journal of Politics*, vol. 27, no.1, February 1965, pp. 109–132; see also Hanrieder, "Compatability and Consensus: A Proposal for the Conceptual Linkage of External and Internal Dimensions of Foreign Policy," *American Political Science Review*, vol. 61, no. 4, December 1967, pp. 971–982; *West German Foreign Policy 1949–1963: International Pressure and Domestic Response* (Stanford, CA: Stanford University Press, 1967); *The Stable Crisis: Two Decades of German Foreign Policy* (New York: Harper & Row, 1970); *West German Foreign Policy: 1949–1979*, edited (Boulder, CO: Westview Press, 1980); *Germany, America, Europe: Forty Years of German Foreign Policy* (New Haven, CT: Yale University Press, 1989).

29. Wolfram Hanrieder, "Compatability and Consensus: A Proposal for the Conceptual Linkage of External and Internal Dimensions of Foreign Policy," *American Political Science Review*, vol. 61, no. 4, December 1967, p. 1977.

30. Robert D. Putnam, "Studying Elite Political Culture: The Case of Ideology," *American Political Science Review*, vol. 65, no. 3, September 1971, p. 651.

31. Rosenau, 1981, p. 50; for a more recent perspective on the importance of systemic factors for foreign policy, see Fareed Zakaria, "Realism and Domestic Politics: A Review Essay," *International Security*, vol. 17, no. 1, Summer 1992, p. 198.

32. See Ole Waever, "Resisting the Temptation of Post Foreign Policy Analysis," in Walter Carlsnaes and Steve Smith, eds., *European Foreign Policy: The EC and Changing Perspectives in Europe* (London: Sage, 1994).

33. John S. Duffield, "Political Culture and State Behavior: Why Germany Confounds Neorealism," *International Organization*, vol. 53, no. 4, Autumn 1999, p. 779; see also Thomas Berger, "The Past in the Present: Historical Memory and German National Security Policy," *German Politics*, vol. 6, no. 1, April 1997, pp. 37–59; see also John S. Duffield, *World Power Forsaken: Political Culture, International Institutions, and German Security Policy After Unification* (Stanford, CA: Stanford University Press, 1998).

34. See Mary N. Hampton, "Institutions and Learning: Explaining Incremental German Foreign Policy Innovation," *European Security*, vol. 5, no. 4, Winter 1996, pp. 543–563.

35. Joe D. Hagan, *Political Oppositions and Foreign Policy in Comparative Perspective* (Boulder, CO: Lynne Rienner, 1993), p. 49.

36. Helen V. Milner, *Interests, Institutions, and Information: Domestic Politics and International Relations* (Princeton, NJ: Princeton University Press, 1997), pp. 9–10; see also Moravcsik, 1993, p. 14.

37. Jack Snyder argues the importance of minority or parochial domestic actors for foreign policy and warns that "narrow interests can overcome their weakness and 'hijack' foreign policy by participating in logrolling coalitions"; see Jack Snyder, *Myths of Empire: Domestic Politics and International Ambition* (Ithaca, NY: Cornell University Press, 1993); for related work, see Arend Lijphart, ed., *Parliamentary Versus Presidential Government* (New York: Columbia University Press, 1992); Vernon Bogdanor, ed., *Coalition Government in Western Europe* (New York: Heinemann Educational Books, 1983), pp. 1–15.

38. To date, research on this relationship in democratic systems has been limited. Blondel and Müller-Rommel have described cabinet government in parliamentary systems as unique since, "practically no other national arrangement . . . requires that governmental decisions be taken by ministers as a group . . . in cabinet government, both in theory and to a large extent in practice, ministers and prime ministers form part of a common enterprise in which they have a share." In a study of this dynamic in Israel, Diskin and Galnoor found that party politics and inter-party policy clusters were important predictors of foreign policy. Later, Blondel and Thiebault examined the relationship between individuals, ministerial roles, and policy domains in Great Britain. In a survey of the role of coalition politics in German and Israeli foreign policy, Kaarbo concluded that the unity of junior and senior parties on specific issues, junior party strategies of influence in the coalition, and the locus of decision making authority were key determinants for foreign policy development. She concluded that while coalition politics is often "crucial for explaining foreign policy," it remains "under-represented in studies of foreign policy and change"; see Jean Blondel and Ferdinand Müller-Rommel, "Introduction," in J. Blondel and F. Müller-Rommel, eds., *Governing Together* (New York: St. Martin's Press, 1993), p. 1; Abraham Diskin and Itzhak Galnoor, "Political Distances Between Knesset Members and Coalition Behavior: The Peace Agreements with Egypt," *Political Studies Quarterly*, vol. 38, no. 4, 1990; see Juliet Kaarbo, "Power and Influence in Foreign Policy Decision Making: the Role of Junior Coalition Partners in German and Israeli Foreign Policy," *International Studies Quarterly*, vol. 40, no. 2, 1996, pp. 501–530.

This approach also was taken by a number of scholars of German politics and society who carefully examined the *innenpolitische* developments that affect foreign policy behavior. Studies by German scholars such as Haftendorn describe some relationship between coalition politics and foreign policy "room to maneuver." More recent scholarship [for example, Boutwell's *The German Nuclear Dilemma* (Ithaca, NY: Cornell University Press, 1990)] has continued the examination of the inter-party politics that can affect foreign policy behavior; for more on the German party system, see Gerard Braunthal, *Parties and Politics in Modern Germany* (Boulder, CO: Westview, 1996); Ludger Kuhnhardt, *Beyond Divisions and After: Eassays on Democracy, the Germans, and Europe* (New York: P. Lang Publishers, 1996); and Walter L. Bühl, "Gesellschaftliche Grundlagen der Deutschen Außenpolitik," in *Deutschlands neue Außenpolitik, Band 1: Grundlagen*, Karl Kaiser and Hanns W. Maull, eds. (München: R. Oldenbourg Verlag, 1995), pp. 175–201; Chrisian Søe, "Not Without Us! The FDP's Survival, Position, and Influence," in P. H. Merkl, ed., *The Federal Republic of Germany at Forty* (New York: New York University Press, 1989), pp. 313–339.

39. For an overview of the political culture literature, see Lucian W. Pye, "Introduction: Political Culture and Political Development," and Sidney Verba, "Conclusion: Comparative Political Culture," in Pye and Verba, eds., *Political Culture and Political Development* (Princeton, NJ: Princeton University Press, 1965), chapters 1 and 12; Robert D. Putnam, *The Beliefs of Politicians: Ideology, Conflict, and Democracy in Britain and Italy* (New Haven, CT: Yale University Press, 1973); David J. Elkins and Richard E. B. Simeon, "A Cause in Search of Its Effect, of What Does Political Culture Explain," *Comparative Politics*, vol. 11, no. 2, January 1979, pp. 127–146; Gabriel Almond and Sidney Verba, eds., *The Civic Culture Revisited*

(Boston: Little, Brown, 1980); and Harry Eckstein, "A Culturalist Theory of Political Change," *American Political Science Review*, vol. 62, no. 3, September 1988; pp. 789–804; see also Thomas U. Berger, "America's Reluctant Allies: The Genesis of the Political Military Cultures of Japan and West Germany," (Ph. D. Dissertation, Massachusetts Institute of Technology, 1991).

40. Pye and Verba, eds., 1965, p. 7.

41. For more on the importance of German political culture, see John S. Duffield, "Political Culture and State Behavior: Why Germany Confounds Neorealism," *International Organization*, vol. 53, no. 4, Autumn 1999, pp. 765–803; Gabriel A. Almond, "The Study of Political Culture," in Dirk Berg-Schlosser and Ralf Rytlewski, eds., *Political Culture in Germany* (New York: St. Martin's Press, 1993), pp. 13–26; Arthur Hoffmann and Kerry Longhurst, "German Strategic Culture in Action," *Contemporary Security Policy*, vol. 20, no. 2, August 1999, pp. 31–49.

42. Thomas Risse-Kappen, "Public Opinion, Domestic Structure, and Foreign Policy in Liberal Democracies," *World Politics*, vol. 43, no. 2, 1991, p. 482; see also Risse-Kappen, ed., *Bringing Transnational Relations Back In: Non-State Actors, Domestic Structures, and International Institutions* (Cambridge: Cambridge University Press, 1995); Susan Peterson, "How Democracies Differ: Public Opinion, State Structure, and the Lessons of the Fashoda Crisis," *Security Studies*, vol. 5, no. 3, 1995, pp. 3–37.

More recently, Mo argued that the impact of public pressure on foreign policy behavior is a function of the distribution of political power between the leader and constituency; see Jongryn Mo, "Domestic Institutions and International Bargaining: The Role of Agent Veto in Two-Level Games," *American Political Science Review*, vol. 89, 1995, pp. 914–924; see also Robin F. Marra, Charles W. Ostrom, and Dennis M. Simon, "Foreign Policy and Presidential Popularity: Creating Windows of Opportunity in the Perpetual Election," *Journal of Conflict Resolution*, vol. 34, 1989, pp. 588–623; see also Susan Peterson, "How Democracies Differ: Public Opinion, State Structure, and the Lessons of the Fashoda Crisis," *Security Studies*, vol. 5, Autumn 1995, pp. 3–37. Douglas Foyle argues that public opinion can constrain policymaking "because of the anticipatory efforts by policy makers to ascertain what the public would accept"; see Douglas C. Foyle, "Public Opinion and Foreign Policy: Elite Beliefs as a Mediating Variable," *International Studies Quarterly*, vol. 41, no. 2, 1997, p. 146; see also Douglas C. Foyle, *Counting the Public In: Presidents, Public Opinion, and Foreign Policy* (New York: Columbia University Press, 1999).

43. See Thomas U. Berger, *Cultures of Antimilitarism: National Security in Germany and Japan* (Baltimore, MD: Johns Hopkins University Press, 1998). This resembles the concept of strategic culture as developed by Jack Snyder, Colin Gray, Yitzak Klein, and others. See Jack Snyder, *The Soviet Strategic Culture: Implications for Nuclear Options*, R-2154-AF (Santa Monica, CA: Rand, 1977); Snyder, *The Myths of Empire: Politics and International Ambition*; Colin Gray, "National Styles in Strategy: the American Example," *International Security*, vol. 6, no. 2, 1981; Colin Gray, *Nuclear Strategy and National Style* (Lanham, MD: University Press of America, 1986); Yitzak Klein, "A Theory of Strategic Culture," *Comparative Strategy*, vol. 10, no. 1, 1991, pp. 3–17.

44. Alexander George, "Knowledge for Statecraft: The Challenge for Political Science and History," *International Security*, vol. 22, no. 1, Summer 1997, p. 47.

45. George, Summer 1997, p. 50; for more information on the utility of the method of structured, focused case comparison, see Alexander L. George and Andrew Bennett, *Case Studies and Theory Development* (Cambridge, MA: MIT Press, forthcoming).

46. Alexander L. George, "Case Studies and Theory Development: The Method of Structured, Focused Comparison," in Paul Gordon Lauren, ed., *Diplomacy: New Approaches in History, Theory, and Policy* (New York: Free Press, 1979).

47. Confidential interview, Presse- und Informationsamt der Bundesregierung, Bonn, 23 September 1998.

48. George, Summer 1997, p. 47.

49. George, 1979, pp. 51–52.

2

The Persian Gulf Crisis and Checkbook Diplomacy

Never again do we want to send our sons to the barracks. And if again somewhere this insanity of war should break out, and if fate should want it that our land becomes a battlefield, then we shall simply perish and at least take with us the knowledge that we neither encouraged nor committed the crime.

—Carlo Schmid, 1946[1]

After the events in the Gulf and against the background of other looming conflicts, we Germans can no longer ignore the question of what we can contribute to peace outside of Europe. We must come to terms with the greater responsibility which we have gained through the overcoming of partition and the regaining of our full sovereignty. This is demanded by our neighbors, and this is demanded by the world.

—Helmut Kohl, 1991[2]

For the foreseeable future Germany will need armed forces. Our goal is to make them superfluous. Until we have reached this goal, German forces must be structured only so that they are capable of territorial defense and to fulfill our alliance obligations. A constitutional amendment that aims at allowing the *Bundeswehr* to participate in military actions [outside the NATO area] is incompatible with our peace and security policy. We reject German participation in military operations under UN command or those sanctioned by the United Nations . . . [but] the Federal Republic of Germany should be able to participate in UN blue-helmet peacekeeping missions.

—SPD Party Congress Resolution, 1991[3]

The crisis in the Persian Gulf that began with the Iraqi invasion of Kuwait in August 1990 became the first serious security challenge for Germany in the post-Cold War era. Even before official German unification in October 1990, the crisis drew leaders into a debate about the country's proper role in the new international order. This chapter explores the evolution of German responses to three strategic dilemmas created by events in the Persian Gulf (Figure 2.1) and how the crises, in turn, shaped domestic political conditions. The pattern of evidence suggests that the Gulf crisis was a crucial catalyst for German leaders to assess domestic constraints and reshape their commitment to international security in the post-Cold War era.[4]

THE IRAQI INVASION OF KUWAIT AND OPERATION DESERT SHIELD

Historical Background

On August 2, 1990, Iraqi military forces invaded and occupied Kuwait on orders from President Saddam Hussein. Within three days, Iraq controlled most of the territory of Kuwait and a staggering 24% of the world's known oil supplies. Western intelligence organizations estimated

Figure 2.1
Strategic Dilemmas in the Persian Gulf

Stages/Dates	Strategic Dilemma	Foreign Policy Response
I. 1990	Iraqi Invasion of Kuwait/ Operation Desert Shield	Checkbook Diplomacy
II. 1990–1991	Threats to Turkey and Israel/ Operation Desert Storm	Logistical Support, Help in Defense of Turkey and Israel
III. 1991	Iraqi Attack on Kurds/ Refugee Crisis Relief	Troop Deployment and Logistical Support

that Iraq had deployed 38 divisions with 540,000 soldiers in the theater of operations, and the force was supported by 700 Iraqi combat aircraft, 4,200 tanks, and 3,100 mobile artillery units.[5] After their rapid victory, Iraqi troops established strong defensive positions in Kuwait and began to consolidate their hold on the region.[6] The war created an immediate refugee crisis, as some 850,000 third-country nationals and 300,000 Palestinians from both Iraq and Kuwait fled to Saudi Arabia and Jordan. The invasion also created a diplomatic crisis when Iraqi authorities ordered the closure of all foreign embassies in Kuwait City and directed that 10,000 western citizens in Kuwait (including 400 Germans) be held hostage as "human shields" until western governments ended their efforts to reverse the invasion.

The international community reacted with surprise and horror at this sudden breach of sovereignty and order in the Middle East, and the Iraqi invasion clearly presented the international community with a major strategic dilemma. Within hours of the invasion, the United Nations (UN) Security Council met for an emergency session to consider the proper response to the violation of international law and norms. The Security Council passed Resolution #660 on August 2, 1990, which condemned the invasion as a violation of international law, demanded the immediate and unconditional withdrawal of Iraqi forces from Kuwait, and called for negotiations between the two governments for a nonviolent resolution of the conflict. Nevertheless, Iraq continued to resist UN efforts in the weeks and months following the invasion, leading to a steady escalation in the intensity and scope of subsequent resolutions. On August 6, the UN Security Council passed Resolution #661, which imposed severe trade sanctions on Iraq and established the foundation for an economic embargo of the country. Later, Security Council Resolution #665 demanded that foreign nationals be allowed to leave the region and that the embassies and missions in Kuwait remain open. Resolution #670 authorized the use of naval force to enforce economic sanctions on Iraq and created a no-fly zone over the region.[7] Other resolutions were directed toward handling the immediate crisis in the theater of war and looked ahead to compensation for financial losses and human rights violations resulting from the invasion.[8]

United States President George Bush took the lead in defining a western response to the invasion in conjunction with the efforts of the UN Security Council. He and his advisers developed a plan to deploy a multinational defense force in Saudi Arabia and neighboring Gulf states to shield the remaining oil-rich regions from further Iraqi aggression, and Bush quickly dispatched the U.S. Rapid Defense Force to the region. Washington also joined forces with the UN in the rhetorical battle against Iraqi aggression. On August 4, 1990, President Bush spoke out on the emerging western consensus that the Iraqi invasion was a blatant violation of international law and must be reversed. Echoing UN Security Council Resolution #660, Bush condemned the invasion and demanded an immediate and unconditional return to the *status quo ante bellum*. To force Iraqi compliance, the United States and its allies stated their willingness to impose economic sanctions on Iraq including an embargo on oil sales. Furthermore, the president pledged to use all necessary means, including military force, to defend against any further aggression in the region.[9] Seeking clarity of understanding, President Bush stated unequivocally, "This [the Iraqi invasion of Kuwait] will not stand."[10] The actions of the Bush administration and the UN Security Council represented a serious, progressive use of a range of instruments of statecraft to achieve a central foreign policy objective.

Western European powers supported the strong policy lines of the U.S. government and UN Security Council. Led by British Prime Minister Margaret Thatcher, members of the European Community (EC) gave their support to U.S. and UN efforts to reverse the events in the Gulf. At an emergency ministerial meeting of the EC on August 10, 1990, representatives issued a press statement on the matter, saying:

In view of the vital European interest in stability, territorial security, and the sovereignty of the states in the Middle East, the European Community calls for the immediate restoration of the sovereignty of Kuwait and full Iraqi compliance with Resolution #662 of the Security Council of the United Nations.[11]

The Gulf Dilemma for Germany

The Iraqi invasion of Kuwait presented the Federal Republic of Germany with a very serious and complicated strategic dilemma at the worst possible time. All German leaders believed the invasion itself was a blatant violation of international law, but efforts by the international community to respond to the crisis posed a complex challenge for the Federal Republic.

On August 11, 1990, President Bush telephoned Chancellor Kohl and personally requested that the German government consider the deployment of troops to the Gulf. Several weeks later, U.S. Secretary of State Baker visited Bonn and again urged Kohl and Genscher to make a "significant contribution to the liberation of Kuwait and freedom in the Middle East."[12] Recognizing that coalition operations in the Gulf would be expensive (with some estimates of $100 billion), Baker and other administration officials proposed that economically stable allies, including Germany, Japan, and Saudi Arabia, share the financial burden of coalition operations by contributing to a special fund. On August 30, 1990, U.S. State Department officials again formally requested a substantial pledge of German financial support.

Like their counterparts throughout the western world, German politi-cal leaders gathered quickly after the Iraqi invasion to consider their response options. Chancellor Helmut Kohl, Christian Democratic Union (CDU); Foreign Minister Hans-Dietrich Genscher, Free Democratic Party (FDP); and Defense Minister Gerhard Stoltenberg (CDU), and other cab-inet officials held their first emergency cabinet meeting regarding the cri-sis on August 2, 1990. The leaders agreed that Germany had significant interests in the Gulf region that were threatened by the Iraqi aggression and regional instability, including access to oil for the European Commu-nity, numerous corporate contracts, and financial ties. According to Gen-scher, cabinet leaders agreed that:

the ambitions of Saddam Hussein were unmistakable. Hussein wanted to make sure that Iraq was the undisputed supreme power in the region. The foundation of his politics, as he had already demonstrated with the invasion of Iran in 1980, was based on aggression. Germany [recognized] that Saddam Hussein posed a threat not only for his country but for the whole region.[13]

The cabinet issued a series of formal denunciations of the Iraqi inva-sion of Kuwait, to support UN Security Council resolutions on the mat-ter, and to provide encouragement for allied efforts. They did not agree, however, about how and when to commit German government resources to respond to this security dilemma. In fact, German foreign policy activism was significantly impeded in 1990 by major developments in domestic politics and serious political disagreements about the proper response to the Gulf crisis.[14]

First, the timing of the Gulf crisis could not have been worse for the Federal Republic of Germany, which was in the middle of unification negotiations with the former East Germany. When Iraq invaded Kuwait on August 2, 1990, German leaders were engaged in several different negotiations with other powers on the process and outcome of unifica-tion, including the Two-Plus-Four conferences, ministry-level talks between representatives of East and West on unification procedures, and end-stage negotiations with occupying authorities still based in Germany after World War II. To complicate matters even further, officials were gearing up for the first all-German elections set for December 1990.[15]

The German government and polity clearly were focused on domestic political maneuverings related to the unification process, and not on international developments in the summer of 1990. Only a few select government agencies and research institutes had begun to consider the implications of unification for foreign policy, and such concerns had not yet been raised to the level of cabinet discussions or *Bundestag* delibera-tions.[16] In fact, Foreign Minister Genscher admitted that the Gulf crisis was initially seen as a "distraction" from more important matters in Ger-many at the time. His preference was for the cabinet to postpone serious deliberations about foreign policy for some time, while the government dedicated its energy and resources to reunification negotiations and policy refinement.[17] He admitted that:

When the Gulf crisis broke out, we were nearing the end of the Two-Plus-Four negotiations with the United States, the Soviet Union, Great Britain, France, and the German Democratic Republic; and only a few weeks remained for suspending the four-power rights and for the negotiation over the bilateral German-Soviet contract. . . . Therefore, my first thought after the Iraqi invasion was whether this event would have any effect on relations between the West and the Soviet Union, which were vital for the German agreement.[18]

Given the urgency of the unfolding crisis, however, German leaders and domestic groups were forced to consider a foreign policy architecture that would guide them firmly and clearly into the post-Cold War era. Leaders did agree that the government must respond in some way to the strategic dilemmas caused by the Iraqi invasion and subsequent U.S. government requests for material and financial assistance for military operations in the Gulf.

At the same time, leaders also agreed that the German Basic Law essentially barred the government from sending troops to the Persian Gulf. In fact, this agreement was a function of Germany's historical foreign policy architecture and an accepted *Verfassungswirklichkeit* (constitutional political reality) that dictated a defensive posture for the German military after World War II. While this represented a fundamental constraint on German foreign policy in the Gulf crisis, the strategic dilemma prompted leaders to debate whether and how to overcome this constitutional and perceptual barrier to the use of force.

At issue was the interpretation of two key sections of the Basic Law as they related to the question of the constitutionality of committing troops outside the NATO area. Articles 24 and 87 of the Basic Law implied, according to the standard political interpretation of the Cold War, that German military action was limited to participation in regional, collective security institutions.[19] According to Article 24, paragraph 2 of the Basic Law:

For the maintenance of peace, the Federation may enter a system of mutual collective security; in doing so it will consent to such limitations upon its rights of sovereignty as will bring about and secure a peaceful and lasting order in Europe and among the nations of the world.

Meanwhile, Article 87 stated:

The Federation shall build up Armed Forces for defense purposes. Their numerical strength and general organizational structure shall be shown in the budget.

. . . Apart from defense, the Armed Forces may only be used to the extent explicitly permitted by this Basic Law.

Most German leaders agreed that these articles of the Basic Law allowed German involvement only in regional collective security defense. This was, of course, consistent with Germany's commitment to NATO area operations through Article V of the NATO Treaty, in which all parties agreed that "an armed attack against one or more of them . . . shall be considered an attack against them all."[20] This interpretation of the Basic Law, allowing for regional collective defense, dominated West Germany's foreign policy architecture during the Cold War and had been confirmed repeatedly by cabinet decisions up through the 1980s (including the CDU/CSU-FDP coalition led by Kohl).[21]

However, the Gulf crisis triggered a new round of elite debates about these questions as they related to the proper German foreign policy response to the dilemma. German leaders disagreed about the constitutionality of participation in collective security operations outside the NATO and through UN peacekeeping missions.[22]

Chancellor Kohl and Defense Minister Stoltenberg recognized from the outset that the Gulf crisis would create an opportunity to address the debate about the constitutionality of out-of-area troop deployment and, perhaps, to reshape Germany's foreign policy profile for the post-Cold War era. Within days of the invasion, Kohl began to hint that his party supported a broader interpretation of the Basic Law that would allow Germany to support operations in the Gulf.[23] Defense Minister Stoltenberg also began to articulate a CDU position that Germany could participate in UN-sponsored collective security operations and peacekeeping ("blue helmet") missions. Both leaders believed that these foreign policy changes were necessary for political reasons and might be realized without amendment to the Basic Law. Instead, they called for a "clarification" of the law in regard to collective security. In mid-August 1990, Kohl decided to try to force the issue of constitutional reinterpretation by publicly floating the idea that if the Western European Union (WEU) agreed to joint action in the Gulf, Germany would take part "within the context of its legal and practical abilities."[24] This was interpreted by many as an invitation for the WEU to take an initiative that would provide Kohl with the political justification for increased German military involvement.[25]

Conservative leaders could not garner support for this stance from Foreign Minister Genscher and other junior party leaders, however. Through repeated public statements, Genscher made it clear that although Germany would support its allies in the Gulf crisis, his party was unwilling to support German military action in the Gulf region for legal reasons. Genscher knew that events in the Gulf put Germany in an awkward position. Consistent with the foreign policy architecture that bore his name, he worked hard to articulate a *Verantwortungspolitik* for Germany in response to the Gulf crisis. Accordingly, Genscher pushed for a diplomatic solution, and later rationalized it in his memoirs:

I primarily favored the diplomatic response to the crisis offered by the UN Security Council. In the clarity of its resolutions, differences between East and West seemed to disappear. The agreement between the United States and the Soviet Union [on Security Council resolutions] was crucial because only through unity and decisiveness could Saddam Hussein be defeated.[26]

Meanwhile, the Free Democrats maintained a strict interpretationist position that Articles 24 and 87 barred Germany from military involvement outside of the NATO area.[27] The only way to resolve these matters, FDP leaders argued, was for the government collectively to consider a change in the Basic Law. An amendment would require a two-thirds majority in both the *Bundestag* and *Bundesrat*, but no one could guarantee such support at the time.[28]

Throughout August 1990, leaders of the major and junior parties in coalition disagreed about the best way to address constitutional constraints on German military action. At the same time, opposition leaders made it clear that they would oppose any attempt to change the constitution to allow German troops to participate in combat operations outside the NATO area. Social Democratic Party (SPD) *Fraktion* leader Hans-Ulrich Klose and Foreign Policy Spokesman Norbert Gansel argued that the Basic Law barred the German government from deploying troops to the Gulf region or any UN operations where they might face potential combat. They argued that the Social Democratic Party would oppose any government effort to deploy troops and would be very zealous in controlling any amendment negotiations.[29]

Disagreement Inside Political Parties

Most representatives of the major political parties in Germany lined up in support of their cabinet leaders. Kohl and Stoltenberg derived support from the Christian Democratic Union for their plan to gradually push for broader interpretations of the Basic Law for political reasons. From the outset, Conservative leaders supported a more liberal interpretation of the "use of force" clauses in the Basic Law, and stressed that it was essential for Germany to stand united with its allies in response to the crisis. CDU security policy spokesman Karl Lamers supported a broader interpretation wrapped in a benign mantle—he suggested that Germany should have the ability to back diplomacy with force, and stipulated that military instruments of statecraft were not going to be the most important.[30]

Some Conservative members of the Christian Socialist Union took even more extreme positions on the question, even though they were aware that they were neither supported by the majority of party members nor by the public. CSU leaders, including Theo Waigel, argued that a unified Germany should be prepared to assume a greater leadership role in world affairs, consistent with that of Great Britain and France. CSU officials argued that all constitutional restraints on German foreign policy activism should be eliminated as relics of a post-World War II reality that no longer held true.

As noted previously, the Free Democratic Party provided support for Genscher's stands on the Gulf crisis throughout the fall of 1990. Party leaders articulated their position that the government should construct an appropriate and forthright response to the crisis, but most stressed the legal barriers to the use of force. Members argued that any serious action would require a fundamental change in the German constitution, which would involve slow and serious deliberations about the future of German foreign policy. In so doing, the FDP was determined to reflect what they perceived as a general public reluctance to get involved in the Gulf crisis.[31]

However, the opposition Social Democratic Party, the Green/Alliance '90 Party, and the emergent Party of Democratic Socialism (PDS), stood united in their opposition to German participation in the Gulf conflict. Their members would not support German troop involvement in any combat operations, even those ostensibly authorized by Chapter VII of the UN Charter. They also agreed that any such action in the future would require a fundamental change in the Basic Law, which they would not support without careful stipulations and boundaries.[32] While there were some differences of opinion between the left and right wings of the SPD on these questions—some leaders of the *Bundestag Fraktion* including Gansel, Klose, and Bjorn Engholm have since admitted that they were personally willing to negotiate with the governing coalition on the matter and perhaps support participation in "blue helmet" UN peacekeeping operations—overall, the party stood firm in its opposition to a troop deployment.[33] Meanwhile, PDS and Green stands on the matter were a function of traditional party orientations—anti-militarist pacifism and a mistrust of government institutions and ambitions. They vocally opposed any talk of the use of force or a projected normalization of the German foreign policy profile.

Uncertainty in the German Polity

The Gulf crisis caught most Germans by surprise. Like their leaders, public attitudes toward the Gulf crisis were characterized by a preoccupation with domestic affairs and the unification process. The average German was confronted by a series of domestic developments in the summer of 1990 that were perceived to be much more important than a distant war. After all, Chancellor Kohl and Soviet leader Mikhael Gorbachev had just reached an historic agreement on unification in July, and a series of related negotiations were underway between East and West Germany and with key allies. Most Germans also were monitoring closely developments in currency union and market stability. Important *Länder* elections were scheduled for October and the first all-German election was set for December 1990.[34]

Nevertheless, the Gulf crisis slowly crept into German public awareness and produced mixed sentiments about a proper German response to the invasion. Public opinion polls conducted in the fall of 1990 indicated that while a majority of Germans supported a multilateral effort to evict Iraqi troops from Kuwait, an even stronger majority opposed German participation in the operation.[35] In a press conference that fall, Genscher characterized German public attitudes as weak. Furthermore, he concluded that the government was in an accordingly weak position both internally and externally given that "the war fit neither the political needs nor the mood of the people."[36]

Results of public opinion surveys about German attitudes began to appear in the media in late August and September, showing that the public exhibited differing viewpoints on the crisis. Some 65% of West German respondents said that the Iraqi invasion of Kuwait was a violation of international law and supported United Nations efforts to reverse this action. Only 28% believed that Germany should participate in any multinational mission to protect the Gulf region through the use of force, while 70% of the public opposed direct German involvement.[37]

The Government Response to the Gulf Crisis

German leaders weighed their options for response to the Gulf crisis and the direct requests for assistance from key allies. A survey of domestic political conditions at the time provided clear guidance for Germany: Cabinet leaders disagreed on the need for (and the constitutionality of) such a troop deployment, parties were deeply divided on the issue, and the German people opposed any consideration of the use of force.

At a key meeting on August 20, 1990, Kohl, Genscher, and Stoltenberg discussed options for a German response to U.S., NATO, and UN pressures for action. They agreed that provisions of the Basic Law prevented Germany from deploying troops to the multinational force in the Gulf and also prevented Germany from participating in any direct way in UN-sponsored military sanctions in the region. They quietly agreed that the government should consider ways to address the constitutionality constraint in the future. Records of that meeting show that German leaders clearly viewed their response to the Gulf crisis through the lens of the crucial and ongoing Two-Plus-Four negotiations.[38]

After several more weeks of internal debate, CDU and FDP cabinet members agreed on a compromise in mid-September 1990. Leaders announced that Germany would provide economic aid to those states most affected by the invasion, and logistical and financial support for the military coalition aligned against Iraqi forces—but they would not deploy troops to the region. Germany followed the lead of other EC members in pledging $2 billion in nonmilitary assistance to countries in the Gulf region including Israel, Egypt, Turkey, Jordan, and Syria. Turkey would also receive about $1.2 billion in military assistance, while Israel received more than $500 million. In time, the German government committed a total of $11.5 billion to the coalition effort, about one sixth of the total cost of the coalition efforts.[39] In addition, the German *Bundeswehr* provided extensive support for the movement of U.S. and British forces to the Gulf including the U.S. VII Corps, and the 7th Armoured Brigade and 1st Armoured Division of the British Army of the Rhine.[40]

This "checkbook diplomacy" met with general approval inside Germany. Cabinet leaders endorsed the action as the right measure for the time, and some members of the opposition SPD and Green/Alliance '90 parties even offered their support for the coalition action. SPD leader Hans-Jochen Vogel stated that the Social Democrats strongly supported any efforts made to stay out of the war and achieve a peaceful resolution. There was broad consensus that financial and logistical support represented the limits of German actions based on established constitutional barriers.[41]

OPERATION DESERT STORM

The German financial contribution to Operation Desert Shield was quite significant, and allied leaders seemed to accept the political and domestic constraints on further German activism in 1990. The international military coalition assembled in the Gulf for the operation included troops from dozens of countries. United States forces in the Gulf alone totaled 200,000 by November, the United Kingdom deployed 35,000 soldiers, France 15,000, and the Arab League had mobilized more than 100,000. Other states, including Pakistan, Morocco, and Bangladesh contributed thousands of troops, while hundreds of troops were sent from Senegal, Niger, Honduras, and Argentina. Material and equipment to support Desert Shield was provided by countries as diverse as Syria, Bangladesh, the Soviet Union, Greece, Canada, and Portugal.[42]

The Persian Gulf crisis intensified in three significant ways from November 1990 to February 1991, prompting a new round of international pressure for German action. First, Iraqi leader Saddam Hussein implemented plans to absorb Kuwait into his country by declaring Kuwait officially the "nineteenth province of Iraq," closing all embassies in Kuwait City, and expelling diplomats and foreign citizens. Furthermore, Iraq resisted all international efforts to challenge these actions, and

Hussein and his Bathist party leadership in Iraq became ever more defi-
ant towards the international community. Iraqi troops occupying Kuwait
were reinforced and resupplied, and they began to develop strong defensive positions, communication and supply networks, and artillery positions for a long military standoff in the region.

Western leaders developed a new consensus that Hussein might have
to be driven out of Kuwait by force. In the UN Security Council, there
was growing agreement among the permanent members (including
unprecedented cooperation between the U.S. and Soviet delegations)
that current resolutions focused on economic sanctions were having little impact on Iraq. On November 29, 1990, diplomats passed the historic
UN Security Council Resolution #678, which authorized member states
to use "all necessary means" to enforce full Iraqi compliance with UN resolutions by midnight on January 15, 1991, if this had not been accom-
plished through peaceful means.[43]

Working with the UN, Bush administration officials also resolved to
turn the tide of events in the Gulf region by threatening to use military
force. On November 8, 1990, President Bush announced a doubling of
U.S. ground forces in the Gulf region to 430,000. This would include the
deployment of two more armored divisions and elements of a third, an
infantry division, a Marine Expeditionary Force, three aircraft carrier battle groups, an additional fourteen fighter squadrons, two bomber
squadrons, and eleven support squadrons. These changes in military
deployments were clearly designed to allow for offensive operations if
Iraq did not comply with UN Security Council resolutions and the
imposed ultimatum for withdrawal of forces from Kuwait.[44]

The Bush administration's decision to change the structure and orientation of the multinational force gathering in the Gulf prompted German
officials to revisit the question of allied support. Just days after the U.S.
decision, Chancellor Kohl traveled to Washington for an official state
visit. President Bush and top officials took the opportunity to pressure the
German government for a renewed (and intensified) commitment to the
multinational force. As before, the chancellor was sympathetic to U.S.
and allied interests in the region, and he pledged that Germany would do
all it could to support the multinational force. As before, Kohl also
informed Bush that Germany had to reckon with significant domestic
political constraints on further action. Nevertheless, Bush administration
officials were satisfied that the German leadership would reconsider its
commitment to the western response to the Gulf crisis.[45]

The crisis in the Persian Gulf also became a challenge to the security of
Turkey and the NATO alliance. As the Iraqi war machine gathered
strength in November and December, western leaders began to recognize
an imminent threat to Turkey, which borders Iraq to the north. Turkey
might become engaged in a spillover of the conventional conflict, they

feared, with more than 500,000 Iraqi soldiers positioned a few hundred kilometers from their border. Intelligence reports surfaced in the fall which suggested that Turkey had become a target for Iraqi intermediate-range ballistic missiles, which could be armed with chemical or biological warheads.

On December 17, 1990, NATO foreign and defense ministers met in Brussels for a special session devoted to security on the southern flank of the alliance. The ministers agreed that Iraq posed a real threat to Turkish security and that NATO allies should be prepared to come to the aid of Turkey if it were attacked by Iraq (consistent with Article V of the North Atlantic Treaty).[46] Concurrent negotiations in NATO's Defense Planning Committee produced an unprecedented agreement by the alliance that Turkish government authorities would have operational control of defense policy if that country was attacked, and negotiators designed contingency plans for pre-positioned troop deployments to Turkey from allied countries. The next day, many of the same leaders convened for a high-level meeting of the European Community in Brussels, where they pledged their support for Turkey in this time of crisis.

Germany was directly affected by the widening of this crisis to Turkey. The Defense Planning Committee contingency for pre-positioned troop deployment included orders for an Allied Command Europe mobile force (AMF) to be deployed within weeks.[47] The AMF contingency had been drawn up years earlier, and included plans for a squadron of German soldiers (consisting of up to 800 troops) to support the deployment of eighteen German fighter jets and air defense units equipped with HAWK and ROLAND missiles. According to the contingency, these troops were to be mobilized and deployed directly to the NATO airbase in Erhac, Turkey, when needed. Like Operation Desert Shield, this contingency created an immediate and serious strategic dilemma for the German government. The Turkish request for military assistance would conflict with differing interpretations of Basic Law Articles 24 and 87. In this case, however, NATO would be requesting military assistance consistent with Article V of the Atlantic Treaty and, customarily, with standing political interpretations of the boundaries of the Basic Law.[48]

When some political leaders expressed hesitation about a German troop deployment in the immediate aftermath of the Defense Planning Committee agreement, Turkish officials went public with their request for German action, stressing the importance of their bilateral relationship with Germany and alliance obligations. Early in the crisis, Turkish President Turgut Ozal publicly stated his wishes that Germany uphold its commitments to the alliance and to Turkey, and stressing themes such as "friendly obligation" and "reasonable requirements" in his rhetoric.[49] By January 1991, however, President Ozal had grown quite impatient and opined that "Germany has become so rich and fat that it has forgotten its fighting spirit."[50] While some leaders remained privately skeptical of the need for the AMF deployment, the German cabinet began deliberating on the question in the winter months of 1990 and 1991.[51]

A third dimension of this strategic dilemma was the revelation that some German firms had been involved in the design and construction of Iraqi chemical and biological laboratories, and had aided in research projects to extend the range of Iraqi ballistic missiles. At the end of 1990, investigators began to unearth information showing that German companies had established legitimate business relationships with Iraqi firms to design and build laboratories that could, potentially, have dual-use capabilities that would enable the production of chemical and biological agents.[52]

The news of the German connection to the Iraqi war machine rocked Bonn and many western capitals. Broadly speaking, this news led to questions about the reliability and loyalty of the German government in the NATO alliance. Germany faced intense criticism and blame for contributing to the development of the Iraqi war machine, and some claimed that Germany shared responsibility for creating the Gulf crisis in the first place. These allegations also directly threatened the special relationship between Germany and Israel that had been established after World War II, because Israel was widely expected to be the primary target of Iraqi ballistic missiles.[53] This development threw a serious new wrinkle in the Gulf crisis for Germany. As Ronald Asmus stated:

When the Germans were confronted with the reality of Iraqi missiles falling on Tel Aviv, it triggered a complex psychological and political reaction that helped produce a major shift in policy. The public revelation that German firms had illegally contributed to the Iraqi military buildup, particularly that German-origin technology had allowed Iraq to expand its chemical weapons stock and to extend the range of its Scud missiles, combined with German historical guilt rooted in the Holocaust, created a political imperative for Germany to act.[54]

These three dimensions of the Gulf crisis did indeed create intense new pressures for Germany to act in the fall and winter months of 1990 and 1991. The United States government stepped up its request for German contributions to a new offensive force structure in the region, and the UN Security Council declared its resolve to use force to overturn the Iraqi invasion of Kuwait. Meanwhile, threats to Turkey demanded attention, and Israel appeared to be in the crosshairs of Iraqi medium-range weapons that had been augmented through indirect German contributions to the Iraqi war machine. The German government recognized the scale of this crisis and debated new ways to bolster regional security.[55]

Domestic Constraints

German leaders struggled to balance internal and external demands in this new phase of the crisis.[56] Chancellor Kohl and Defense Minister Stoltenberg repeatedly reminded the international community of Germany's past financial pledges to the crisis response, also indicating that they would support further German activism. Consistent with past deliberations, Kohl quietly favored a broader interpretation of the Basic Law and a reasonable German military and financial commitment to respond to the Gulf crisis. There is evidence to suggest that Kohl and Stoltenberg dominated cabinet discussions of Germany's obligation to Turkey through the NATO alliance, indicating that they felt obligated to provide the requested assistance through the AMF.[57] Not all Conservative leaders agreed with this position, however. In late January, German President Richard von Weizsäcker responded to international pressure for troop deployments to the Gulf region by jokingly questioning whether "the world really wants to rediscover how well German soldiers can fight?"[58]

Hans-Dietrich Genscher was again a pivotal player in foreign policy decision making, walking the tightrope between external and internal demands. Genscher was extremely conscious of how important this crisis was in terms of East–West and alliance relations, and he attempted to quietly steer German foreign policy activism without disrupting the status quo. After some deliberations, Genscher supported the deployment of the *Luftwaffe* squadron and 200 soldiers for the mobile force, and was later convinced to support air defense units to be deployed from Germany to Turkey and Israel. The foreign minister was extremely concerned about the allegations of German involvement with the Iraqi war machine, particularly in the context of the threat of genocide against Israel.[59] Genscher also felt it imperative that Germany commit some form of assistance to Turkey consistent with Article V of the NATO treaty, and he did not relish the thought of his country as the sole defector from alliance commitments if Turkish security were actually threatened. In an interview in early February 1991, Genscher reflected on this fragile balance of internal and external pressures for action:

German foreign policy is holding course. Holding course means for us, above all, standing at Israel's side in this deathly threat in historic and moral responsibility . . . we are helping Israel with the desired defense weapons. Germany affirmed its unrestricted solidarity with the allies who are fighting on behalf of the community of states. This solidarity is expressed not only by words. We are carrying our share in the common burdens. The constitutional restriction which still exists concerning our military participation in UN actions is certainly not an expression of a lack of responsibility and shirking. This restriction was well-founded for a divided country as a consequence of our history. . . . Holding course also means that no one has reason to doubt Germany's reliability in the alliance. Our soldiers who are stationed in Turkey as an expression of our solidarity with our alliance partner must be protected.[60]

Among political parties, this intensification of the Gulf crisis produced a serious reconsideration of German foreign policy latitude, but it also exposed a series of divisions within all major party organizations. Chancellor Kohl and key Conservatives expressed solidarity with the West and support for a more serious German contribution to regional security, but some members of the Christian Democratic Union opposed this course. Foreign policy speaker for the CDU/CSU *Fraktion*, Karl-Heinz Hornhues, argued on the floor of the *Bundestag* that "it must be clear that the unified Germany is a normal state and should accept its responsibility in the international community." CDU and CSU officials made it clear that the Basic Law need not be amended to allow the deployment of German troops to such UN-sponsored operations in the future, and they left little room for negotiation of new constraints on the German use of force.[61] Meanwhile, CDU General Secretary Volker Rühe spoke out in opposition to Genscher's policy of appeasement of U.S., NATO, and Turkish interests in the Gulf crisis, arguing that Germany must assert its own foreign policy stand on the question.[62]

The Free Democrats also debated whether Germany should respond to deeper obligations in the Gulf region.[63] While Genscher supported the basic German obligations to the NATO alliance and dominated party discussion on the matter, there was disagreement in the ranks. Several leaders of the FDP, including Otto Graf Lambsdorff, publicly questioned the grounds on which the government could decide to deploy German troops to the region.[64] In an interesting attempt to split the party on the question, Lambsdorff contended that there would be a technical difference between a missile and ground attack against Turkey, and only the latter would necessitate German troop deployments consistent with NATO obligations.[65]

Some of the most interesting debates about the proper German response to the latest provocations in the Gulf region occurred inside the opposition Social Democratic Party. The SPD traditionally had provided support for collective security and UN initiatives, but the establishment of a military force in the Gulf region for possible offensive operations presented them with a real conundrum. Moderate members of the SPD, led by *Fraktion* Chairman Hans-Ulrich Klose, argued that Germany must demonstrate its solidarity for the coalition in the Gulf.[66] Former Chancellor Willy Brandt also declared that Germany should be represented in the Gulf.[67] Meanwhile, party leader Oskar Lafontaine condemned the government plan to send German troops to Turkey, opposed the financial pledges of support, and challenged the very principle of the coalition use of force to eject Iraqi forces from Kuwait.[68] SPD Party Chairman Hans-Jochen Vogel interpreted this as German support for offensive military operations outside the NATO area, something expressly forbidden by the Basic Law.[69] He articulated the position of many opponents to government action in a *Bundestag* speech on January 31, 1991:

With regard to the Gulf conflict, I say that the reasons that we rejected military action before the expiration of the ultimatum and advocated the continuation of sanctions have not been refuted so far. The foreseeable dangers and the risks that were and are connected with military action have by no means been warded off. The decisions of the government that were made after 15 January 1991, were not what we wished and advocated for. . . . The participation of German soldiers in the Gulf War is out of the question. We reject it because our constitution does not permit it.[70]

In an interesting reference to the external pressures for Germany to act, he added:

I state very clearly here—and this is also addressed to NATO Secretary General Manfred Wörner: Whether the Federal Republic can and will participate in military measures on the basis of UN resolutions is its decision alone. This cannot be decided by the Turkish president or the NATO Secretary General. . . . We reserve the right to take all appropriate steps to preserve this position which is a crucial principle of parliamentary democracy.[71]

Gerhard Schröder, SPD Prime Minister of Lower Saxony, also became an outspoken opponent of government action, sharing Vogel's resentment of the international pressure that had been focused on Germany for some time. Schröder publicly lashed out at British criticism of German foreign policy in a very undiplomatic statement:

I find the United Kingdom a great place and because the pubs close at 10:30 pm, then I have to watch a lot of stupid movies on television, movies that made me angry because of the way in which we Germans were portrayed as especially warlike and bellicose. . . . I didn't find this right and I don't think it is an accurate portrayal of the Germans. But now, now when the majority of Germans are saying 'We are against war,' this isn't right either. You know what really makes me mad about this British campaign—and I find it undignified—is the way in which we react in Germany, namely in a subservient fashion as if they were right. They are not right, and the English are using this conflict to work through some other problems that they have. I think it is really time that we say to them, and I am happy to do this: Why don't you organize a rational social welfare society and then we can talk to one another as Europeans on an equal basis, including controversial questions such as these.[72]

While sharply critical, Schröder spoke for many Germans in the winter of 1990–91 who were afraid of being drawn into an expensive and potentially dangerous conflict without a clearly articulated definition of national interests.

Threats to Israel divided the Social Democratic Party and the political left in Germany. The opposition had long stood against the use of force and in favor of humanitarianism and diplomacy. Now they were faced with a threat to Israel that seemed partially sponsored by German firms, presenting a terrible contradiction in policy options. As the crisis intensified, opposition leaders were presented with the difficult choice between supporting the use of force, and supporting Israelis against potential genocide from ballistic missiles tipped with biological or chemical agents.

Schröder again spoke out on why he and key SPD leaders refused to change their minds about the necessity of the Gulf War in light of direct threats to Israel:

I said no because I was simultaneously being asked to support Israel and to support war. I am not in favor and can not be in favor of war. . . . The logic of war must be understood. War means that when Saddam Hussein uses chemical weapons, on the other side, on the side of the allies, the use of nuclear weapons will be discussed, and when one thinks it through to its logical conclusion, the use of nuclear weapons can not be excluded. This, however, would be a scenario in which all of the Middle East, including Israel, would be destroyed.

Faced with this Faustian dilemma, several prominent leftist intellectuals, including Jürgen Habermas, singer Wolf Biermann, and writer Hans Magnus Enzensberger, broke ranks with the anti-war movement and publicly supported the use of force in the Gulf War.[73] Key Green Party leaders, including Petra Kelly, Joschka Fischer, and Micha Brumlik, also offered to support Israel in light of the magnitude of Iraqi threats and contended that the use of force might be necessary in a larger effort to "liberate Kuwait from evil."[74]

From November 1990 to January 1991, there was widespread public opposition to German involvement in the Persian Gulf conflict—and public resistance seemed to grow as the shadow of war loomed larger. The symbols of German opposition in the late fall of 1990 were anti-war demonstrations in major cities, public opinion polls, and a few stories of dissent inside the German military. Public protests steadily gathered momentum throughout this period, and an estimated 200,000 Germans gathered in Bonn on January 26, 1991, for one of the largest protests of the Gulf crisis.[75] At the same time, a January 18, 1991 poll conducted by the German Infas Institute found that 79% of Germans believed that the use of force against Iraq was wrong. Another survey conducted the same week found that 68% of Germans feared that the fallout from the destruction of chemical and nuclear facilities could threaten German cities.[76] At the same time, public support for NATO had reached an historic low—with only 53% of Germans believing that the alliance was essential for German security.[77] Finally, as an extension of growing public opposition to the war, stories began to appear in the media about dissent inside the ranks of the German military. In one instance, several

Luftwaffe officers who had been ordered to deploy to Turkey as part of the AMF went public with their opposition to government action. They claimed the deployment was unconstitutional because Turkey had not been attacked and "Germany might be acting provocatively in sending warplanes there."[78]

In retrospect, experts have suggested that western perceptions of the German public's intense opposition to the war were shaped mostly by a vocal minority of opposition and intense media coverage. There is some evidence to support this interpretation in the surprisingly rapid turn-around in popular sentiment that occurred during the last two weeks of January 1991. Public opposition seemed to evaporate after the onset of the air war in the Gulf, when Iraqi forces began launching intermediate-range Scud missiles against neighboring countries, including Israel. In this, citizens of the world witnessed their worst nightmares, with intense media coverage of Israeli citizens huddled in sealed rooms with gas masks, fearing that the next strike on Tel-Aviv would include chemical or biological warheads. Put simply, many experts believe that these strikes provoked a sea change in German public opinion about the necessity of the use of force in the Gulf region.

Suddenly, marches that had originally been scheduled to oppose the use of force in the Gulf War became marches in support of Israeli security and highly critical of the newly revealed German connection to the Iraqi military machine. Germans now felt a more serious sense of responsibility for events in the Gulf.[79]

By late January 1991, one survey of German citizens showed that 71% approved of allied military action against Iraq, and only 21% were opposed.[80] Victory for the western coalition was forecast by 82%, and 57% of Germans now supported the strong financial contribution to the allied effort as the right and proper response to this strategic dilemma.[81] By early February 1991, an Institute for Demoskopie survey found a strong majority of Germans in favor of the use of military force to eject Iraqi troops from Kuwait. The poll also found that 56% of Germans strongly favored or favored the deployment of *Bundeswehr* troops to Turkey as part of NATO obligations, while 35% were opposed or very opposed.[82]

The Gulf crisis also prompted a deeper reflection in the polity about Germany's role in international politics. Polls in the spring of 1991 found a steady pro-American sentiment, with 70% of Germans supporting a strong bilateral relationship. In 1991, 69% of Germans said that they believed NATO to be essential for their security, up from 53% the year before.[83] At a broader level, 59% of respondents said that "Germany should pursue a more active role in world affairs." An astonishing 88% of respondents favored German support for UN humanitarian operations in 1991, and 58% said that Germany should participate in UN peacekeeping missions.[84]

The Government Response to the Crisis

This phase of the Gulf crisis presented the German government with a set of complex issues and decisions. As leaders surveyed international conditions in January and February 1991, they observed intense pressures for a stronger German response to the crisis in requests from the United States to support the allied coalition forces, challenges to NATO in Turkey, and serious threats to Israeli security through Scud missile attacks. However, as leaders surveyed domestic conditions in the spring of 1991, they saw lingering differences of opinion inside the cabinet, division in the major party organizations, and shifting popular opinion about the use of force. The Gulf War was clearly a seminal event in the evolution of German foreign policy.

Officials agreed that Germany should respond to the intensifying Gulf crisis (and impending war) by adopting a set of common principles, including:[85]

1. close joint cooperation with the United States on a solution to the crisis;
2. German dependability and loyalty to key allies;
3. support for, but not participation in the use of force for the restoration of the peace and the independence of Kuwait;
4. compensation for the absence of troops in a "comparatively high, nonmilitary operation to support the defense of the alliance";
5. special efforts to support the security of Israel due to historical responsibility;
6. the Gulf crisis should not be allowed to endanger the German unification process and cooperation with the Soviet Union.[86]

Government leaders used these principles to respond the Gulf crisis on three levels. First, Germany stepped up its support for the United States and the allied coalition in the Gulf. Cabinet leaders agreed to increase their support for coalition operations in the Gulf and to dramatically ease restrictions on U.S. military activity in bases in Germany. The U.S./NATO Rhein-Main airbase in Frankfurt had already become one of the most important installations supporting the coalition deployment in the Gulf, and Germany pledged to continue their logistical support for operations.[87]

The government agreed to the transfer of *Bundeswehr* troops for support operations outside the immediate theater of operations. The Defense Ministry announced in early February 1991 that German naval forces would be moved from the English Channel and Atlantic Ocean operations to the eastern Mediterranean to cover NATO operations in that sector while U.S. forces were forward deployed to the Gulf and Red Sea. This eastward deployment would include 2,200 sailors in a flotilla of seventeen ships including frigates, destroyers, and support vessels. According to the ministry, the mission was to "participate in NATO's broad-ranging sea reconnaissance and to secure international shipping routes and thereby continue its training." Later, eleven ships and 900 sailors from two minesweeping flotillas, normally assigned to the English Channel, were transferred to operations in the Persian Gulf.[88]

In January and February 1991, German officials announced significant increases in their financial and material contributions to the coalition war effort. Bonn contributed $6.5 billion in cash and in-kind deliveries to support Operation Desert Storm, equal to approximately 12% of all war costs. $300 million of this contribution was direct payment for the chartering of civilian aircraft to deploy troops to the Gulf region during the last days of the force structure buildup. During the spring, Germany also contributed $500 million to Great Britain and $200 million to France to support the costs of the war. German officials also announced an increase in humanitarian relief aid for states in the theater that were affected by the war and economic sanctions, including Jordan, Egypt, Turkey, and Israel. In terms of material support, Germany provided the allied coalition with 70 "Spürnpanzer Fuchs" reconnaissance vehicles designed to detect radiation, chemical, or biological agents on the battlefield. In addition, Germany donated more than 4,000 transportation vehicles and large amounts of ammunition for tanks and artillery.[89]

Germany's declaration of solidarity with the NATO alliance and Turkey comprised the second level of its response to the crisis. After weeks of internal debate, the cabinet announced on January 2, 1991, that Germany would respond to the Turkish and NATO requests for assistance by deploying 18 Alpha-Jet fighters and more than 200 German soldiers to a NATO airbase in Erhac, Turkey, for the duration of the crisis.[90] This was presented to the German polity as a natural extension of their commitment to NATO, but the move actually contributed to serious disagreements inside and outside the government. Several leaders of the FDP, including Otto Graf Lambsdorff, publicly questioned the grounds on which the government had made its decision. Meanwhile, leaders of the SPD proclaimed their opposition to the deployment as a violation of the Basic Law and as "the wrong decision," with Green Party leaders also condemning the move.[91] As a compromise, the Defense Ministry did stipulate that Germans would not be deployed to areas of potential conflict and would not be ordered into conflict by Turkish or NATO commanders without prior consent by the German government and NATO alliance.[92] In addition, Germany agreed to the deployment of Roland and Hawk anti-aircraft missile units, as well as about 800 troops to protect airfields in Turkey with AMF deployments.[93] Three reconnaissance planes with 125 ground personnel were also forward deployed to the base.[94]

Finally, the German government strengthened its support for Israel. The revelations of ties between German industry and the Iraqi war machine served to change public attitudes inside Germany and cemented the resolve of government leaders to support Israeli security at all costs. In January 1991, the government announced that it would provide almost $200 million in humanitarian aid to Israel and would deploy Fuchs reconnaissance vehicles and Patriot missile defense batteries to Israel for the duration of the conflict.[95]

Genscher and Kohl made a series of public statements describing Germany's commitment to Israeli security and sovereignty, and a number of political leaders from across the political spectrum joined the government in this expression of solidarity. Iraqi forces eventually fired 39 missiles at Israeli civilian targets in January and February 1991, with Tel Aviv taking the largest number of hits. As predicted, this created a political crisis and the Israelis were determined to retaliate. Instead, some 15% of total Desert Storm operational resources became devoted to finding and destroying mobile Scud launchers.[96] Finally, in an interesting twist, Foreign Minister Genscher traveled to Israel as a sign of Germany's commitment to her ally, but he did not enjoy the public reception he had anticipated. Genscher was instead met by angry protests and heckling (which received a great deal of coverage by the German media). Upon his return, the German cabinet approved another $600 million in defense assistance for Israel that included chemical and biological warfare protection. Later, the government announced a plan to finance Israeli acquisition of two submarines and several air defense systems. Kohl and Genscher had clearly demonstrated German support for Israeli security at this crucial point in the crisis.[97]

German financial and material contributions were significant in the Persian Gulf War, which began on January 16, 1991, with massive air assaults against Iraqi command and control facilities, infrastructure, and defensive positions in the theater.[98] Coalition forces quickly gained air supremacy and implemented a coalition sortie rate averaging 2,000 flights per day.[99] The ground war began on February 22, 1991, after 39 days of air assaults. Operations were based on coalition strategies for "maneuver and envelopment."[100] A cease-fire was declared on February 27, 1991.[101]

Looking back, the Gulf War clearly had a profound effect on the German debate about a new security policy construct. The quick coalition victory served, in fact, to undermine much of the domestic political opposition to a German presence in future multilateral operations. Other factors also helped to bring about a change in the domestic political climate in Germany. The achievement of unification facilitated renewed strength in foreign policy behavior and shifted attention away from the long-awaited unification process. Also, the CDU-CSU/FDP governing coalition won a combined majority of support in the December 1990 national elections, providing further political room to maneuver.

THE KURDISH REFUGEE CRISIS AND OPERATION PROVIDE COMFORT

Historical Background

The international community celebrated the defeat of Iraq and the withdrawal of Iraqi occupation forces from Kuwait in February and March 1991, but the crisis in the Persian Gulf was not yet over. The Kurdish refugee crisis represented an unforeseen consequence of shifting balances of power in the region, and a foreshadowing of future strategic dilemmas for Germany and its western allies.

In late February 1991, members of Kurdish and Shi'ite minorities in Iraq began uprisings against government forces, designed to achieve regional autonomy by taking advantage of perceived Iraqi military weakness. Shi'ite groups had long attempted to secure autonomy for themselves in the southeastern part of Iraq, and this struggle had played out well before, during, and after the Iran–Iraq War (1980–1988). However, in a surprisingly rapid and efficient manner in the wake of the Gulf War, Saddam Hussein dispatched surviving divisions of the Republican Guard to the region to end the uprising. The Kurdish uprising in northern Iraq quickly became a central concern for the international community in the weeks after the Gulf War, and eventually drew western powers into the region once again.

As a culturally distinct ethnic national group, the Kurds shared a common religion in Islam, a common Persian dialect, and a common historical experience—centuries of conflict with nearby groups, empires, and state governments.[102] By 1991, some 25 million Kurds lived in the mountainous region north and east of the Tigris and Euphrates Rivers basin, which included the contiguous areas of Turkey, Iran, Iraq, and Syria.[103] In 1991, 4.5 million Kurds lived in Iraq, constituting about 23% of the total Iraqi population.[104] Since the founding of the Iraqi state in 1920, however, Kurdish groups had skirmished with government forces in the north in regular attempts to define an autonomous region for themselves.

The Iran–Iraq War (1980–1988) provided the Kurds of northern Iraq with the opening they had been waiting for, and in 1987 they rallied forces and launched a full-scale guerrilla war. The Iraqi military response to the Kurdish uprising was swift and strong. Iraqi officials publicly defined an area in the northern part of their country, which included more than 2,000 villages, that they declared henceforth open to direct, indiscriminate attacks. In one of the more brutal moves in the war, Iraqi officials issued orders in June 1987 that included two points:

1. The corps commanders shall carry out sporadic bombardments using artillery, helicopters, and aircraft, at all times of the day or night, in order to kill the

largest number of persons present in those prohibited zones, keeping us informed of the results.

2. All persons captured in those villages shall be detained and interrogated by the security services and those between the ages of 15 and 70 shall be executed after any useful information has been obtained from them.[105]

Tens of thousands of Kurds died in this campaign, including large numbers of fatalities from chemical weapons attacks that were ordered by Saddam Hussein.[106]

During the Persian Gulf crisis, and concurrent with the buildup of Operation Desert Shield, several Kurdish groups began planning for another partisan war against Iraqi forces. These plans were supported by U.S. intelligence agencies, and western governments encouraged two key factions of Kurdish partisan groups in northern Iraq to join forces: the Kurdish Democratic Party (KDP) and the splinter rival group, the Patriotic Union of Kurdistan (PUK). Given the proper alignment of circumstances, they might be able to defeat Iraqi forces and declare an independent Kurdistan in northern Iraq.

In mid-March 1991, Kurdish groups in northern Iraq publicly declared their desire for political autonomy and their willingness to fight for it. As promised, key Kurdish factions banded together, proclaimed a federated state, established a parliamentary body, and declared their wish to be rid of the Iraqi troops.[107] Instead of accepting the loss of regional influence, however, Saddam Hussein ordered 30,000 soldiers from the Republican Guard to crush the rebellion. Kurdish partisans engaged the troops but were generally ill-prepared to confront armored assaults and attacks from the air.[108] By the end of March, hundreds of thousands of Kurdish civilians were forced to flee the fighting while partisans attempted desperate holding actions. By early April 1991, the fight was effectively over, and more than 500,000 Kurdish refugees from Iraq were huddled at the Turkish border; another million flooded into Iran after harrowing trips through the mountainous border region.[109] Within three weeks, more than 2.5 million Iraqi Kurds had fled the violent repression of the Republican Guard and sought shelter, food, and protection in the north.

The western response to the brewing humanitarian crisis was aided by the significant western military force already deployed to the region and by the presence of the international press. Television news cameras began documenting the refugee crisis almost immediately, supplying the world with images of a pending humanitarian catastrophe.[110]

On April 5, 1991, the United Nations Security Council passed Resolution #688 which insisted that "Iraq allow immediate access by international humanitarian organizations to all those in need of assistance in all parts of Iraq."[111] The resolution also established a no-fly zone in the northern sector of Iraq, to be enforced by an allied air operation, and they banned the presence of any Iraqi military personnel in the protected area. In some ways the resolution was historic—it provided for a protection zone for humanitarian relief operations in northern Iraq (in direct violation of Iraqi sovereignty), and it provided the Kurds with temporary, *de facto* regional autonomy. In so doing, it set a precedent for future operations.

In conjunction with the UN Security Council resolutions, the Bush administration began to explore the proper response to the conflict. Secretary of State James Baker traveled to the border region between Turkey and Iraq and met directly with Kurdish refugees who described their personal tragedies and pled for western assistance.[112] Soon thereafter, Bush and Baker announced that the U.S. government would lead Operational Provide Comfort, a relief mission designed to deal with short- and long-term concerns of the Kurdish population in the region. The government announced that it would deploy 10,000 soldiers to the region and create a defensive line around the Iraqi city of Mosul in the north. The U.S. government and key allies also formally declared a "no-fly zone" for Iraqi fixed- and rotary-wing aircraft north of the 36th parallel.

At the outset, Bush again returned to the practice of "rolodex diplomacy" that had been so effective in assembly of the Gulf War coalition.[113] The president contacted Helmut Kohl and Hans-Dietrich Genscher in early April 1991, and personally requested German participation in the humanitarian relief operations in northern Iraq, Turkey, and Iran.[114] On April 16, German and U.S. officials met to discuss the dangerous situation for the Kurds, and President Bush publicly called for a widening of the relief operation to include troop contingents from multiple governments.[115]

Domestic Conditions

The Kurdish refugee crisis was somewhat different from the previous strategic dilemmas in the Persian Gulf, and the German government began to consider direct participation in Operation Provide Comfort almost immediately. Chancellor Kohl saw the events of March and April 1991 in a different light than Operations Desert Shield and Desert Storm. This time, he believed, the crisis seemed to meet the standing definition of criteria suitable for the deployment of German forces outside the NATO area. Kohl believed that it would represent a classic UN blue-helmet peacekeeping mission, sanctioned through Security Council resolutions and carried out with the consent of the Turkish and Iranian governments. In a speech before the *Bundestag*, Kohl asserted that Germany had greater responsibility to respond to this humanitarian crisis:

A united Germany must assume more responsibility in the realm of security under a European roof, and also of course in the contact of the United Nations. I am in favor of making this possible this year. It is obvious that we will accept the responsibilities that arise from our membership in the United Nations. This means that we must also be willing to participate in military actions in the context of the United Nations for the preservation or re-establishment of peace as well as the maintenance of international law.[116]

Kohl and key Conservative leaders agreed, however, that in order for Germany to identify its future role in dealing with international security issues and its future identity and role in Europe, it was essential for the Basic Law to allow Germany to participate in future military actions.[117] In March 1991, Kohl argued publicly that "Germans can no longer ignore the question of what we can contribute to peace outside of Europe. We must come to terms with the greater responsibility which we have gained through the overcoming of partition and the regaining of our full sovereignty . . . this is demanded by the world.[118]

Kohl's solution was to consider ways to widen the existing interpretation of German foreign policy latitude that would allow future German deployments abroad without domestic constraints. In this debate, Kohl's position was public and clear:

"I have clearly stated my preference before that a land with the stature of Germany with its 80 million people can take a greater position in world politics and greater responsibility in United Nations activities."[119]

Conservatives were also quite aware that key segments of the polity, including SPD, PDS, and Green/Alliance '90 Party leaders, opposed any amendment to the Basic Law that would allow a wider interpretation of government latitude on the use of force question. This was a particular concern given the fact that amendment to the Basic Law would require a two-thirds majority in both houses of the German parliament—including the *Bundesrat*, where the SPD had established control through regional constituency elections.

Defense Minister Gerhard Stoltenberg supported German participation in Operation Provide Comfort and a more liberal interpretation of the Basic Law. A close political ally of Kohl's, he said in an interview from early 1991:

Iraqi aggression against the small sheikdom of Kuwait has made it clear that the end of the Cold War does not necessarily mean the arrival of permanent peace. Peace in Europe does not automatically translate into peace for Europe. The increasing international intertwinement of states has reduced the physical distances also in times of crisis and conflict. Events in distant regions can rapidly affect one's own security either through a destabilization of the international order or through the direct endangering of the basis for our economic and social order. The increasing proliferation of weapons of mass destruction and modern, long-range weapons systems has placed the direct military threats to Europe from beyond the continent into the realm of the feasible.[120]

Conservative leaders clearly had considered more liberal interpretations of the Basic Law for some time, and the Gulf War experience seemed to crystallize their resolve to implement changes. Other cabinet leaders were, however, more circumspect in their assessments of the timing and need for change.

Hans-Dietrich Genscher had spent much of the winter repeating his conviction that the German government could not deploy troops to participate in Operations Desert Shield and Desert Storm because of restrictions in the Basic Law. During the time of the crisis concerning Turkish security, Genscher had even hesitated to offer German support for a NATO defense plan against a threat he did not believe existed. However, the brewing humanitarian crisis of the Kurds seemed to strike a different chord in the foreign minister. Once a stalwart opponent of troop deployment outside the NATO area except for rare UN blue-helmet operations, Genscher began to develop a new political position in the spring. By April 1991, Genscher had gone public with his conversion to the belief that Germany should be able to participate in future collective security operations outside the NATO area, so long as the government immediately adopted amendments to the Basic Law to allow such actions. Genscher made the argument that German participation in Operation Provide Comfort was essential, given the scale of the humanitarian crisis, but he remained equally firm in his conviction that a change in the Basic Law was a necessary precondition. In a mid-April speech before the *Bundestag* in support of German involvement, he said:

The world is witness to immeasurable sorrow in Iraq. There, people were killed, persecuted, and expelled. In the mountains people starve and freeze to death, children die in the arms of their parents . . . the dreadful fate of the Kurdish groups in the south of the country evokes our revolt and our compassion. Kurds and other groups in Iraq are threatened by annihilation and downfall. The state community is allowed to remain silent . . . what happens in Iraq is no longer an inner issue of this country, it is attempted genocide.[121]

On April 19, 1991, Genscher visited Turkey to conduct diplomatic talks on the proper solutions to the crisis. While in Ankara, Genscher publicly stated the intentions of the cabinet to help deal with this crisis through German participation in Operation Provide Comfort. All evidence suggests that the Gulf War experience convinced him that "German blue-helmet forces would be acceptable in the future."[122] In early April, Genscher appealed for *Bundestag* support for the operation through personal communications to key members of the Security and Foreign Policy committees.[123] Throughout this period, Genscher maintained that the governing coalition should agree to amendments of the Basic Law before committing to any significant deployment of forces. In May, he predicted that the government would make an effort to change the Basic Law so that participation of German armed forces within the context of actions of the United Nations would be possible without question (and without differentiating between the types of missions that could be supported).[124]

The emergence of a general consensus in the cabinet for German participation in Operation Provide Comfort was reflected by governing party leaders. Conservative leaders seemed quite open to the possibility; indeed, some had argued in favor of military action throughout the Gulf conflict. CDU party leader Volker Rühe had been outspoken in his support:

It is self-evident that the main task of the German armed forces will continue to be the maintenance of peace in Europe. But a consequence of the growing responsibility of our country must be that German forces in multinational units will also help secure peace, promote freedom, and implement international law. At stake is much more than the image of our country in the international community. At stake is the basic question of our identity as a reunified, sovereign country and whether in the long run we want to continue to differ from similar democracies in Europe. It is also a question of the future of Europe. Whoever wants to build a unified Europe cannot insist on a Sonderrolle for Germany in such key foreign policy questions. I am convinced that if we Germans continue to adopt a different stance than our European neighbors in the long run on this issue, this will have major consequences for the European unification process. Europe can only function and bring its interests to bear if the tasks of the community go beyond a common economic and monetary union and include common foreign and defense policy.[125]

German participation in Operation Provide Comfort was met with general acceptance inside the cabinet and the major parties in government, but there were vocal opponents who saw the mission less as an urgent humanitarian crisis demanding western attention, and more as a symbol of the widening latitude of the federal government. The question of German participation in the Kurdish operation essentially split the opposition Social Democratic Party. Left-wing members of the organization viewed participation as unconstitutional and as a dangerous trend toward more intensive German military engagements in operations around the world. According to one high-ranking government official, those that were convinced that any out-of-area troop deployment into potential combat zones was strictly prohibited by the Basic Law determined that the Kurdish relief mission was "the first step on the path of sin."[126]

In September 1990, most SPD delegates had rejected this step toward "sin" at a special party congress, where they voted down an initiative that would have allowed unlimited German participation in blue-helmet peacekeeping missions. A number of leading SPD officials opposed the use of military force in the Gulf at the time, insisting that economic sanctions should have been given more time to work. As conditions changed in the Gulf region, so too did attitudes in the Social Democratic Party. By the time of the May 1991 special party congress, the SPD leadership was divided. *Fraktion* leaders and moderates in the party who were concerned about foreign policy priorities, including Hans-Ulrich Klose, Karsten Voigt, Bjorn Engholm, and Norbert Gansel, called on the party to shift its position to support *Bundeswehr* participation in UN collective security organizations (so-called "Chapter VII missions").[127] Meanwhile, left-wing leaders of the party refused to consider the possibility of German military deployment outside of strictly blue-helmet peacekeeping operations. At the end of the special congress in May 1991, the SPD reached a shallow compromise in the agreement that German troops could participate in UN blue-helmet peacekeeping missions that met key criteria, including established cease-fire, consent of the warring parties, operational control by the UN, sanctioning by the UN Security Council, and the involvement of other European governments in the operation.[128] The compromise resolution on security policy won by a relatively narrow margin (230–179). It read:

For the foreseeable future Germany will need armed forces. Our goal is to make them superfluous. Until we have reached this goal, German forces must be structured in terms of their size, doctrine, structure, and armaments so that they are capable of territorial defense and can fulfill our alliance obligations. They must be reduced so that they do not constitute a threat yet continue to function as war prevention. We rejected the expansion of the tasks of NATO and the WEU to include possible use of their troops outside the NATO area and the creation of a Rapid Reaction Force for this purpose. A constitutional amendment that aims at allowing the *Bundeswehr* to participate in these or other actions is incompatible with our peace and security policy. We reject German participation in military operations under UN command or those sanctioned by the United Nations. At the same time, the Federal Republic of Germany must be able to participate in peace-keeping missions in the context of blue-helmet missions.[129]

Even this seemingly benign statement from the opposition SPD was only forged through great debate and compromise—a reminder of just how strong the resistance of the left was to any enlargement of the role of the *Bundeswehr*.[130] Party debates about German involvement in Operation Provide Comfort were as divided as the opinions of the opposition parties. It was clear that the Gulf War experience had a profound effect in shaping public attitudes about what Germany could and should do in the world, but it was not clear to leaders in Bonn just how far the public was willing to go to support greater German activism in world affairs.

Consistent with trends that developed during the Gulf conflict, surveys showed that about 60% of Germans believed that the Gulf War had been necessary and proper.[131] However, at the same time, polls found that a majority of Germans were opposed to amending the Basic Law to allow the use of *Bundeswehr* troops outside the NATO area.[132] In an excellent study of public attitudes toward foreign and security policy questions at this time of transition, Ronald Asmus found that such issues confronted the political culture of reticence that had served the German polity so well throughout the Cold War. He pointed out that the very idea of German military action outside the NATO area stood in direct conflict with the political culture of reticence and forced a kind of foreign policy cognitive dissonance on many Germans. This condition reflected itself in public opinion polls at the time which found that Germans would support diffuse descriptions of military responses to humanitarian crises, but that they were equally reluctant to support the deployment of the *Bundeswehr* when presented with specific contingencies. Overall, some 59% of Germans supported the development of a more active international role.[133] German public opinion was clearly in transition, and the government leadership could not count on a majority in support of significant actions.

The Government Acts

In the aftermath of the Gulf War, cabinet leaders believed they had enough domestic support for two major actions. First, the government announced in March 1991 that it would respond to specific requests for post-war assistance from the UN Security Council and the United States by deploying a group of five minesweepers and two support ships to the Persian Gulf.[134] These ships would coordinate with allied efforts to locate and destroy any remaining mines that had been deployed during the war, thus making the gulf safe for commerce once again.[135] Several weeks later, Germany offered heavy transport helicopters and personnel to support post-war UNIKOM (the UN Iraq–Kuwait Observer Mission) and the UN Special Commission (UNSCOM) investigation of Iraqi nuclear, biological, and chemical weapons, and ballistic missile facilities.

Second, German leaders decided in early April 1991 to deploy 600 *Bundeswehr* soldiers to the affected areas of Turkey and Iran to assist in the massive humanitarian relief effort for 2.5 million Kurdish refugees. On April 12, 1991, German units were first deployed to Turkey and Iran, where they established large tent shelter areas, began water purification projects, and provided food and sanitation for segments of the refugee population.[136] Logistical support for this German mission included *Transall* military transport aircraft, the forward deployment of twenty *Luftwaffe* helicopters to Iran, and a number of other support aircraft. In Iran, small supply depots were also constructed and staffed by German soldiers.[137] In mid-April, the government announced that the Federal Republic would deploy a medical corps to Iran and Turkey as part of the international relief effort.[138] Several teams of doctors tended to the tens of thousands of refugees in the border area between Turkey and Iran. Together with the German and International Red Cross, *Bundeswehr* soldiers established camps in the mountainous border region that aided more than 130,000 Kurds. Together with financial contributions, German support for the Kurds amounted to nearly 2.6 billion DM, or one third of all provided by the EC.[139]

Kohl, Stoltenberg, and Genscher all said that such actions were possible in the wake of the Gulf War because of an unprecedented level of elite consensus for action. Kohl celebrated the new spirit of German foreign policy activism that spring in a speech in Berlin, where he said that Germans could "no longer ignore the question of what we can contribute to peace outside of Europe. . . . We must come to terms with the greater responsibility which we have gained through the overcoming of partition and the regaining of our full sovereignty."[140] While these moves suggested a new level of flexibility, Kohl and other Conservative leaders were aware of lingering opposition inside and outside the government that would present legal obstacles to any attempt to actually participate in future Gulf War-like operations. This was evidenced by the FDP's continued insistence on constitutional changes to allow future operations, and by a general public reluctance to become involved in such operations. One opinion poll conducted in May 1991 found that even after the coalition victory in the Gulf region, 72% of the public remained opposed to German participation in future UN peacekeeping operations.[141]

CONCLUSION

The Gulf War and its aftermath presented a series of strategic dilemmas to western powers, and it was certainly also a foreshadowing of the conflicts of the 1990s. The German government was able to fashion a response to the Persian Gulf crisis that demonstrated a commitment to international security, but that did not jeopardize coalition relations or require a change in the constitution. While the chancellor clearly wanted to become more actively involved, he and his supporters were constrained by domestic political opposition. In the end, Germany's support for Operations Desert Shield and Desert Storm helped the coalition to defend Saudi Arabia, to adequately prepare for an offensive against Iraqi forces in Kuwait, and to successfully conduct the air and ground wars in January and February 1991. The German government had paid more than DM 17 billion in helping to fight the war, not including the costs of the deployments in the eastern Mediterranean and Turkey. In the spring of 1991, Chancellor Kohl confidently assessed the German role in the crisis as follows: "We have dedicated ourselves to the side of freedom, law, and justice during the Gulf conflict, using such means as were available in accord with our constitution. The world should recognize this achievement."[142] But one expert, Ronald Asmus, has pointed out that German actions in the Gulf were more representative of dependent foreign policy. He concluded:

What was perhaps most striking in the German debate was the almost total lack of any discussion about German strategic interests in the Gulf and how they should guide policy. Instead, the terms were set by such issues as whether Germans "owed" the United States political support in the Gulf in return for American support during the unification process, or whether Germany's historical obligation toward Israel required it to act in a specific fashion. . . . It was the rare voice that spoke out that Germany's own interests were at stake in the Gulf and that the country had to find ways to defend them, the restraints of the Basic Law notwithstanding.[143]

NOTES

1. From Carlo Schmid, *Errinerungen* (1979), p. 490, as quoted in Donald Abenheim, *Reforging the Iron Cross: The Search for Tradition in the West German Armed Forces* (Princeton, NJ: Princeton University Press, 1988), p. 43. Carlo Schmid was one of the fathers of the Basic Law.

2. Kohl's speech transcript reprinted in *Bulletin*, no. 33, 22 March 1991, p. 1451.

3. See the Resolution on Foreign, Peace, and Security Policy, Bremen Party Congress, Presseservice der SPD, 31 May 1991.

4. Klaus Kinkel, "Peacekeeping Missions: Germany Can Now Play Its Part," *NATO Review*, vol. 5, October 1994, p. 3.

5. Lawrence Freedman and Efraim Karsh, "How Kuwait Was Won: Strategy in the Gulf War," *International Security*, vol. 16, no. 2, Fall 1991, pp. 5–41; see also Christopher Bellamy, "Arithmetic of Death in the Wake of the Gulf Conflict," *Independent*, 20 March 1991, p. 1.

6. See Freedman and Karsh, Fall 1991, pp. 5–41; see also Theo Sommer, "Wie sich der Knotenschürzte," *Die Zeit*, 18 January 1991, p. 1.

7. Burns H. Weston, "Security Council Resolution 678 and Persian Gulf Decision Making: Precarious Legitimacy," *American Journal of International Law*, vol. 85, no. 3, July 1991, pp. 516–535.

8. Lawrence Freedman and Efraim Karsh, Fall 1991, p. 7; see also Testimony of William Webster, Director of the Central Intelligence Agency, 5 December 1990, U.S. House of Representatives, Hearings before the Committee on Armed Services, *Crisis in the Persian Gulf: Sanctions, Diplomacy, and War* (Washington, DC: U.S. Government Printing Office, 1991).

9. Susan Willett, *The Gulf Crisis: Economic Implications* (London: Brassey's/Centre for Defence Studies, University of London, November 1990); Clyde R. Mark, *Iraq: U.S. Economic Sanctions* (Washington, DC: Congressional Research Service, 22 January 1991).

10. Thomas Wittke, "Verbündete wünschen stärkere außenpolitische Rolle Bonns," *General-Anzeiger*, 14 December 1990, p. 4.

11. Hans-Dietrich Genscher, *Errinnerungen* (Berlin: Siedler Verlag, 1996), p. 905.

12. Ibid., p. 914.

13. Ibid., p. 900.

14. Sommer, *Die Zeit*, 18 January 1991, p. 1.

15. Ronald D. Asmus, *Germany After the Gulf War*, RAND Note #N-3391-AF, (Santa Monica, CA: RAND, 1991), p. 9.

16. Interview with Helmut Kohl, German RFTV—Satellit 1; transcript in Bundespresse Agentur Material, 16 August 1990.

17. Interview with Hans-Dietrich Genscher, German RFTV, 23 August 1990; transcript in Bundespresse Agentur Material, 23 August 1990.

18. Genscher, *Errinnerungen*, 1996, pp. 903–904.

19. Grundgesetz für die Bundesrepublik Deutschland, Bundeszentrale für politische Bildung, Bonn, October 1990, p. 53.

20. John Reed, *Germany and NATO* (Washington, DC: National Defense University Press, 1987).

21. Robert Leicht, "Wann darf der Helm blau oder grün sein?" *Die Zeit*, 6 December 1991, p. 9.

22. Confidential interview, Konrad Adenauer Stiftung, Sankt Augustin, 9 June 1996.

23. It is important to note that this was a reflection of Kohl's leadership style. For a comprehensive survey of his approach to the chancellorship, see Clay Clemans and William E. Patterson, eds., "The Kohl Chancellorship," a Special Issue of *German Politics*, vol. 7, no. 1, April 1998.

24. Kohl, as quoted in Christoph Bluth, "Germany: Towards a New Security Format," *The World Today*, vol. 8, no. 11, November 1992, p. 197.

25. R. W. Appleman, "German Leader Signals Change in Defense Policy," *New York Times*, 29 May 1991, p. 1A; Author gained perspective on this from confidential interview, Bundeshaus (Bundestag Legislative Offices), Bonn, 21 June 1996.

26. Genscher, *Errinnerungen*, 1996, p. 912.

27. "Das wird ein schwieriges Jahr," *Der Spiegel*, 5 January 1991, pp. 16–21.

28. "Ich habe Kurs gehalten," *Der Spiegel*, 4 February 1991, p. 24; FDP Bundeshauptausschuß, "Liberale Außenpolitik," p. 8; and "Beschluß des Bundeshauptausschusses der FDP vom 25.05.91 in Hamburg (Auszug)," *Stichworte zur Sicherheitspolitik*, June 1991, p. 39.

29. "SPD: In den Wolken," Der Spiegel, 4 February 1991, p. 37; "Außenpolitik: Normale Rolle," *Der Spiegel*, 11 March 1991, pp. 22–23; Narbert Gansel, "Reformen in Sicherheitspolitik," *Der Spiegel*, 11 March 1991, p. 5.

30. "Deutschlands Verantwortung," Außenpolitischer Kongreß, pp. 9–10; see also Lamer's statement in the *Rheinischer Merkur*, 10 May 1991, p. 6.

31. "Beschluß des Bundeshauptausschusses der FDP vom 25.05.91 in Hamburg (Auszug)," *Stichworte*, June 1991, p. 39.

32. Confidential interview, Bundeshaus (Bundestag Legislative Offices), Bonn, 19 June 1996.

33. "SPD: In den Wolken," p. 37; "Außenpolitik: Normale Rolle," 11 March 1991, pp. 22–23; and Gansel, "Reformen in Sicherheitspolitik," p. 5.

34. See Asmus, *Germany After the Gulf War*, 1991.

35. Confidential interview, Columbus, Ohio, 29 April 1993.

36. Statement of Foreign Minister Genscher on the meeting of the WEU and EPZ with respect to the situation at the Gulf, *Bulletin*, no. 102, 25 August 1990, pp. 858–860.

37. "Wir haben die Faust geballt," *Der Spiegel*, no. 36, 1990, pp. 176–180; see also "Gezisch am Nachmittag," *Der Spiegel*, no. 48, 1990, pp. 29–31.

38. Genscher, *Errinnerungen*, 1996, p. 907.

39. "Golfkrise: Geschäft des Lebens," *Der Spiegel*, no. 51, 1991, pp. 136–142; see also Ronald D. Asmus, *Germany in Transition: National Self-Confidence and International Reticence*, N-3522-AF (Santa Monica, CA: RAND, 1992), p. 14; "Kohl Urges Berlin as Unified Capital," *New York Times*, 24 April 1991, p. 7A.

40. Genscher, *Errinnerungen*, 1996, p. 910.

41. *Der Spiegel*, 6 February 1991, p. 47.

42. "Das Augenblickliche Kräftverhältnis am Golf," *Frankfurter Allgemeine Zeitung*, 11 January 1991, p. 4.

43. Freedman and Karsh, *International Security*, Fall 1991, p. 8.

44. See "U.S. to Send 700 More Tanks," *International Herald Tribune*, 9 November 1990, p. 1; and "Bush Adds to Gulf Build-up," *International Herald Tribune*, 9 November 1990, p. 1.

45. The chancellor again expressed strong support for the coalition mission at the CSCE conference of November 19–20; Press and Information Office of the German Government, *Bulletin*, no. 71, 22 November 1980, p. 622; see also Alan Riding, "Western Europe Urges Air Embargo Against Iraq," *New York Times*, 19 September 1990, p. A3.

46. See Reed, *Germany and NATO*, 1987.

47. *Der Spiegel*, 5 January 1991, p. 41.

48. "Deutsche Bomben auf Baghdad," *Der Spiegel*, vol. 5, 1991, pp. 22–24; confidential interview, Deutsche Gesellschaft für Auswärtige Politik, Bonn, 19 June 1996; see also confidential interview, Bundesministerium der Verteidigung, Bonn, 11 July 1996.

49. Thomas Wittke, "Verbündete wünschen stärkere außenpolitische Rolle Bonns," *General-Anzeiger*, 14 December 1990, p. 4.

50. Ozal quoted in *Der Spiegel*, 28 January 1991, p. 14.

51. See Karl Kaiser and Klaus Becher, "Deutschland und der Irak-Konflikt," *Arbeitspapiere zur Internationalen Politik*, vol. 68 (Bonn: Forschungsinstitut der Deutschen Gesellschaft für Auswärtige Politik, February 1992), pp. 30–33; see also *Der Spiegel*, 5 January 1991.

52. Ernst Tugendhat, "Der Golfkrieg, Deutschland, und Israel," *Die Zeit*, 1 March 1991, p. 8.

53. Lily G. Feldman, *The Special Relationship between Israel and West Germany* (London: Unwin Hyman, 1984).

54. Ronald D. Asmus, *German Strategy and Opinion After the Wall, 1990–1993*, (Santa Monica, CA: RAND, 1994), 1994, p. 63.

55. Wolf Biermann, "Damit wir uns missverstehen: Ich bin für diesen Krieg am Golf," *Die Zeit*, 1 February 1991, p. 6.

56. Robert Leicht, "Kein Kurswechsel im Kriegsgetümmel," *Die Zeit*, 15 February 1991, p. 1; see also Christopher Bertram, "Die Deutschen im Zwielicht," *Die Zeit*, 8 February 1991, p. 8.

57. "Der will schlicht überleben," *Der Spiegel*, 7 January 1991, pp. 18–20.

58. *Die Zeit*, 8 February 1991, p. 4.

59. Interview with Hans-Dietrich Genscher by Richard Kiessler and Paul Lersch in Bonn, "I Have Stayed the Course," *Der Spiegel*, 4 February 1991, pp. 22–25; reprinted in FBIS-WEU, 91-024, 5 February 1991, p. 13.

60. Hans-Dietrich Genscher, "Kurs halten heißt Flagge zeigen," *Welt am Sonntag*, 3 February 1991, p. 6.

61. Confidential interview, Bundeshaus (Bundestag Legislative Offices), Bonn, 22 June 1996; see also "Die CDU/CSU drängt auf eine Änderung des Grundgesetzes," *General-Anzeiger*, 19 February 1991, p. 3.

62. "Die CDU/CSU drängt auf eine Änderung des Grundgesetzes," *General-Anzeiger*, 19 February 1991, p. 3.

63. Genscher, *Erinnerungen*, 1996, p. 913.

64. "Warum sollen wir nicht dabeisien?" *Der Spiegel*, 11 February 1991, pp. 27–30.

65. *Der Spiegel*, 28 January 1991, p. 14.

66. "In den Wolken," *Der Spiegel*, no. 6, 1991, pp. 36–39.

67. Interview with Willy Brandt, *Der Spiegel*, 11 February 1991, p. 21.

68. "Den Ernstfall nicht gewagt," *Der Spiegel*, 11 February 1991, pp. 25–27; see also the speech of then leader of the SPD caucus Hans-Jochen Vogel, "Mäßiger Start in schwieriger Zeit," *Das Parlament*, 8/15 February 1991, pp. 4–5.

69. Interview with Hans-Jochen Vogel, German SAT Television, 18 January 1991.

70. "Statement of SPD Chairman Hans-Jochen Vogel in the Bundestag," 31 January 1991; transcript reprinted in FBIS-WEU, 91-022, 1 February 1991, p. 9.

71. Ibid.

72. Schröder interview with Henryk M. Broder, *Der Spiegel*, 29 April 1991, pp. 26–31.

73. "Wir haben die Faust geballt," *Der Spiegel* 36, 1990, pp. 176–180; see also Wolf Biermann, "Damit wir uns missverstehen: Ich bin für diesen Krieg am Golf," *Die Zeit*, 1 February 1991, p. 6.

74. "Schwieriges Jahr," pp. 23, 28; Hans Magnus Enzensberger, "Hitler's Wiedergänger," *Der Spiegel*, 4 February 1991, pp. 26–28.

75. "Operation Wüstensturm; zweiter Golfkrieg—Allierten gegen Irak: Friedensbemühungen," *Archiv der Gegenwart*, no. 2, 17–28 January 1991, pp. 35266–35267; see also "Zahl der Kriegsdienstverweigerer auf rund 30,000 gestiegen," *Stichworte*, March 1991, p. 46.

76. "Umfragen zum Krieg," *Die Zeit*, 25 January 1991, p. 16.

77. Asmus, *German Strategy and Opinion After the Wall, 1990–1993*, 1994, pp. 60–61.

78. "Operation Wüstensturm; zweiter Golfkrieg—Allierten gegen Irak: Friedensbemühungen," *Archiv der Gegenwart*, no. 2, 17–28 January 1991, pp. 35266–35267; see also Elizabeth Pond, *Beyond the Wall* (Washington, DC: The Brookings Institution, 1993).

79. Anson Rabinbach, "German Intellectuals and the Gulf War," *Dissent*, Fall 1991, pp. 459–463.

80. ZDF Politbarometer for February and March 1991, Forschungsgruppe Wahlen, Mannheim.

81. "The Mood in January," *Süddeutsche Zeitung*, 29 January 1991, p. 10.

82. "EMNID-Institut Umfrage—Bedeutung der Bundeswehr seit Golfkrise wesentlich höher eingeschätzt," *Stichworte zur Sicherheitspolitik*, February 1991, Bundesministerium der Verteidigung, Pressemitteilung 38, 8 February 1991, Bonn.

83. Asmus, *German Strategy and Opinion After the Wall, 1990–1993*, p. 60.

84. Ibid., p. 61.

85. Statement of Chancellor Kohl on the situation in the Gulf region and in Lithuania, *Bulletin*, no. 4, 15 January 1991, pp. 1–3.

86. Genscher, *Errinerungen*, 1996, p. 921.

87. *Süddeutsche Zeitung*, 14 September 1990, p. 1; see also Ferdinand Protzman, "Bonn, Heeding Critics in U.S., Will Provide Planes and Ships for the Gulf Effort," *New York Times*, 15 September 1990, p. 5A.

88. Berlin ADN Report, 31 January 1991; reprinted in FBIS-WEU, 91-022, 1 February 1991, p. 13.

89. Les Aspin, Chairman House Armed Services Committee, "Sharing the Burden of the Persian Gulf: Are the Allies Paying Their Fair Share?" 8 April 1991.

90. Genscher, *Errinerungen*, 1996, p. 858; "Das wird ein schwieriges Jahr," *Der Spiegel*, 28 January 1991, pp. 22–23; Helmut Kohl, "Fünf Jahre EUREKA," *Bulletin*, no. 73, 25 June 1991, p. 591.

91. "Warum sollen wir nicht dabeisien?" *Der Spiegel*, 11 February 1991, pp. 27–30.

92. See statements of government spokesman Dieter Vogel, *Stichworte*, January 1991, pp. 22–23; Gerhard Stoltenberg interview for "Im Brennpunkt," German RFTV; transcript from BPA, 4 February 1991, p. 203.

93. Helmut Kohl, "Bundeswehr im Mittelmeer," *Stichworte*, February 1991, p. 32.

94. Berlin ADN Report, 31 January 1991; reprinted in FBIS-WEU, 91-022, 1 February 1991, p. 13; see also Hans-Dietrich Genscher, "Der will schlicht überleben," *Der Spiegel*, 7 January 1991, p. 19; "Der Himmel schließt sich," *Der Spiegel*, 21 January 1991, p. 20; "Bemühungen der Bundesregierung zur friedlichen Lösung der Golfkrise," *Bulletin*, no. 2, 10 January 1991, pp. 5–6.

95. "Die totale Beistandschaft," *Der Spiegel*, 11 February 1991, pp. 32–33.

96. Martin Navias, *Saddam's Scud War and Ballistic Missile Proliferation* (London: Brassey's/Centre for Defence Studies, University of London, 1991), p. 21.

97. Asmus, *German Strategy and Opinion After the Wall, 1990–1993*, 1994, p. 16.

98. "Das Augenblickliche Kräftverhältnis am Golf," *Frankfurter Allgemeine Zeitung*, 11 January 1991, p. 4; see also *International Herald Tribune*, 3 January 1991, p. 4.

99. Freedman and Karsh, *International Security*, Fall 1991, pp. 24–26.

100. "Vietnam mit gutem Ende," *Der Spiegel* 10, 1991, pp. 157–164; see also Bob Woodward, *The Commanders* (New York: Simon and Schuster, 1991).

101. Hans-Dietrich Genscher, "Erklärung der Bundesregierung zur jüngsten Entwicklung in der Golfregion," *Bulletin* 20, 23 February 1991, p. 137.

102. Ted Robert Gurr and Barbara Harff, *Ethnic Conflict in World Politics* (Boulder, CO: Westview Press, 1994), p. 30.

103. Ibid., p. 30.

104. Thomas G. Weiss and Cindy Collins, *Humanitarian Challenges and Intervention: World Politics and the Dilemmas of Help* (Boulder, CO: Westview Press, 1996), p. 75.

105. Quote from documents captured in the 1991 Kurdish uprising; quoted by Aryeh Neier, "Putting Saddam Hussein on Trial," *New York Review*, 23 September 1993, p. 47.

106. P. W. Galbraith and C. Van Hollen, Jr., *Chemical Weapons in Kurdistan: Iraq's Final Offensive, A Staff Report* (Washington, DC: Senate Committee on Foreign Relations, 1988).

107. David McDowall, *The Kurds: A Nation Denied* (London: Minority Rights Publications, 1992).

108. Volkhard Windfuhr, "Wer hofft, der wird siegen," *Der Spiegel*, no. 15, 1991, pp. 174–175.

109. Larry Minear, U. B. P. Chelliah, Jeff Crisp, John Mackinlay, and Thomas G. Weiss, *United Nations Coordination of the International Humanitarian Response to the Gulf Crisis 1990–1991*, Occasional Paper 13 (Providence, RI: Thomas J. Watson Jr. Institute for International Studies, 1992), p. 1.

110. "Es Wird nur noch Asche sein," *Der Spiegel*, no. 15, 1991, pp. 168–176.

111. Mehrdad R. Izady, *The Kurds: A Concise Handbook* (Washington, DC: Taylor and Francis, 1992); see also Philip G. Kreyenbroek and Stefan Sperl, eds., *The Kurds: A Contemporary Overview* (London: Routledge, 1992).

112. "Durchbruch im Minenfeld?" *Der Spiegel*, no. 16, 1991, pp. 166–167.

113. "Schwarzkopf Pascha in Baghdad," *Der Spiegel*, no. 17, 1991, pp. 162–164.

114. Ian Johnstone, *Aftermath of the Gulf War: An Assessment of UN Action.* (Boulder, CO: Lynne Rienner, 1994); see also "Schwarzkopf Pascha in Baghdad," *Der Spiegel*, no. 17, 1991, pp. 162–164.

115. Genscher, *Erinnerungen*, 1996, p. 922.

116. Kohl's speech transcription in *Bulletin*, no. 64, 6 June 1991, p. 24962.

117. Confidential interview, Bundeshaus (Bundestag Legislative Offices), Bonn, 21 June 1996.

118. Kohl's speech transcript reprinted in *Bulletin*, no. 33, 22 March 1991, p. 1451.

119. Debate on Amending the German Basic Law, German RFTV, 1 March 1991; text transcript from the BPA, 1 March 1991, p. 8.

120. Stoltenberg speech, "Die wachsende Verantwortung des vereinten Deutschlands," *Europäische Sicherheit* (EWK/WWR), no. 3, 1991, p. 137; see also Genscher, *Erinnerungen*, 1996, p. 928.

121. *Deutschland Nachrichten*, 21 April 1991, p. 3.

122. *Stuttgarter Zeitung*, 20 February 1991, p. 3; Speech reprinted in *Bulletin*, Press and Information Office of the German Government, 3 March 1991, no. 135.

123. Hans-Dietrich Genscher, "Humanitäre Hilfe der Bundesrepublik für die Irakischen Flüchtlinge—Erklärung der Bundesregierung über die Lage im Irak und die Situation der irakischen Flüchtlinge, insbesondere der Kurden," 20. Sitzung des Bundestages am 17 April 1991; reprinted in *Stichworte zur Sicherheitspolitik*, May 1991, Bundesministerium der Verteidigung, Bonn.

124. Hans-Dietrich Genscher, "Liberale Außenpolitik für das vereinte Deutschland," *Leiteantrag für den Bundeshauptausshuss der FDP*, Hamburg, 25 May 1991.

125. Volker Rühe, "Die weltpolitische Verantwortung des geeinten Deutschlands," *CDU-Dokumentation*, no. 17, 1991, p. 9.

126. Author confidential interview #4, Kanzleramt, Bonn, Germany, 11 June 1996.

127. "SPD: In den Wolken," *Der Spiegel*, 4 February 1991, p. 37; "Außenpolitik: Normale Rolle," 11 March 1991, pp. 22–23; Gansel, "Reformen in Sicherheitspolitik," p.5.

128. Confidential interview, Bundeshaus (Bundestag Legislative Offices), Bonn, 19 June 1996.

129. See the Resolution on Foreign, Peace, and Security Policy, Bremen Party Congress, Presseservice der SPD, 31 May 1991.

130. "Bundeswehr: tolerant, charakterfest," *Der Spiegel*, 3 June 1991, pp. 20–23.

131. EMNID poll on the Bundeswehr and the Gulf War, Stichworte, February 1991, pp. 36–37; "Angst vor dem Krieg am Golf," *Süddeutsche Zeitung*, 29 January 1991, p. 10.

132. ZDF Politbarometer for February and March 1991, Forschungsgruppe Wahlen in Mannheim; for more polling data from this period, see "EMNID-Institut Umfrage—Bedeutung der Bundeswehr seit Golfkrise wesentlich höher eingeschätzt," *Stichworte zur Sicherheitspolitik*, February 1991, Bundesministerium der Verteidigung, Pressemitteilung 38, 8 February 1991, Bonn.

133. Asmus, *German Strategy and Opinion After the Wall, 1990–1993*, 1994, p. 61.

134. Karl-Heinz Kamp, "The German Bundeswehr in Out-of-Area Operations: To Engage or Not to Engage?" *The World Today*, August–September 1993, pp. 165–168.

135. Dieter Vogel, "Minenräum der Bundesmarine im Gebiet des Persischen Golfs," *Bulletin*, no. 26, 13 March 1991, p. 192.

136. Francis M. Deng, *Protecting the Dispossessed: A Challenge for the International Community* (Washington, DC: Brookings Institution, 1993).

137. Statement of Foreign Minister Genscher on the state in Iraq and the situation of the Iraqi refugees, especially the Kurds, *Bulletin*, no. 38, 18 April 1991, p. 278; see also "Möglichst unauffällig: Die ersten deutschen Soldaten sind im UNO-Einsatz—im Kambodscha," *Der Spiegel*, 1 June 1992, pp. 125–128.

138. "Focus of Kurdish Aid to Shift to Iran," statement to the press by Government Spokesperson Dieter Vogel, as quoted in *Deutschland Nachrichten*, 24 April 1991, p. 1.

139. "Außenminister Hans-Dietrich Genscher nahm in einem Interview mit dem ZDF für die Sendung "Mittagsmagazin," am 8 April 1991; Auswärtiges Amt, Pressemitteilung, no. 1081/91, 8 April 1991; see also Kamp, *The World Today*, August–September 1993, pp. 165–168.

140. Kohl, as quoted in Ronald D. Asmus, *Germany's Geopolitical Maturation*, RAND Issue Paper (Santa Monica, CA: RAND, February 1993), p. 22.

141. *Politbarometer in Deutschland*, Reports nos. 731 and 732, February 1991.

142. Statement of German Chancellor Helmut Kohl addressed to the Bundestag, *Bulletin*, no. 28, 14 March 1991, p. 209; see also Kohl, press conference, "Herausforderungen und Chancen der Außen- und Innenpolitik," *Bulletin*, no. 21, 1 March 1991, p. 141.

143. Asmus, *Germany After the Gulf War*, 1991, p. 4.

3

Peacekeeping and Humanitarian Relief Operations in Somalia

Germany has a growing responsibility in the world and our forces must operate in multinational units to help secure peace, promote freedom, and implement international law. Much more than our image in the international community is at stake, rather it is the basic question of our identity as a reunified, sovereign country.

—Volker Rühe, 1992[1]

Blue-helmet operations of the *Bundeswehr* are important for the maintenance of peace and order in Somalia. But unification means that we will need ten years to find a new German identity, during which time we would like to quietly solve our own problems and not intervene in other lands. This government would be better off if it did not get involved in overseas adventures.

—Gerhard Schröder, 1993[2]

The humanitarian crisis in Somalia represented a new foreign policy challenge for Germany that put the elite's post-Gulf War compromise on the use of force to the test. By the summer of 1992, deteriorating conditions in Somalia meant mass starvation and indiscriminate violence, and Western powers developed a plan for intervention and peacekeeping in the country. This chapter explores the evolution of the German response to the humanitarian crisis in Somalia (Figure 3.1) and how such events, in turn, shaped domestic political orientations.

CIVIL WAR AND FAMINE IN THE HORN OF AFRICA

Historical Background

Somalia is strategically located in the Horn of Africa, bordering on the Red Sea and the Indian Ocean. Somalia gained its independence in 1960, but the country experienced a number of difficult periods in the transition to a post-colonial identity. In 1969, Siad Barre took power and ruled Somalia for more than twenty years. Barre adopted legislative and administrative reforms threatening civil and political rights that had been institutionalized in the Somali Constitution of 1960. In the interests of "national security," the Barre regime instituted a series of very rigid laws and punished violators with long prison sentences and the death penalty.[3]

The population of Somalia is divided along ethnic, tribal lines into two key groups, the Samal and the Sab. In the 1980s and early 1990s, the Samal majority included a number of clan groups living mainly in the northern part of Somalia, and these clans were further divided into sub-clan and family groups. The Sab minority included two clan groups that were concentrated more in central and southern Somalia. In 1988, clan members from the Samal majority began to publicly challenge the authority of Siad Barre, a Sab. They claimed that Barre had become a dictator with too much power and that he did not respect the rights or needs of the Samal. Samal clan groups joined to form a political unit, the Somalia National Movement (SNM), and began to foment unrest throughout the entire country.

Figure 3.1
Strategic Dilemmas in Somalia

Stages/Dates	Strategic Dilemma	Foreign Policy Response
I. 1992–1993	Civil War and Famine/ Operation Restore Hope	Slow Deployment of Troops and Support
II. 1993–1994	Mission Creep and the Breakdown of Relief Operations	Phased Withdrawal of Troops

Barre ordered a severe military crackdown on the Samal group's actions in the north in May 1988. Government troops destroyed hundreds of northern villages, killing an estimated 5,000 civilians from the Issaq clan of the Samal tribe. This event sparked a widespread civil war and caused the breakdown of national infrastructure that led to famine and humanitarian tragedy. After the crackdown, Barre desperately tried to hold on to power by rallying support from the Sab and linking the government with clan groups, including the Somali National Front (SNF). Meanwhile, Samal tribe members from the SNM joined with other clans to form military units, including the Somali Patriotic Front (SPF) and the United Somali Congress (USC).[4] By 1990, the civil war had produced a complete breakdown in infrastructure, including agricultural production and distribution.

On January 25, 1991, President Siad Barre and his supporters fled Mogadishu, leaving the country without a national government.[5] Two prominent leaders, Mohammed Farah Aideed and Ali Mahdi, seized power for the United Somali Congress and promised to share political control of the government. Unfortunately, personal and political differences soon led to a breakdown in these arrangements, leading to the most intense period of the civil war in the fall of 1991. Mogadishu was devastated by intense combat in its streets, and there seemed little hope for a peaceful resolution to the political crisis in Somalia.[6]

The Humanitarian Crisis Prompts an International Response

The crisis in Somalia slowly came to international attention during the fall and winter months of 1991–92. Members of the Western media began to report the makings of a humanitarian catastrophe—a product of famine, regional political instability, civil war, and indiscriminate violence against civilian populations. UN officials and Western governments began to consider ways for the international community to respond to the country's most immediate concerns of a widespread hunger and famine. As the crisis intensified in 1992, so did Western media coverage of its effects on civilians.[7]

In April 1992, UN diplomats brokered a tentative cease-fire arrangement with the warring clans in Somalia and obtained pledges to allow humanitarian relief operations in the countryside. On April 24, 1992, the UN Security Council passed Resolution #751, which created the UN Operation in Somalia (UNOSOM). This operation would deploy 4,200 blue-helmet peacekeepers to deliver food to the needy, monitor the cease-fire in Mogadishu, oversee the demobilization and disarmament of warring clans, and generally "assist in national reconciliation." UNOSOM troops included blue-helmet contingents from Pakistan, Canada, Malaysia, and other countries.[8]

At first, UNOSOM was highly effective in delivering food aid to key sectors of Mogadishu and the surrounding countryside, but it soon became clear that there was simply not enough relief aid nor enough personnel to make the mission a complete success. Relief convoys that left Mogadishu for the surrounding countryside were regularly attacked by warring clans and the food aid taken by military units. In the fall of 1992, with continued threats of the breakdown of civil order and occasional breeches of the cease-fire agreement, UN Secretary General Boutros-Ghali approached the Security Council to consider new options for the mission including: a continuation of the peacekeeping mission as UNO-SOM (which seemed a losing proposition), the abandonment of UNO-SOM's missions other than centralized food relief provision, or the augmentation of the mission to include the use of force to establish and maintain a secure environment for relief operations. Government representatives debated these options for several weeks.

UN Security Council member states made a decisive commitment to action on December 3, 1992. Resolution #814 created a new, militarized form of relief operations in Somalia, labeled UN Operation in Somalia II (UNOSOM II). This mission authorized the use of "all necessary force" to secure the delivery of humanitarian aid to the people of Somalia. UNO-SOM II would be the largest peacekeeping operation (at 33,000 troops) and the most expensive operation (approximately $1.5 billion) in the history of the UN.[9] This was clearly an historic decision given its scope and profile—it would be a humanitarian relief mission at the barrel of a gun, a Chapter VII mission in Chapter VI clothing. Boutros-Ghali himself admitted that this type of mission would explore the boundaries of UN power, capabilities, and authority. He described it simply as "an opportunity to test new ideas about peacemaking and peace enforcement."[10]

In conjunction with UN Security Council action, the Bush administration announced that U.S. forces would form the military vanguard of the new relief mission, named "Operation Restore Hope." The mission was designed with a number of lofty goals including the social, political and economic reconstruction of Somalia.[11] Together, the Bush administration, key allies, and UN officials finalized plans for Operation Restore Hope and UNOSOM II, and considered ways to build an international consensus in support of the mission. U.S. diplomats began strongly encouraging Germany to provide financial contributions for Somali relief operations, and several officials used backchannels to encourage Germany to deploy soldiers to Somalia for UNOSOM II. United Nations officials lobbied Germany and other governments to participate in the peace operation. In January 1993, UN Secretary General Boutros-Ghali visited Bonn and directly lobbied Kohl, Kinkel, Rühe, and top German parliamentary leaders to consider the deployment of German troops as part of UNOSOM II. He stressed the importance of a German role by stating publicly that the world "needs Germany to be fully responsible and engaged in peace-keeping, peace enforcement, and peace making." NATO Secretary General Manfred Wörner called for Germany to participate militarily in international peace missions. At a special conference with German political leaders, he warned that "if the past practice of foreign policy restraint continued, Germany's role in the alliance could be seriously damaged."[12]

The first German response to this crisis was reflective of past lessons about foreign policy latitude. Kohl and his new Foreign Minister, Klaus Kinkel, made high profile commitments of support in July 1992 for non-military humanitarian relief efforts—increasing the number of relief flights as well as the volume of food shipments into Somalia from airbases in Kenya and Tanzania. In late August 1992, Kohl ordered the deployment of four German Transall transport planes to Mombasa, along with 44 soldiers from the *Luftwaffe*. These planes began the regular delivery of emergency food aid shipments into Mogadishu's airport, and food and supplies were delivered to those in need.[13] At the end of October 1992, *Luftwaffe* transport planes even began to airdrop food pallets to needy Somalis who lived in remote regions of the country. The air delivery of relief supplies to Somalia continued through March 1993, with German soldiers flying 655 sorties and delivering thousands of tons of needed supplies.[14]

Facing continued violence in Somalia and greater international pressure on Germany for action, however, Chancellor Kohl followed the U.S. lead by announcing on December 18 that he wanted to deploy *Bundeswehr* troops to the multilateral peacekeeping efforts in Somalia. He said that based on preliminary negotiations with the foreign and defense ministries, the government believed that Germany could deploy a battalion of 1,600 soldiers to Africa to participate in Operation Restore Hope and UNOSOM II.[15] The chancellor explained that German engineers, medical personnel, telecommunications specialists, and security forces would be deployed in a remote section of Somalia where, it was promised, "there would be no threat of combat."[16] This commitment of troops to a peacekeeping mission would be possible, according to Kohl, because an agreement had been worked out within the governing coalition to deploy the troops "legally and under the existing constitution."[17]

Domestic Constraints on the German Response to Somalia

With his public pledge to deploy *Bundeswehr* soldiers to Somalia as part of the UNOSOM II relief operation, Helmut Kohl had laid his political cards on the table. It was by no means certain in December 1992 that the chancellor could actually assemble a political consensus to legitimate this action, however. A multidimensional obstacle blocked Kohl's preferred course of action. First, key cabinet officials recently had climbed on the bandwagon for a more liberal interpretation of Basic Law restrictions on the use of force, but there was no absolute consensus on the matter. Second, there were serious standing disagreements between major party organizations over the constitutionality of troop deployment outside the NATO area, and the FDP and SPD had demanded a constitutional amendment as a precondition for any such deployments. Finally, public attitudes toward the mission were mixed and very dynamic. This would be a difficult consensus to build in a shifting international and domestic political environment.

Kohl approached the task of consensus building by casting the Somalia mission in a broader context of new German responsibilities in the post-Cold War era. At a special conference on security in February 1993, Kohl said that Germany must actively be engaged in world politics in spite of the potential risks. Somalia provided a unique strategic opportunity, and he argued:

We must be engaged in the main mission of the United Nations to promote world peace and international security. Every country should provide support for the Somalia mission to the best of its abilities . . . [because] we have responsibilities that go along with our rights as members of the organization.[18]

The chancellor drew support for the military operation from top officials in the Defense Ministry. Volker Rühe had become Kohl's fourth defense minister in April 1992, after years of experience in the administration of the CDU party organization. Even before taking office, Rühe had allied himself with key strategic thinkers in the ministry who saw the future of the *Bundeswehr* in expanded commitments to international security.[19] Regarding Somalia, Rühe announced in December 1992 that he had ordered preparations to send *Bundeswehr* soldiers, communications troops, medical staff, and engineers to participate in the relief effort. Rühe stated his personal opinion that the Somalia mission would be constitutional and the proper response to a moral imperative for action. He urged that "the German government must take speedy, practical steps [because] Somalia cannot wait for the solution of our constitutional problems."[20]

Kohl's pledge for troop deployments to Somalia was also supported by Chief of Staff of the Federal Armed Forces Klaus Naumann.[21] Like Rühe, Naumann supported the need for a humanitarian relief mission in Somalia and believed in expanding the traditional role of the *Bundeswehr* in light of the collapse of the Cold War consensus on European defense.[22] In fact, Naumann had authored an internal document in early 1992 that called for the expansion of German security interests within existing constitutional parameters. When the so-called "Naumann Paper" was leaked to the press, however, critics claimed that this was the beginning of a resurgence of German nationalism and accused the military leadership of "megalomania."[23] Nevertheless, Naumann's position was eventually to prove very important in the broadening of Germany's foreign and security policy.

Kohl's new foreign minister, Klaus Kinkel, walked a tightrope between support for the Somalia operation in principle, and the concerns of the left Liberals that such actions would violate the Basic Law. Kinkel (FDP) became foreign minister in April 1992, in the wake of the retirement of Hans-Dietrich Genscher. A former justice minister and special assistant to Genscher, Kinkel was inclined to follow the course set by his mentor to: recognize international imperatives for German action; allow broader short-term interpretations of the constitutionality of out-of-area troop deployments in the cabinet; and demand in exchange Conservative long-term support for an amendment to the Basic Law to deal with this issue. In fact, even before Kohl's pledge for German engagement in UNOSOM II, Kinkel had negotiated with cabinet and party leaders to establish a common government position on the matter. He followed up on these pledges and claimed international responsibility for Germany in many public forums during the winter months of 1992–1993. At a speech on German–American cooperation, for example, Kinkel said that he supported the Somalia mission because Germany had "an important responsibility as partners of the United States and an important role to play in regional and global affairs."[24] Privately, however, Kinkel was lobbying key Conservatives to consider an amendment to the Basic Law to allow such missions (within limits) in the future.[25]

Debates inside the cabinet regarding the constitutionality of deploying German troops to Somalia were a microcosm of broader disagreements among the major party organizations. As in the case of the Gulf War, different interpretations of Articles 24 and 87a of the Basic Law caused turmoil and debates among German political leaders over decisions concerning the use of force.[26] Kohl and Rühe accurately represented the interests of most members of the CDU/CSU party organization, which supported a more liberal interpretation of the Basic Law, and argued that there was no need for a constitutional amendment for the deployment of German forces in humanitarian missions abroad. On the more extreme end of the party's security policy platform, some Conservatives were on the record in support of future German participation in both multinational peacekeeping and peace-making operations under the auspices of the UN, NATO, or even the Western European Union (WEU).[27]

Conservative leaders were challenged in their position by both the junior party in coalition government (the FDP), and the main opposition party (the SPD), but there were important differences between these parties' positions. The FDP leadership, following the guidance of elder statesman Hans-Dietrich Genscher and new party leader Klaus Kinkel, developed a fairly sophisticated political strategy on the issue.[28] First, the FDP leadership made it clear that they supported a fairly broad range of potential deployments of German support for international security in the twenty-first century. FDP leaders believed in German participation in Chapter VI peacekeeping operations, and most grudgingly supported Chapter VII contingencies in line with Conservative viewpoints. However, they demanded that an amendment to the Basic Law be considered as a fundamental precondition to adopting such a broader role in international relations.[29] At the time, Party Chairman Otto Lambsdorff stated that "the FDP would agree to the [Somalia] mission if it meant providing humanitarian aid in a limited territory" consistent with the boundaries of peacekeeping, but he had serious reservations about the deployment because of the possibility of violence involving UN peacekeepers and "unexpected political complications that could occur in the course of the war."[30]

The Social Democratic Party took a firm public line regarding the Somalia dilemma, but in private the issue divided the party leadership. Publicly, SPD leaders opposed the Somalia deployment, stating it was a violation of the constitution, and they demanded that the government enter into negotiations to amend the Basic Law. Minister President of Schleswig-Holstein, Bjorn Engholm, announced that the party would contest any action taken by the government in the Federal Constitutional Court.[31] Engholm said that the SPD did support blue-helmet peacekeeping missions under Chapter VI of the UN Charter—based on the preconditions of a UN Security Council resolution and a vote of approval by the *Bundestag*—but they were unwilling to consider a broadening of the latitude for the use of force.[32]

Behind the rhetoric, however, lay a great deal of internal party maneuvering and negotiation on the matter. In September 1990, representatives at an SPD Party Congress had rejected a resolution calling for unconditional party support for German participation in peacekeeping missions.[33] By 1992, Hans-Ulrich Klose, leader of the SPD *Bundestag Fraktion*, continued to argue that the party was opposed to any type of deployment in Somalia without an amendment to the Basic Law, but suggested that a properly authorized Somalia mission would be "one which his party would support."[34] Klose warned that "in the light of the growing number of political and military crises all around the globe, it will be increasingly impossible to draw a sharp distinction between peacekeeping and peacemaking, and that Germany could eventually be drawn into a conflict.[35] Meanwhile, Norbert Gansel, the chief foreign policy spokesman for the SPD, argued that the party should support the deployment of *Bundeswehr* soldiers for humanitarian operations even without amending the constitution.[36] He publicly criticized the SPD for not being able to reach a joint resolution with other parties that would support the *Bundeswehr*'s participation in military deployments. Finally, Gerhard Schröder, the Minister President of Lower Saxony, said that peacekeeping was an essential mission of the *Bundeswehr*, but that such questions had become too politically complicated. He opposed German involvement in combat operations and said that Germany required "ten years to find a new identity, during which time we would like to solve our own problems in quiet and not intervene in other lands."[37] He added that the "government would be better off if it did not get involved in overseas adventures before the Constitutional Court decision."[38]

Public attitudes were quite mixed during the debates over the proper course of action in Somalia. Surveys of German attitudes toward the Somalia deployment, negotiations inside the government on interpretation of the Basic Law, and German responsibility in international affairs were conducted throughout 1992 and 1993. In the summer of 1993, for example, 53% of Germans said that they would support the Somalia mission, and 56% said that they thought a Constitutional Court review of the Somalia deployment was reasonable. A strong majority, 62%, agreed that some sort of negotiated settlement between the government and the opposition to amend the Basic Law would be significant.[39]

German public opinion reflected that of the cabinet and party positions at the time. Most Germans believed that their country should act in response to international humanitarian crises like Somalia, but they disagreed over the constitutionality of such action and the limits on German engagement overseas. One survey conducted in 1992 found that 62% of respondents felt that "Germany should pursue a more active role" in international affairs, but by 1993 that figure had dropped to 57%. When asked about various possible deployments of troops abroad, 95% of Germans said that they supported some role in humanitarian missions, 53% favored participation in UN peacekeeping missions, 50% of Germans supported the deployment of the *Bundeswehr* in peace missions led by NATO, but only 18% said that Germany should participate in future Gulf War-like operations sanctioned by the UN.[40]

Not only was the public's opinion mixed on the Somalia deployment, but there were also reports of dissent within the military ranks on the issue. Several *Bundeswehr* soldiers from the 26th Airbone division stationed in Berlin reportedly protested to their superior officers about the mission when it became more apparent that they would be shipped out to Somalia.[41] One editorial by Helmut Oplethal, appearing in the *Frankfurter Rundschau* in May 1993, suggested that the military viewed the operation somewhat differently than did the leadership in Bonn. He said that military leaders feared that the location of the German deployment, around Belet Uen, Somalia, was less stable than the government claimed, that the need for military forces to deliver humanitarian aid in Somalia had diminished in recent months, and that nongovernment organizations might be better suited to deal with the humanitarian dimensions of the mission than the military. In a sweeping critique, Oplethal explained the skeptics' position:

This operation could be called humanitarian to some extent, but it does not work without military coercion, which the German soldiers must avoid. However, Bonn should not abuse the tortured Somalia as an exercise field for Bonn's tests of power and as a place for the telegenic self-presentation of a very disputed new role of the *Bundeswehr*.[42]

Germany Responds to the Crisis in Somalia

The German government responded to the crisis in Somalia and international appeals for support for the humanitarian relief operation on two levels. First, Conservative leaders realized that they must appease domestic political opponents of any *Bundeswehr* deployment to Somalia by entering into negotiations on amending the Basic Law. These talks soon collapsed, but the political concession from the right for negotiations was highly significant. Second, cabinet leaders moved forward with plans to deploy 1,600 *Bundeswehr* soldiers to Somalia as part of the UNOSOM II relief mission, and they put forward a cabinet initiative for vote in the *Bundestag* in April 1993.

Government leaders decided in late December 1992 that they should participate in inter-party negotiations on the question of amendment to the Basic Law. While key Conservatives were reluctant to open this political can of worms—and continued to insist that the Basic Law did not prevent German troop deployments in humanitarian operations abroad—they came to view the negotiations as politically necessary. Their junior coalition partner, the Free Democratic Party, had taken a stand on the question, stating their opposition to the deployment without first making real progress towards amending the Basic Law. In exchange for their willingness to enter into the negotiations, the CDU/CSU obtained a valuable concession from the FDP—the government position on amending the Basic Law would include a clause allowing German participation in future peacemaking operations with the UN, NATO, or even the WEU. Conservatives attempted to sugar-coat this clause for the opposition by suggesting that such actions outside the norm would require a two-thirds majority vote of support from the *Bundestag*.[43]

Party leaders met in Bonn in January 1993 to discuss their respective ideas on amending the Basic Law. The government proposal included several key clauses:

1. Germany could participate in peacekeeping operations authorized by UN Security Council resolutions, or within the framework of regional agreements in accordance with the UN Charter as long as Germany remained a member.
2. Germany could participate in peace-making operations based on Chapters VII and VIII of the UN Charter and in accordance with Security Council resolutions.
3. Germany could exercise the right of collective self-defense in terms of Article 51 of the UN Charter together with other countries within the framework of alliances and other regional agreements to which Germany belonged.

4. Government plans for troop deployments under the authority of the UN would require a simple majority vote in the *Bundestag*. Government plans for military operations in conjunction with alliances and regional organizations would require a two-thirds majority in the *Bundestag*.[44]

Government leaders argued that this amendment proposal struck the right balance between responsibility to the international community and parliamentary limitations on government action. At the same time, CDU/CSU negotiators made it clear during the talks that they did not view such a change as absolutely necessary, and that they would ensure that Germany was engaged in future military operations within the frameworks of the UN, NATO, and even the WEU.[45] As if to punctuate this strong stand, Defense Minister Rühe announced on January 6, 1993, that "the German government must take speedy, practical steps to deploy troops for UNOSOM II. Somalia cannot wait for the solution of our basic problems."[46]

According to Hans-Ulrich Klose, head of the SPD *Bundestag Fraktion*, the party was prepared to amend the constitution to enable the deployment of the *Bundeswehr* in Somalia. Representatives at the special conference categorically rejected the Conservative proposal to allow future peacemaking operations through the amendment to the Basic Law.[47] SPD party representatives concluded that the government proposal was simply unacceptable. They viewed the widening of contingencies for German troop deployment abroad as a very dangerous precedent and a violation of basic norms in foreign and defense policy. Some left-wing members of the party attacked the government position and claimed that Conservatives were attempting to "re-imperialize" the *Bundeswehr*. These concerns were echoed by key representatives of the Green/Alliance '90 group and other critics of the government. On January 15, 1993, the SPD went public with its opposition to the government proposal for amending the Basic Law. They advanced an initiative in the *Bundestag* for a narrow amendment, but it failed after its first reading because of government opposition.[48]

The international climate changed dramatically from December 1992 to April 1993, while the German government seemed unable to reach any serious compromise over the constitutionality of troop deployment to Somalia. International peacekeepers were sent to Somalia and generally found little resistance or threat of violence. Within weeks, U.S., British, French, Turkish, Pakistani, and Malaysian troops had all been deployed to Somalia without incident. In late March 1993, the UN Security Council passed Resolution #814, which broadened the operation's objectives to include political reconciliation, economic and social reconstruction, and disarmament. In a letter to the members of the German cabinet just two weeks later, the UN Secretary General urgently requested the deployment of German troops in the peacekeeping mission.[49]

Meanwhile, Kohl, Rühe, and other Conservative leaders tried to convince Foreign Minister Kinkel and the FDP that the end of the bipolar international structure meant an end to the German conception of a military role only for defensive purposes. They finally achieved this in April by emphasizing the international demands for German action in Somalia.[50] On April 21, 1993, the cabinet decided to forward an initiative to the *Bundestag* for approval of German troop deployments to Somalia. As before, government spokesmen pledged that the troops would be deployed solely for humanitarian relief operations in a part of central Somalia that was free of violence.[51] Cabinet leaders immediately launched a television and media blitz and ensured that the government proposal would receive a fair hearing from the leadership in the *Bundestag*.[52] Kinkel presented the government plan for German participation in UNOSOM II. Kinkel provided a detailed account of the plans for the operation and persuasively defined the Somalia question in the largest context of German responsibility for international security in the post-Cold War era:

The United Nations have been able to free themselves through the discontinuation of the East–West conflict from their decades of paralysis in the truest sense of the word. For the first time the odd situation exists that this organization turns into what their founding fathers had in mind, namely, the role of the central peace-guardian of mankind. We must, whether we want to or not, come to a political and constitutional consensus that allows us to contribute to peace. Despite our legal limitations, we can look back for a long time at our remarkable balance of German participation in the humanitarian peace missions of the United Nations. All of these actions are similar to each other. It is always about helping people in need and to protect them from violence and human rights abuses. . . .

We have made a decision in the cabinet this morning. We have determined after a tiring examination that no constitutional law barriers oppose this use, and despite certain changes in the responsibility profile, the action fits in the framework of our decision on December 17, 1992. It takes place in a pacified area. The Secretary General of the UN assures us that the action purely serves humanitarian purposes. German foreign policy has always been, and remains, a policy of peace.[53]

The cabinet plan soon generated a broad base of support in the legislature, and the deployment initiative received a majority of support for the German mission to Somalia.[54] At the same time, representatives of the opposition SPD and Green/Alliance '90 parties spoke out against the mission, voted against *Bundestag* authorization, and pledged to challenge the initiative in the German Federal Constitutional Court.

"MISSION CREEP" AND THE BREAKDOWN OF UNOSOM II

The United Nations relief mission to Somalia was the largest and most expensive operation ever undertaken by the organization. It involved more than 33,000 troops from 17 different countries in a massive effort to deliver relief supplies to those in need, disarm warring clan groups, and bring order and stability to the war-torn country.

In late April 1993, as soon as the *Bundestag* vote was taken authorizing the German deployment to Somalia, the Defense Ministry issued orders for an advance unit under Major General Georg Bernhard, deputy commander of the *Bundeswehr* Third Corps, to deploy to central Somalia. Within days, 60 more German soldiers shipped out to Somalia, including telecommunications experts, engineers, transport and logistical officers, and infantry. These troops aided the advance unit in establishing a base of operations near Belet Uen, a remote town in central Mogadishu. Infantry soldiers deployed to Somalia came largely from the 23rd Mountain Infantry Brigade in Bad Reichenhall, while many of the engineers and transport troops came from the First Corps based in Münster.[55]

The largest deployment of German soldiers began in late June and early July 1993, and troops immediately began to establish supply lines and base operations in central Somalia. The first German supply ship, the M.S. *Beerberg*, arrived with needed materials for the ground troop deployment on July 3, and the first supply convoy from the port reached German troops in Belet Uen on July 9.[56] Troops also began joint efforts with a neighboring Italian brigade to build an airstrip for transport flights directly to central Somalia.[57]

By late summer, 1,700 German soldiers were committed to the UNOSOM II operation, engaged in a wide variety of tasks. The priority for the mission was logistical support for neighboring military garrisons and direct assistance for the native population. German troops staffed and directed regular supply convoys from ports in Somalia to other garrisons in the central region of the country. Engineers worked on bridge and road repair projects.[58] Together with Italian troops, the Germans worked on water purification projects and storage and distribution systems. They also began maintenance on supply roads, combat air bases, and supply points.[59] By the end of 1993, the German troops had purified approximately 14 million liters of water, delivered 6,000 tons of supplies, and logged more than 580,000 kilometers in transport operations.

German troops helped with the reconstruction of schools and the Belet Uen hospital. Teams of engineers repaired roads, drilled a series of water wells for local citizens, secured irrigation canals and dams in the region, and repaired city administration buildings in the vicinity. In Belet Uen's hospital, medical teams saw 7,500 patients and conducted some 350 operations.[60] German forces even assisted in civil reconstruction by educating local citizens about the need for representative elections for city administration, and the new city administration was installed in a ceremony at the German base camp on October 28, 1993.[61]

Mission Creep

For German soldiers, the Somalia mission took on a relatively routine atmosphere. By August 1993, German media sources were reporting that soldiers were satisfied that they were helping to meet the needs of Somalis and were surprised by the generally warm reception they had received.[62] However, this experience was somewhat unique, as other units in the multinational force began to come under fire from armed Somali clan groups.

Most experts cite "mission creep" as the fundamental problem that began to unravel the tranquillity of the mission in Somalia. *Mission creep* refers to the expansion of the *raison d'être* of military operations, and commanders have warned of its consequences for centuries. In the case of Somalia, the UN and leaders of the major players in UNOSOM II began to assume greater authority concerning issues of peace, stability, and security in Somalia than had originally been mandated. UN Security Council Resolution #814 of March 26, 1993, is often cited as a classic example of mission creep. This resolution was designed to provide a broad mandate for humanitarian operations in Somalia, but many critics have suggested that it was simply too broad. The resolution authorized the peacekeepers to "assume responsibility for the consolidation, expansion, and maintenance of a secure environment throughout Somalia." This mandate provided the authorization that some national units sought to begin to seize weapons caches of the various warring clans. Instead of providing stability through forced disarmament, UN actions were interpreted instead as taking sides with one clan against others.[63]

In June 1993, this conflict turned to bloodshed. Somali clan fighters ambushed and surrounded a convoy of Pakistani peacekeepers, and more than 40 soldiers were killed. The international response to attacks on UN troops was swift and serious. On June 6, 1993, UN Security Council Resolution #837 reaffirmed the mandate of the UNOSOM II mission and authorized UN and national military commanders to take all necessary measures to maintain the peace. This resolution was interpreted as a mandate for the troops to attempt to locate, arrest, and punish those who sponsored attacks on peacekeepers, and Mohammad Aideed became the prime suspect for the ambush on the Pakistanis.[64] On June 12, 1993, a UN assault force including soldiers from eleven different countries carried out a retaliatory raid against the forces of rebel leader Mohammed Farah Aideed. More than 200 persons were arrested including a deputy to Aideed. This ambush, revenge attacks, and the threat of further violence became a pivotal issue in Germany, and was the foundation for the SPD challenge of the Somalia deployment in the German Constitutional Court.[65]

These moves were sufficient to convince Aideed that the international community had allied with his rival, Ali Mahdi. One expert on this subject, Michael Inacker, has noted that Aideed's perception of bias on the part of the UN had historical ties to U.S. support for Siad Barre in the 1980s and the support of Boutros-Ghali (when he was a diplomat working for the Egyptian government). Somali attacks on UN peacekeepers escalated again in August and September 1993, making life much more tense for soldiers serving the UNOSOM II mission. Most German operations occurred without incident, but some soldiers actually were pinned down in a crossfire during a skirmish between rival clans near the Mogadishu airport on July 14, 1993.[66] Clashes between peacekeepers and Somali clan groups between June and September 1993 claimed the lives of 46 UN peacekeepers and an estimated 400 Somali nationals.[67]

As the international peacekeeping mission turned its attention to the hunt for Aideed in the late summer of 1993, critics began to warn that the military was suffering mission creep and that resources were not being well spent. In July 1993, the UN Undersecretary General for Humanitarian Affairs, Jan Eliasson, reported to the Economic and Social Council in Geneva that only 15% of the $166 million pledged to the UN for humanitarian assistance in Somalia had yet been provided. He complained that the international community was spending "ten dollars on military protection for every dollar of humanitarian assistance."[68]

Critics who warned about a potentially disastrous mission creep proved correct. On October 3, 1993, U.S. soldiers participating in the UNOSOM II mission carried out a bold daylight raid to capture top generals from the Aideed clan. U.S. Major General Thomas Montgomery ordered this infiltration in downtown Mogadishu, with the support of Cobra and Blackhawk helicopter gunships.[69] The mission quickly turned to tragedy when two of the helicopters were shot down, and U.S. soldiers became engaged in a bloody, day-long firefight on the streets of Mogadishu. By the time UN armored personnel carriers arrived at the scene to rescue the soldiers, eighteen had been killed and another seventy-five wounded.[70]

The Mogadishu tragedy would have important repercussions for Germany and its involvement in Africa. Just days after the clash, one of the posts of the Italian garrison north of Belet Uen (neighboring the Germans) came under fire and the German camp was placed on high alert status for almost one week. Perceptions of new threats to the camp were heightened by the coincidental timing of the death of Germany's first peacekeeper abroad. Just two weeks after the U.S. Ranger tragedy in Mogadishu, German Medical Staff Sergeant Alexander Arndt was shot in Phnom Penh, Cambodia, by an unknown assailant on a motorcycle. Arndt was the first German soldier ever to be killed in a UN peacekeeping mission, and his death had serious implications for German political leaders.[71]

Critics saw the October 3 attack, counterattack, and its aftermath as a dangerous outgrowth of mission creep. Political leaders saw it as a watershed for the UN mission in Somalia. Within forty-eight hours, President Bill Clinton gave an Oval Office address to the nation, announcing that U.S. forces would be withdrawn from Somalia by March 1994.

The Breakdown of Domestic Consensus in Germany

German leaders had established a consensus in support of the deployment of the *Bundeswehr* in early 1993, and the mission was considered quite successful through October of that year. Deadly clashes between UN peacekeepers and the warring clans in Mogadishu, culminating in the events on October 3, fundamentally changed most views of the operation. These events apparently convinced many Western leaders that the UN mission in Somalia was simply too dangerous and costly, and what followed in Germany was an interesting series of stages of response: from disbelief, to retrenchment, to an emerging consensus for a relatively rapid withdrawal from Somalia.

Helmut Kohl first had dealt with the question of whether the Somalia mission was worth the anticipated casualties in the summer of 1993, in the wake of attacks on Pakistani peacekeepers. At the time, Kohl agreed that the situation in Somalia deserved some concern, but said that the German government felt strongly about the imperative to deliver humanitarian aid to those in need. The chancellor had pledged German support for the mission, and he was sensitive to Germany's international image on the matter. In July, Kohl stated that "just because there were a few unexpected problems, German troops would not back down."[72]

In the wake of the October 3 tragedy, the death of Sergeant Arndt in Cambodia, and President Clinton's announcement of the U.S. withdrawal from the mission, Kohl recognized a great deal of pressure for German retrenchment. Nevertheless, the chancellor held firm in the first few weeks of October that Germany should continue its role in UNOSOM II and not cave in to the opposition SPD's demand for the immediate and complete withdrawal of *Bundeswehr* soldiers from Somalia.[73] The week of October 11, the chancellor, defense minister, and foreign minister all agreed that there was "absolutely no need for withdrawing the soldiers immediately," and they stressed that the Constitutional Court ruling provided them with a legal foundation to continue the operation. Kohl argued that Germany should not plan to withdraw its forces while key allies remained in the country. To assuage growing domestic concern, Kohl's press spokesman stated that the chancellor was "of the opinion that one should rethink the deployment of German soldiers in Somalia."

According to the spokesman, the chancellor regretted that there were "now people who claim that the Germans must withdraw because the Americans are withdrawing," especially because, "Germany had gained a particularly high reputation" from participation in the humanitarian relief effort.[74]

Foreign Minister Kinkel had always maintained a somewhat tentative, wait-and-see attitude regarding the operation, and he had continued to personally lobby the government to find a negotiated settlement to the Basic Law amendment question. Once serious fighting had erupted between UN peacekeepers and Somalis, Kinkel felt that the mission had taken on a dangerous new profile and publicly expressed his concerns about the constitutionality of peace-making in this context.[75]

Meanwhile, the defense minister made it clear that he supported the decision to move forward with the operation. Rühe had visited the soldiers in Somalia in July 1993 and was satisfied that they were in a relatively safe and remote region of the country.[76] Like his counterparts in the cabinet, Rühe recognized the October collapse of international consensus and the need to reconsider the deployment, however. On October 19, Rühe announced that he would explore the issue of withdrawal of troops from Somalia at a meeting of NATO leaders in Travemünde. He stressed his desire to coordinate German actions with the allies present in Somalia, including France, Italy, Belgium, and Norway, but hinted that the *Bundeswehr* "would not be the last unit to switch off the light" on UNOSOM II.[77]

The erosion of party support for the mission began with the SPD and Green/Alliance '90 opposition. The governing council of the SPD had repeatedly appealed to the German government to not send the main *Bundeswehr* contingent to Somalia in light of the June 1993 attacks. From June to November 1993, they contended that the mission had grown beyond the original plan for peaceful humanitarian relief and that there was simply no governing authority for the operation. In the wake of the October attack, SPD party leader Günter Verheugen declared the Somalia mission a "failure" and demanded an immediate withdrawal of German troops from the operation. Verheugen claimed that the UN had become "a party to the war in Somalia," and therefore, a humanitarian operation by the *Bundeswehr* under these conditions was "pure illusion."[78]

The Free Democratic Party also began to rethink the Somalia mission in the wake of the attacks. While the junior coalition partner had toed the major party line during the early stages of the operation, it was clear to any serious observer that FDP support for UNOSOM II was tentative at best. Klaus Kinkel had carefully maintained the wait-and-see approach through the spring and summer of 1993, and the spiral of tragedy in Somalia seemed to convince skeptical FDP party members that the operation should not continue in its present form. In advance of the October attack, Jürgen Koppelin, an FDP defense expert, had warned that German soldiers in Somalia might have to be recalled should new fighting erupt in the area where they were stationed.[79] At the same time, FDP Secretary General Hoyer warned that while there was "no reason to lose one's nerve for the operation" at the time, Germany should "negotiate with its allies on a rapid and peaceful withdrawal from Somalia."[80]

Public attitudes toward the Somalia deployment seemed to follow the government's lead in the fall of 1993. While 58% of those polled said that Germany should be able to serve in missions under the UN flag, only 53% supported the Somalia deployment.[81] In September 1993, the Institute for Demoskopie polled Germans on their attitudes regarding the danger of the operation: 51% said that they believed German troops should be withdrawn from Somalia if they "were to come under fire from rebels in the country."[82]

Germany Responds to the Breakdown of UNOSOM II

The deadly attacks on UN peacekeepers in Somalia called attention to the danger of such deployments, and leaders in capitals throughout the world had to struggle with the proper response to the attack. For most western leaders, the idea of further involvement in the Somali civil war was no longer an option. President Clinton's announcement that U.S. troops would be "honorably withdrawn" in a timely manner from Somalia set a precedent that many allies soon followed. In fact, Clinton faced much of the same erosion of domestic political consensus for the Somalia deployment as did German leaders in the wake of the October attack. Congressional leaders, driven by polls indicating that the majority of Americans were now opposed to the operation, put a great deal of pressure on the president and his cabinet to ensure that an honorable withdrawal would take place in a timely manner.[83]

For Germany the question was no longer *whether* soldiers should be removed from Africa, but rather *how* and *when*? According to secondary sources, Kohl and Rühe decided in late November 1993 that the *Bundeswehr* should be withdrawn from Somalia starting in February 1994 and ending before April.[84] German leaders adopted this plan after a series of talks with the Pentagon in Washington, and U.S. Secretary of Defense Les Aspin promised Rühe the United States could protect the withdrawal of German forces via the Mogadishu airport until March 31, 1994—but not a day longer.[85] On December 20, 1993, the German cabinet discussed the plans for a military withdrawal and announced that troops would be out of Somalia by the end of March.[86]

German troops began the long road home from Somalia in January 1994. Engineers and soldiers began to dismantle their camp near Belet Uen in February, and the entire base of operations was vacated and left to local Somali authorities on February 28, 1994. The last contingent of

170 soldiers left Mogadishu for Djibouti on March 18, 1994.[87] A Defense Ministry assessment of involvement in the UNOSOM II mission calculated that some 4,500 German soldiers (including air lift and naval federation) had participated in the operation, and total estimated costs were DM 310 million.[88]

Defense Minister Rühe was upbeat as he greeted soldiers returning from the Somalia operation at an airbase in Germany. He proudly concluded:

You have in the last months fulfilled a significant assignment, assisting people in need. In just ten months, German soldiers worked as blue-helmet peacekeepers and fulfilled their duties. . . . The engagement for UNOSOM II was a military operation and it was supported by military logistics in Djibouti, Kenya, at sea, and at home. You have fulfilled your duties in an efficient and effective way. . . . We must now consider the lessons of this operation for the future. We must strengthen the capabilities of the United Nations, and many governments must work together to support multilateral actions.

Everything that we did in Somalia was for humanitarian good. Your operation in Somalia was an investment in humanity, and also in the future of the *Bundeswehr*. Germany has proven its capabilities to be a responsible member of broader society. We are prepared for growing responsibilities in the world. . . . I thank you for your true service. You have not only fulfilled your duty as soldiers. You were also roving ambassadors for our land and were a credit to Germany's reputation in the world.[89]

This characterization of the mission was to have a profound influence on the future development of German foreign policy responses to humanitarian tragedies.

NOTES

1. Volker Rühe, "Die weltpolitische Verantwortung des geeinten Deutschlands," CDU-Dokumentation, no. 17 (Bonn: Pressemitteilung, 1991), p. 9.

2. Bela Anda interview with Gerhard Schröder, "Blauhelmeinsatz Kanzlerkandidate SPD," *Bild*, 19 April 1993, p. 1.

3. *A Government at War with Its Own People: An Africa Watch Report* (New York: The African Watch Committee, January 1990).

4. See Terrence Lyons, *Somalia: State Collapse, Multilateral Intervention, and Strategies for Political Reconstruction* (Washington, DC: The Brookings Institution, 1995).

5. The African Watch Committee, p. 45.

6. Lyons, *Somalia*, pp. 22–23.

7. Ramesh Thakur, "From Peacekeeping to Peace Enforcement: The UN Operation in Somalia," *The Journal of Modern African Studies*, vol. 32, no. 3, December 1994, pp. 387–410.

8. See David Rawson, *The Somali State and Foreign Aid* (Washington, DC: Foreign Service Institute of the U.S. Department of State, 1993).

9. Bundesministerium der Verteidigung, Informationsstab Referat Öffentlichkeitsarbeit, "Information zur Sicherheitspolitik: Beteiligung der Bundeswehr an Missionen der Vereinten Nationen, 1992 bis 1994," February 1995, pp. 16–17.

10. Samuel Makinda, "Somalia: From Humanitarian Intervention to Military Offensive." *The World Today*, vol. 5, October 1993, p. 184.

11. Ibid., p. 186.

12. "Wörner Urges FRG Role in Peacekeeping Missions," *Berlin DDP*, 8 January 1993; reprinted in FBIS-WEU, 93-006, 11 January 1993, p. 10.

13. Klaus Kinkel, "Peacekeeping Missions: Germany Can Now Play Its Part," *NATO Review*, vol. 5, no. 3, October 1994, p. 4.

14. Wolfgang Wagner, "Abenteuer in Somalia," *Europa-Archiv*, Folge 6, 1994, pp. 151–159.

15. *Frankfurter Allgemeine Zeitung*, 17 December 1992, p. 1; see also "Kohl Seeks to Send up to 1,500 Troops on Somalia Mission," *New York Times*, 18 December 1992, p. A1.

16. See "Kinkel: UN Needs to Become Powerful Instrument of New World Policy," *This Week in Germany*, 25 September 1992; and Craig R. Whitney, "UN Asks Bonn to Send Troops as Peacekeepers," *New York Times*, 10 January 1993, p. A1.

17. Ibid.

18. Helmut Kohl, "Die Sicherheitsinteressen Deutschlands," transcript of speech presented on 6 February 1993; reprinted in *Bulletin*, Presse- und Informationsamt der Bundesregierung, no. 13, Bonn, 10 February 1993, p. 101.

19. "Schneisen Schlagen," *Der Spiegel*, 46, 1992, pp. 26–27.

20. "Eine regelrechte Psychose," *Der Spiegel*, 21 December 1992, pp. 18–19.

21. See "Naumann: Bundeswehr ist bequem und überheblich geworden," *Suddeutsche Zeitung*, 4 May 1992; see also interview with Naumann in *Financial Times*, 13 July 1992; "GröBenwahn der Generäle" *Der Spiegel*, 6 April 1992, pp. 18–21.

22. "Zickzack nach Afrika," *Der Spiegel*, 1, 1993, pp. 27–28.

23. See Quentin Peel, "Confusion Reigns in Bundeswehr," *Financial Times*, 17 February 1993. The annual report of the parliamentary ombudsman on defense, released in March 1992, mentioned cases of *Bundeswehr* commanders' extreme frustration with the political leadership's restructuring effort, as well as its guidance on German operations in Turkey and Iran. See "Scharfe Kritik an Stoltenberg," *Süddeutsche Zeitung*, 13 March 1992; "Sinn und Aufgaben der Streitkräfte," *Frankfurter Allgemeine Zeitung*, 13 March 1992, p. 1.

24. Klaus Kinkel, "Die Rolle Deutschlands in der Weltpolitik," *Bulletin*, Presse- und Informationsamt der Bundesregierung, no. 18, s. 141, Bonn, 3 March 1993, p. 141.

25. "Zickzack nach Afrika," *Der Spiegel*, 1 January 1993, pp. 27–28.

26. Karl-Heinz Kamp, "The German Bundeswehr in Out-of-Area Operations: To Engage or Not to Engage?" *The World Today*, vol. 4, p. 167.

27. Confidential interview, Bundeshaus (Bundestag Legislative Offices), Bonn, 20 June 1996; see also John S. Duffield, "German Security Policy after Unification; Sources of Continuity and Restraint," *Contemporary Security Policy*, vol. 15, no. 3, December 1994, pp. 170–198.

28. "Kinkel Renews Call for Out-of-Area Amendment," Berlin ADN Radio; reprinted in FBIS-WEU, 93–110, 10 June 1993, p. 10.

29. Duffield, "German Security Policy," pp. 170–198.

30. *Süddeutsche Zeitung*, 23 April 1993, p. 2.

31. "Tagesschau," Deutschefernsehen ARD, interview transcript from 17 December 1992, BPA, Presse- und Informationsamt der Bundesregierung, 17 December 1992.

32. Karl-Heinz, Kamp "German Bundeswehr in Out-of-Area Operations: To Engage or Not to Engage?" *The World Today*, vol. 49, 1993, pp. 165–168.

33. "Zur Discussion um einen Bundeswehr-einsatz in Somalia," debate televised on German television ARD, 23 December 1992, transcript from BPA, 23 December 1992; see also Resolution on Foreign, Peace, and Security Policy Passed at the Bremen Party Congress, Presseservice der SPD, 31 May 1991.

34. FBIS-WEU-92-240, "SPD Supports Bundeswehr Role," 14 December 1992, p. 23.

35. FBIS-WEU-92-239, "SPD Urges New Party Policy," 30 November 1992, p. 14.

36. FBIS-WEU-92-240, "SPD Supports Bundeswehr Role," p. 37.

37. Bela Anda interview with Gerhard Schröder, "Blauhelmeinsatz Kanzlerkandidate SPD," *Bild*, 19 April 1993, p. 1

38. Anda interview with Schröder, 1993, p. 1. In this same interview, Schröder was asked whether he would run for chancellor in 1994. He replied, "I am not searching for a new job, but I would not rule out something in the future."

39. "INFAS-Umfrage zum Einsatz der Bundeswehr in Somalia sowie zur allgemeinen Beteiligung an UN-Einsätzen," television broadcast on Rückspiegel, MDR 3, 15 May 1993.

40. Ironically, public opinion surveys from 1992 and 1993 also showed that German attentions were not focused on the crisis in Somalia. Germans who were asked to define areas of vital national interest responded that Eastern Europe was most important (69%), Russia was of concern (66%), as were relations with the United States (64%)—while Africa was barely of public concern at the time. Another dimension of public attitudes regarding humanitarian crises was reflected in opinion surveys of "the greatest threats to German vital interests" in 1993: 78% of Germans answered "another Chernobyl" disaster, 69% worried about the spread of ultra-nationalist movements, 63% feared proliferation of rogue states, 48% feared Islamic fundamentalism, and 43% feared immigration problems. A significant domestic political culture of foreign policy reticence was reflected in the surveys; for more on this, see Ronald D. Asmus, *German Strategy and Opinion after the Wall, 1990–1993* (RAND: Santa Monica, CA, 1994), pp. 17 and 63.

41. "Bundeswehr Soldiers Reportedly Refuse Somalia Service," Berlin ADN, 7 May 1993; reprinted in FBIS-WEU, 93-087, 7 May 1993, p. 14.

42. Helmut Oplethal, "Somalia is Not the Issue," *Frankfurther Rundschau*, 14 May 1993, p.3.

43. Franz-Josef Meiers, "NATO's Peacekeeping Dilemma, *Arbeitspapere zur Internationalen Politik*," vol. 94, Forschungsinstitut der Deutschen Gesellschaft für Auswärtige Politik, May 1996.

44. Kamp, *The World Today*, 1993, pp. 165–168.

45. Confidential interview, Kanzleramt, Bonn, 13 June 1996; see also Wolfgang Schlör, *German Security Policy*, Adelphi Paper #277, June 1993, p. 11.

46. *Süddeutsche Zeitung*, 7 January 1993, p. 1.

47. FBIS-WEU-92-240, "SPD Supports Bundeswehr Role," p. 446.

48. *Frankfurter Allgemeine Zeitung*, 20 January 1993, p. 1.

49. Nina Ruge, "Boutros-Ghali: UN Needs Bundeswehr in Somalia," interview with UN Secretary General, Bonn, 23 June 1993.

50. "FDP Presidium Agrees to Bundeswehr Mission in Somalia," *Süddeutsche Zeitung*, 23 April 1993, p. 14.

51. "Erste Information über den Einsatz der Bundeswehr im Rahmen der Vereinten Nationen in Somalia und wichtige Hinweise für die Pressearbeit," Mitteilungen an die Presse, Der Bundesminister der Verteidiung, Bonn, 21 April 1993.

52. "Beschluß der Bundesregierung zur Unterstützung von UNOSOM II in Somalia," *Bulletin*, Presse- und Informationsamt der Bundesregiergun, 32, 23 April 1993, p. 280.

53. Klaus Kinkel, Bundestag Sternographischer Bericht 151 session, Bonn, 21 April 1993.

54. "Auch Verluste," *Der Spiegel*, 24 April 1993, p. 33; see also *Deutschland Nachrichten*, 25 June 1993, p. 1.

55. Michael J. Inacker, "Infantry, Tanks, Command Structure: Bundeswehr Plans for Somalia Mission," *Welt am Sonntag*, 10 January 1993, p. 6.

56. Material für die Presse, "Hintergrundinformationen und Leistungsdaten zum Einsatz des Deutschen Unterstützungsverbandes in Somalia," Bundesministerium der Verteidigung Presse-amt, Bonn, 23 March 1994.

57. Erich Wiedemann, "Ganz Normaler Auftrag," *Der Spiegel* 30, 1993, pp. 110–112.

58. Material für die Presse, "Hintergrundinformationen und Leistungsdaten zum Einsatz des Deutschen Unterstützungsverbandes in Somalia," Bundesministerium der Verteidigung Presse-amt, Bonn, 23 March 1994.

59. Bundesministerium der Verteidigung, Informationsstab Referat Öffentlichkeitsarbeit, "Information zur Sicherheitspolitik: Beteiligung der Bundeswehr an Missionen der Vereinten Nationen, 1992 bis 1994," February 1995, pp. 4–5.

60. For an interesting, journalistic description of life in the Somalia deployment, see Bodo Kirchhoff, "Staub in allen Briefen," *Der Spiegel* 30, 1993, pp. 160–165.

61. Bundesministerium der Verteidigung, *Weißbuch 1994* (Bonn: Bundesministerium der Verteidigung, 1994).

62. For personal accounts of soldiers involvement in the Somalia mission, see "Berichte beteiligter Soldaten"; Bundesministerium der Verteidigung, Informationsstab Referat Öffentlichkeitsarbeit, "Information zur Sicherheitspolitik: Beteiligung der Bundeswehr an Missionen der Vereinten Nationen, 1992 bis 1994," February 1995, pp. 16–17.

63. Samuel M. Makinda, "Somalia: From Humanitarian Intervention to Military Offensive," *The World Today*, vol. 49, no. 10, October 1993, pp. 184–186.

64. Michael J. Inacker, "Infantry, Tanks, Command Structure: Bundeswehr Plans for Somalia Mission," *Welt am Sonntag*, 10 January 1993, p. 6; "Interview mit UN-Generalsekretär Boutros-Ghali über die Toten beim umstrittenen Somalia-Einsatz, einen ständigen Sitz im Sicherheitsrat für Deutschland und Mißmanagement und Korruption bei der Weltorganisation," *Die Stern*, 30 September 1993.

65. Ramesh Thakur, "From Peacekeeping to Peace Enforcement: The UN Operation in Somalia," *The Journal of Modern African Studies*, vol. 32, no. 3, 1994, pp. 387–410.

66. Material für die Presse, "Hintergrundinformationen und Leistungsdaten zum Einsatz des Deutschen Unterstützungsverbandes in Somalia," Bundesministerium der Verteidigung Presseamt, Bonn, 23 March 1994.

67. Samuel M. Makinda, "Somalia: From Humanitarian Intervention to Military Offensive," *The World Today*, vol.49, no. 10, October 1993, pp. 184–186.

68. Africa Confidential, vol. 34, no. 15, 30 July 1993, p. 2; see also *The Indian Ocean Newletter*, 31 July 1993, p. 2.

69. Makinda, October 1993, pp. 184–186.

70. For a detailed account of the tragic event on October 3, 1993, see Michael R. Gordon and John H. Cushman, "Record Contradicts Clinton on Somalia," *New York Times*, 19 October 1993; Michael R. Gordon with Thomas L. Friedman, "Details of U.S. Raid in Somalia: Success So Near, a Loss so Deep," *New York Times*, 25 October 1993; Rick Atkinson, "U.S. Expedition in Somalia: The Making of a Disaster," *International Herald Tribune*, 31 January 1994; see also Jonathan T. Howe, "The United States and the United Nations in Somalia: The Limits of Involvement," *The Washington Quarterly*, vol. 18, no. 3, Summer 1995, pp. 49–62; and John Gerard Ruggie, "Peacekeeping and U.S. Interests," *The Washington Quarterly*, vol. 17, no. 4, Autumn 1994, especially pp. 181–182.

71. *Das Bild*, 18 October 1993, p. 2; reprinted in FBIS-WEU, 19 October 1993, p. 26.

72. FBIS-WEU-93-139, "Kohl defends Bundeswehr Mission in Somalia," 22 July 1993, p. 34.

73. Heinrich Schenemann, "Bonn Now Questions Scope of Somalia Mission," *Welt am Sonntag*, 17 October 1993, pp. 1–2; reprinted in FBIS-WEU 93-200, 19 October 1993, p. 27.

74. Schenemann, 17 October 1993, p. 27. This was supported by information drawn from confidential interview, Bundeshaus (Bundestag Legislative Offices), Bonn, 20 June 1996.

75. "Kinkel Renews Call for Out-of-Area Amendment," Berlin ADN Radio; reprinted in FBIS-WEU, 93-110, 10 June 1993, p. 10.

76. "Pressekonferenz: Urteil des Bundesverfassungsgericht zum Bundeswehreinsatz in Somalia," Presse- und Informationsamt der Bundesregierung, Bonn, June 23, 1993.

77. "Rühe Has Not Coordinated Himself with the Chancellor," *Frankfurter Allgemeine Zeitung*, 19 October 1993, pp. 1–2.

78. Heinrich Schenemann, "Bonn Now Questions Scope of Somalia Mission," *Welt am Sonntag*, 17 October 1993, pp. 1–2; reprinted in FBIS-WEU 93-200, 19 October 1993, p. 27.

79. "Somalia Troops Recall Possible," Berlin ADN, 15 June 1993; reprinted in FBIS-WEU, 93-113, 15 June 1993, p. 27.

80. "Waigel Calls for Reexamination of Somalia Mission," *Frankfurter Allgemeine Zeitung*, 20 July 1993, pp. 1–2.

81. "INFAS-Umfrage zum Einsatz der Bundeswehr in Somalia sowie zur allgemeinen Beteiligung an UN-Einsätzen," television broadcast on *Rückspiegel*, MDR 3, 15 May 1993.

82. EMNID Umfrage für den Spiegel, Eric Wiedemann, "Ganz Normaler Auftrag," Der Spiegel 30, 1993, p. 111.

83. "Withdrawal—But How?" *Frankfurter Allgemeine Zeitung*, 8 October 1993, p. 1.

84. Material für die Presse, "Hintergrundinformationen und Leistungsdaten zum Einsatz des Deutschen Unterstützungsverbandes in Somalia," Bundesministerium der Verteidigung Presse-amt, Bonn, 23 March 1994; see also "Zu Einsätzen der Bundeswehr im Rahmen der UNO," Presse- und Informationsmt der Bundesregierung, Referat Außen- und Sicherheitspolitik, July 1994.

85. "Somalia: Withdrawal to Start as Early As February," *Bild am Sonntag*, 28 November 1993, p. 5; reprinted in FBIS-WEU 93-228, 30 November 1993, p. 18.

86. "Bundeswehr to Leave Somalia by 31 March," Hamburg DPA, 20 December 1993, radio report transcript in FBIS-WEU 93-243, 21 December 1993, p. 20; see also interview with Volker Rühe, *Zweite Deutsche Fernsehen*, 20 December 1993, transcript printed in FBIS-WEU 93-243, 21 December 1993, p. 20.

87. Bundesministerium der Verteidigung, Informationsstab Referat Öffentlichkeitsarbeit, "Information zur Sicherheitspolitik: Beteiligung der Bundeswehr an Missionen der Vereinten Nationen, 1992 bis 1994," February 1995, pp. 4–5.

88. "Bundesminister der Verteidigung Volker Rühe zu den Kosten des Einsatzes des Deutschen Unterstützungsverbandes in Somalia vom Mai 1993 bis März 1994," Bundesministerium der Verteidigung, Bonn, 28 February 1994.

89. Bundesministerium der Verteidigung, Material für die Presse, "Ansprache des Bundesministers der Verteidigung Volker Rühe, anläßlich der Begrüßung und Außerdienststellung des deutschen Unterstützungsverbandes Somalia am 23 März in Köln-Bonn, Bonn, 23 March 1994.

4

Diplomacy and Delay: Responding to the Civil War in the Former Yugoslavia, 1991–1994

> The experience of our most recent history, namely the period of the National–Socialist dictatorship with an inhuman and destructive regime and the regime of injustice of a different kind in the former German Democratic Republic, really establishes a special responsibility for German foreign policy to actively promote peace and human rights in the international realm.
>
> —Helmut Kohl, 1992[1]

The civil war in the former Yugoslavia presented some of the most serious strategic dilemmas ever faced by leaders of the Federal Republic of Germany. In fact, some high-ranking German officials have contended that the crisis in the Balkans was *the* primary catalyst for German foreign policy restructuring and changing domestic political alignments in the post-Cold War era.[2] This chapter explores the evolution of German responses to three dilemmas created by the civil war in the former Yugoslavia (Figure 4.1) and how such crises, in turn, shaped domestic political orientations at several levels. I explore a pattern of evidence that

Figure 4.1
Strategic Dilemmas in the Former Yugoslavia, 1991–1994

Stages/Dates	Strategic Dilemma	Foreign Policy Response
I. 1991–1992	Croatia and Slovenia Secede/ Seek Diplomatic Recognition	Immediate Recognition, Pressure EU to Follow
II. 1992–1993	WEU Enforcement of Embargo/ Adriatic Monitoring	Limited Commitment of Navy and Air Force
III. 1993–1994	Operation Deny Flight/AWACS Deployment Over Bosnia	Debate and Reluctant Staff Commitment

suggests that German leaders both reacted to and consciously used developments in the civil war in Yugoslavia as leverage to circumvent domestic constraints and reshape their commitment to international security in the post-Cold War era.[3]

THE OUTBREAK OF CIVIL WAR: RECOGNITION OF CROATIAN AND SLOVENIAN INDEPENDENCE

Historical Background

The modern crisis in Yugoslavia is a function of a century of upheaval in the Balkans. The assassination of Archduke Franz Ferdinand in the streets of Sarajevo by a Serbian nationalist in 1914 effectively ignited the fires of World War I. After the war, the Kingdom of the Serbs, Croats, and Slovenes was created from the remains of the Ottoman and Habsburg Empires. The first leader of the unified country, King Alexander, changed the name of the country to Yugoslavia, but was unable to resolve the simmering rivalries among the three nationalities in the region. He, too, was killed by an assassin in 1934.[4]

Germany became entangled directly in Balkan affairs in 1941, when Hitler ordered the invasion and occupation of the region. The *Wehrmacht* maintained control of some parts of the country with the support of Croatian nationalist groups, called "Ustashes." German occupation authority was not absolute, and soldiers regularly skirmished with resistance groups including the Serb nationalists, called "Chetniks," and Communist partisans, led by a former locksmith named Josip Broz.[5]

In 1945, Josip Broz Tito emerged as the victor in the resistance against Nazi occupation and became the popular ruler of a newly liberated Yugoslavia. Tito orchestrated the development of a special Yugoslav form of Communism that was independent of the Soviet Union, and banned all other political parties. Under his "Tito Constitution" of 1974, Yugoslavia was established as a federal state consisting of six republics and two autonomous regions, to be governed by a collective federal presidency with rotating political authority.[6] Tito's approach to dealing with ethnic nationalist differences in the Balkans was heavy-handed. Officially, Tito preferred to stifle the expression of differences through determined support for political mantras such as "Brotherhood and Unity" and severe punishment for those who dared to express differences based on ethnicity. Unofficially, regional differences became institutionalized in the 1970s, however, and Tito's death in 1980 created an opening for a liberalization of the system that included free market economics and democratization.[7]

In 1990, leaders of the Yugoslav federation lifted the old Communist regime's ban on political parties and allowed the first multiparty elections in the republics in April. New political organizations, including the nationalist Croatian Democratic Union (HDZ), the Serbian Radical Party, and the Slovene Christian Democrats, were established, and the former Communist Party was renamed the League of Communists of Yugoslavia.[8] In Croatia, the HDZ emerged victorious in the elections (with $4 million in financial backing from the Croatian émigré community in Germany and other European countries). Croatia's president, Franjo Tudjman, was given a popular mandate for his agenda to create a state that would be identified with the Croatian "nation" and one in which he refused to grant strong minority rights to the 600,000-strong Serb population.[9] Other elections in 1990 also transformed the political landscape of Yugoslavia, as Slovenia, Bosnia–Herzegovina, and Macedonia elected noncommunist governments.[10]

Communist leaders maintained power in only two provinces, Serbia and Montenegro, but these regional strongholds were significant. Slobodan Milosevic, President of the Serbian Republic, interpreted the liberalization of politics in the region as a challenge to the power of the federal government and a threat to Yugoslavia's national security.[11] These threats also seemed to rekindle age-old ethnic nationalism in the region during this crucial period of transition. Subsequently, Milosevic began to mobilize Serbian nationalist sentiment and increased official and unofficial rhetorical attacks against Croatians, Muslims, Albanians, and other nationalities—all of whom he believed were threatening the centralization of Yugoslav political authority. At the same time, new leaders in Slovenia and Croatia opposed Milosevic's demands for a return to the centralization of the system, and preferred a loose confederation of states in the Balkans. While the presidents of the six Yugoslav republics met repeatedly to discuss the future of the federation throughout 1990 and 1991, there was little progress in negotiations.[12] One expert who observed this downward spiral of events said that "the single most important reason for the dissolution of Yugoslavia was the inability of this multinational country (including the Muslims, the Serbs, and the Croats) to solve the national question" at this critical point.[13]

The Federation of Yugoslavia dissolved on June 25, 1991, when the governments of the Republics of Slovenia and Croatia declared their independence. This was interpreted by many in the West as a natural response to the centrifugal political forces in the region, to the interplay of economic and social conditions in the various republics, and to the demands by Serbian leaders for a return to the centralization of the old Yugoslavia.[14] It should be noted that Germany's special historical relationship with the two republics complicated its perception of the move. Serbia and Montenegro's response to these declarations was less circumspect, however. They declared war on the secessionist republics and demanded they return to the federation.[15]

Fighting broke out within twenty-four hours of the original declaration, pitting the Serbs first against Slovenia.[16] This conflict lasted ten days, during which time the Yugoslav National Army (JNA) suffered a series of embarrassing defeats, and the Slovenes quickly won *de facto* independence. The war between Croatia and Serbia, however, was much more intense. By the fall of 1991, Serbian irregulars and troops from the JNA had driven native Croats out of more than 30% of Croatian territory. Serbian naval and artillery forces also bombarded Dubrovnik and Vukovar, historic cities along Croatia's Dalmatian coast. After six months of fighting, Croatian and Serbian negotiators agreed to a cease-fire and the imposition of United Nations (UN) peacekeeping troops in a buffer zone in the spring of 1992. All told, the Serb–Croat conflict lasted almost a year and claimed some 10,000 lives. The war in Croatia was over, but Serbian forces soon turned their attention to Bosnia.[17]

Germany Confronts the Crisis in the Balkans

The Croatian and Slovenian declarations of independence and the subsequent civil war in the Balkans presented the West not only with its first European security crisis in the post-Cold War era but also with a major strategic dilemma. The German government was affected by these developments almost immediately. Germany experienced a major influx of refugees seeking asylum after the crisis began in June 1991, and concerns grew about the potential spillover of the conflict into other areas.[18] In this initial phase of the conflict, Chancellor Kohl and key leaders believed that they had domestic support for a series of diplomatic initiatives designed to stop the violence.

The primary focus of diplomacy throughout 1991 and early 1992 was the question of recognition. Should the German government and other Western nations support the legitimacy of the Croat and Slovenian claims of independence through formal recognition? Germany's answer to this question was somewhat complicated by historic ties to the two republics and the occupation experience during World War II. For the first few months after the republics' declarations of independence, Germany stood firm with the positions of the United States and the European Community (EC) that Yugoslavia should be kept together through diplomatic negotiations. At a European Council meeting in Luxembourg in late June 1991, Western diplomats agreed that a fragmentation of the Yugoslav federation would produce a complex mix of new challenges for economic and security relations in the region. The Council recommended that Slovenia and Croatia suspend their move toward independence for three months—a time frame that would allow for continued negotiations on a new institutional arrangement. In a press statement at the end of the conference, Chancellor Kohl offered strong support for the efforts of the European Council and urged all parties to participate in negotiations to restore the Yugoslav federation.[19]

European governments continued their efforts to broker a peace settlement throughout the summer and fall. At a special meeting of the Conference on Security and Cooperation (CSCE) in Europe in July 1991, Jacques Poos, one of three European foreign ministers to serve as an EC mediator, confidently asserted that the CSCE and other organizations would negotiate a peaceful settlement of the crisis and proclaimed: "This is the hour of Europe."[20] In this same spirit, German leaders worked with EC partners to guarantee the participation of Croatia and Slovenia in the EC's peace conference at The Hague on September 7, 1991.[21] When that cease-fire fell apart, NATO leaders gathered in Rome in early November 1991, where they pledged to support a common foreign policy response to the crisis and to continue their push for a diplomatic settlement.[22] Later that month, German leaders encouraged the EC to increase the pressure on the Serbs by imposing economic sanctions against all of the republics of Yugoslavia in November 1991. Economic aid was summarily suspended for Yugoslavia, weapons deliveries were halted, and an oil embargo plan was implemented.[23]

While the West officially remained in support of a restoration of the federation in Yugoslavia, German leaders began to consider a very different foreign policy response to the crisis—full diplomatic recognition of Croatia and Slovenia.[24] The logic for this redirection was two-fold. First, German leaders were more willing than some other Europeans to identify Serbia as the aggressor in this conflict and Croatia and Slovenia as victims. This was based on historic ties to the republics and German perceptions of contemporary developments. German leaders had pushed the EC to establish the sanctions and embargo programs on all Yugoslav republics with the intent to stop Serbian aggression. Key conservatives were interpreting the violence in the former Yugoslavia not as the product of rash Croatian actions, but rather as the result of an aggressive Serbian President Slobodan Milosevic and the Serb-dominated Yugoslav army.[25] In early December, Germany suspended the parts of the bilateral

German–Yugoslav transport agreement that applied to Serbia and Montenegro, communicating the message that Serbia was now the focused target of German actions and that Germany was now willing to take unilateral steps.[26]

Second, this redirection was considered in the context of European politics. By late summer, Foreign Minister Genscher was arguing publicly in Bonn that changing the political mindset on recognition might enable the German government to assume the lead on a matter of common concern to its European partners.[27] By September, Genscher had stated his preference that Germany recognize Croatian and Slovenian independence. On several occasions in October and November, Genscher even warned that Germany would do so unilaterally if necessary.[28] At WEU conference meetings in November and December 1991, other European leaders were unwilling to consider the recognition of Croatia and Slovenia, and remained determined to restore the Yugoslav federation. Debates at these meetings focused on whether or not to support the deployment of European peacekeeping forces as a way to intervene in the conflict between Croatia and Serbia. While Kohl and Genscher remained interested in WEU dialogue, the consideration of potential combat missions further drove them to pursue the diplomatic route of recognition.[29] These developments were important precursors to a shift in German foreign policy.[30]

Domestic Conditions and the Recognition Question

By early December 1991, it appeared that the German government was poised to change direction on the recognition question, and Chancellor Kohl and Genscher surveyed their base of domestic support. They were heartened to find that most cabinet leaders were supportive of diplomatic recognition as the best course of action. In fact, Kohl and key conservatives had been working behind the scenes to build support for recognition for some time. According to the memoirs of Kohl's closest foreign policy advisor, Horst Teltschik, the German government had been in secret negotiations with the Croatian government regarding diplomatic relations since 1990. Teltschik confessed that he met with a personal emissary of Croatian President Tudjman in August 1990 to discuss recognition, and that he had carried out this diplomacy "without the knowledge of the Foreign Office."[31] Thus, it was no surprise inside the government when the Republic of Croatia opened a foreign office in Stuttgart in February 1991 as a preliminary step toward greater cooperation with Germany.[32]

Foreign Minister Genscher was instrumental in bringing about this redirection of German foreign policy, but the diplomatic record shows that he only had joined those in favor of recognition in the summer of

1991. Genscher's visit to Yugoslavia in the last days of June seemed to strengthen his personal resolve to push for the EC's joint recognition of Croatia and Slovenia.[33] The experience convinced him that Serbia was the clear and undisputed aggressor in the conflict, and he drew parallels between past German aggression and the perils of appeasement in World War II. By the fall of 1991, Genscher was convinced that Europe could not stand by and allow history to repeat itself.[34]

Kohl and Genscher also sought support for the recognition of Croatia and Slovenia from the major party organizations. Both the Christian Democratic Union (CDU) and Christian Socialist Union party organizations were supportive of a shift to an open recognition policy. In fact, key leaders in the CDU, including Alfred Dregger, had been quite critical of European plans to restore the federation from the outset, on the grounds that they were no longer realistic.[35] Volker Rühe, then the CDU General Secretary, stated in a press conference that it was not defensible to judge Yugoslavia differently when "we achieved the unity and freedom of our country through the right of self-determination."[36] The FDP also expressed their support for recognition, acknowledging the growing public sentiment against the escalating violence in the Balkans.

Surprisingly, the government even garnered support for unilateral recognition from key leaders in the opposition Social Democratic Party (SPD). Like Genscher, Norbert Gansel, chief foreign policy spokesman for the SPD, traveled to the Balkans in 1991 and was personally transformed by the experience. He returned to suggest that the SPD change its position on the conflict. Gansel argued that he saw no willingness on the part of any faction in the conflict to compromise, thus a policy of pressing for the continued Yugoslav federation seemed increasingly useless.[37]

Public attitudes toward the conflict in the former Yugoslavia also underwent a slow transformation from June to December 1991. At first, the conflict generated little interest for most Germans. An INFAS public opinion survey conducted in July 1991 found that 34% of the respondents felt that independence for the two states would be a dangerous fragmentation of European politics, but 39% believed that the independence of Slovenia and Croatia was the "only guarantee of democracy in the region." In a related response pattern, 54% of Germans felt that the war would be isolated to the Balkans, while 28% felt that the war might threaten European security. Perhaps the most telling question posed in the July survey found that 41% of Germans "trusted the European Community completely" in dealing with the conflict, and 51% at least "trusted" the EC to respond properly.[38] A poll conducted in late july 1991 by the survey group Forsa-Institut found that only 33% of respondents were prepared to grant political asylum to refugees from the Yugoslav war, while a full 67% believed the government should reject the asylum claims.[39]

Heightened media coverage of the dramatic unfolding of events in the Balkans began to change public attitudes about German foreign policy responses to the conflict. By August 1991, less than two months into the war between Croatia and Serbia, EC sources estimated that some 300 noncombatants had already been killed and 50,000 refugees driven from their homes.[40] The Yugoslav army's attack on Dubrovnik and the siege of Vukovar reminded Westerners of the horrors of World War II.[41] At the same time, most of the German media were decidedly pro-Croatian and highly critical of what was interpreted as Serbian aggression.[42] The Bavarian network, *Bayerishe Rundfunk*, provided focused coverage of the situation in the former Yugoslavia that was strongly influenced by the Catholic Church. One expert on the situation argued that the net effect of this interest group–media linkage was that "Croatia had a pipeline into the German media that distorted German public opinion."[43]

Human rights activists and interest groups representing Croatian émigrés also were instrumental in changing the tide of domestic support for a stronger German foreign policy line. Ethnic Croats living in Germany were significant players. Of the 750,000 ethnic Yugoslavs in Germany living in Germany in 1991, more than 600,000 were of direct Croatian descent. Croatian émigrés also were an important support base for the Christian Socialist Union party in Bavaria, and were well aware of the leverage of the CSU in the governing coalition in Bonn. In Bavaria, home to hundreds of thousands of Croatian émigrés, interest groups sponsored large public rallies and began to lobby the German government more heavily for official recognition of Croatia. Throughout the summer and fall, groups of thousands demonstrated in Munich for German recognition of Croatian sovereignty, and the protests gained strength and media attention as the months wore on.[44]

The Government Acts

Domestic conditions were favorable as Genscher and Kohl planned for a foreign policy redirection, and they began a campaign to win support for recognition of Croatia and Slovenia. First, they worked behind the scenes to build consensus among European leaders for more focused foreign policy initiatives that would move toward a definition of the Serbs as the aggressors in the conflict. However, they faced an uphill battle and drew increasing criticism, even from their friends.[45] Meanwhile, Genscher increased the intensity of his public statements that Germany would recognize Croatia and Slovenia unilaterally if necessary. Kohl made several contacts with leaders of the Balkan region, promising Tudjman that Germany would recognize Croatia and would attempt to orchestrate an EC joint recognition strategy at the upcoming Maastricht Summit.[46]

On December 11, 1991, German cabinet leaders decided to recognize the independence of Croatia and Slovenia outside of an established EC framework. They drew legitimacy for this decision from a careful study of international legal implications of recognition that was drafted by a respected international lawyer, as well as an initial promise from the Italian government that it also would support independence. German leaders also claimed that European foreign ministers had agreed at their fall council meeting to set up a two-month deadline for the end of the conflict—a deadline now broken by continued Serbian aggression.[47]

Germany's European partners expressed surprise at this sudden move, and some were outraged. Critics charged that the German government had acted rashly, and that this move threatened the Maastricht Summit, where the EC would consider the Treaty on European Union. At the Maastricht Summit, German government representatives began to lobby for standards for the recognition of new countries like Croatia. On December 16, 1991, with an unusual amount of arm twisting and muscle flexing, Germany persuaded all eleven EC member states to agree on a new set of criteria and the establishment of a commission to review member states.[48] German leaders also were able to secure EC support for joint recognition of Croatia and Slovenia, but European leaders required that all member states postpone that recognition until January 15, 1992. European leaders celebrated this achievement of the Maastricht Summit—a natural extension of the commitment by all member states to the establishment of a Common Foreign and Security Policy (CFSP).

However, German leaders decided only days after the summit that there was simply too much international *and* domestic political pressure to wait for an official EC recognition of Croatia and Slovenia. Kohl believed that his promise to Croatian President Tudjman to move forward with timely recognition obligated him to move quickly. Germans perceived that a democratic ally was under attack from totalitarian Serbia, and Kohl was determined to make a diplomatic stand counter to the challenge. Cabinet leaders also perceived increasing public pressure for Germany to act.[49] Accordingly, the German government announced that it would recognize Croatia and Slovenia on December 23, 1991. This clearly was not intended to renege on the commitment to the Maastricht Summit, but German leaders effectively did just that. Almost as an afterthought, press statements from the German government indicated that they would delay the exchange of ambassadors (the last formal step in establishing normal diplomatic relations) until January 15, 1992, in compliance with pledges made at Maastricht.[50]

When the German government formally recognized Croatian and Slovenian independence on January 15, 1992, ethnic Croats celebrated in the streets of Munich and other German cities. In Bonn, one group of ethnic Croats held aloft a large sign which said: "God and Genscher Saved Us." A song composed to praise Germany for its aid to Croatia, entitled "Danke Deutschland," was a big hit on Croatian radio. Later, Croatian government officials announced their plans to erect a statue honoring Genscher for publicly leading the charge on recognition.[51] This German foreign policy decision was not the end of the story of the crisis in the Balkans, but rather the beginning. The recognition of Croatia and Slovenia was the precursor to an expanded civil war in the Balkans.[52]

MILITARY MONITORING OF THE EMBARGO AGAINST SERBIA AND MONTENEGRO

April 1992 marked a turning point in the crisis in the former Yugoslavia and the onset of a new strategic dilemma for the West. Government negotiators for Croatia and Serbia agreed to a cease-fire in the spring, and negotiated a peaceful settlement to their differences. Croatia would be granted its independence, and the warring factions would pull back from the front lines to create buffer zones allowing the deployment of the new UN Protection Force (UNPROFOR). As the peacekeeping deployment began, Serbian and Croatian diplomats agreed on a post-war stability pact.

However, April 1992 also marked the beginning of a new conflict in the Balkans—the war in Bosnia. This conflict began when Serbian soldiers from the Yugoslav National Army (JNA) crossed the Drijna River in eastern Bosnia and joined forces with Bosnian Serb irregulars. The Serbs attacked towns and villages in eastern Bosnia and soon surrounded Sarajevo, the capital. The cordon around Sarajevo, and subsequent efforts to break the resistance of Bosnian Muslim forces defending the capital city, created a visible symbol of Serbian aggression in the war—and a classic strategic dilemma for Western leaders.

As the extent of the Yugoslav conflict spread rapidly, the international community increased its efforts to deal with the conflict. UN Secretary General Boutros-Ghali began to make more vocal appeals for a strong international community response to Serbian aggression in Bosnia. This time, however, the call was for Germany to consider much more than simple diplomatic efforts to resolve the situation. On July 6, 1992, the Secretary General presented Germany with an official request for greater logistical support for UNPROFOR operations, and hinted at the possibility of a need for *Bundeswehr* participation in a shoring-up operation in the region. NATO leaders also were engaged in high-level negotiations over a stronger Western response to the crisis.[53]

On July 15, 1992, NATO Secretary General Manfred Wörner announced that alliance warships would begin patrolling the Adriatic to cut off any flow of goods banned by the UN to Serbia or Montenegro. NATO leaders and Bush administration officials began back-channel negotiations with European governments for a strong show of resolve in response to the conflict.[54] Wörner presented Germany with an official request for military assistance in the monitoring mission for the embargo.

Domestic Conditions and the Adriatic Deployment

Chancellor Kohl and key conservative leaders recognized immediately that these requests from the UN and NATO presented Germany with a distinct strategic opportunity. Always conscious of the need to maintain domestic support, however, Kohl began systematically to survey his support base for a heightened German commitment to the challenge.

German foreign policy was shaped by an interesting series of events at the elite level. In early April 1992, Hans-Dietrich Genscher resigned from office after eighteen years of service. Genscher's decision was based on both personal needs (he had suffered two heart attacks in recent years), and in response to growing domestic and international criticism that his move to recognize the independence of Croatia and Slovenia was a major diplomatic blunder.[55] After some internal debate inside the FDP, Justice Minister Klaus Kinkel was named as Genscher's successor.[56] Kinkel had prior government experience as Genscher's executive assistant, in another key position in the Foreign Ministry, and as head of German foreign intelligence operations. Critics charged that he was a foreign policy novice.[57]

Additionally, Volker Rühe was named to succeed Gerhard Stoltenberg as Defense Minister. Experts suggested that new leadership in the two top foreign policy posts in the German government granted Kohl and the CDU/CSU greater leverage in policy development, but in the long run the change in leadership signaled a new generation and direction for German foreign policy.

Kohl knew that he had the support of key Conservative leaders at the party level. Karl-Heinz Hornhues, Chairman of the CDU/CSU Foreign Affairs Committee of the *Bundestag*, not only offered his public support for a German commitment of troops to the region, but also pledged his support for future deployments of *Bundeswehr* troops for peacekeeping operations.[58] Johannes Gerser, deputy chairperson of the CDU/CSU *Fraktion*, went so far as to state that German military action should be undertaken in a "precisely aimed strike at the Serbian air forces, airports, and missile bases, with the participation of German forces."[59] In response to the specific request for German support for NATO and WEU embargo monitoring missions, Hornhues, Gerser, and others became outspoken supporters of German action.[60]

Strong Conservative support for German participation in NATO operations in the Balkans was not sufficient to guarantee action, however.

Foreign Minister Kinkel and key leaders of the FDP went on record expressing concerns about any such deployment without prior consideration of the constitutionality of such an initiative. Kinkel argued publicly that the FDP was concerned about military involvement in the region mainly because of "historical reasons."[61]

The opposition parties confronted similar dilemmas when considering the deployment question. The issue created public rifts in the Social Democratic opposition between general party membership and the *Fraktion*. An SPD expert on foreign policy, Karsten Voigt, declared in a July 1992 press release that the deployment of German troops to the Adriatic would be unconstitutional, and warned that the government should not consider the request without a prior change in the Basic Law. Voigt went on to criticize this move as being evidence of a larger government plan to expand the role of the *Bundeswehr* on a global scale. Echoing this sentiment, *Fraktion* leader Hans-Ulrich Klose said that this government plan was clearly unconstitutional and implored the SPD to challenge it before the Federal Constitutional Court.[62] SPD leaders were particularly critical of the timing of any particular government action in response to the UN and NATO requests, given that the parliament had recessed for the summer.

Green and Alliance '90 party members also wrestled with the proper response to the deteriorating situation in the Balkans. Helmut Lippelt, a key member of the federal governing board for *die Grünen*, acknowledged that the crisis presented his party with a special challenge. He admitted that the "Greens are in a moral dilemma. On the one hand we are against military deployments, and on the other hand, for instance, military protection of food transports is absolutely necessary—and with that, one already says yes to force." He went on to say that the images of the crisis, especially media coverage of "starvation camps and ethnic cleansing," forced the Green Party to ask whether they could "still counter these forms of fascism with the means of pure pacifism, which permits easy retreats."[63]

Public attitudes toward the deployment question were also significant. As the salience of the deployment question increased in 1992, so did the frequency of public opinion surveys on the matter. In a survey conducted by the *Süddeutsche Zeitung*, a popular German newspaper, 65% of all German respondents said they opposed participation in a joint European effort to enforce a cease-fire in Yugoslavia.[64] A related poll found that 38% of respondents believed Germany should "only use troops for self defense and in the context of NATO area[s]," 44% said "use them for defense and in NATO area[s] and for the UN as blue helmets for peacekeeping without combat." Finally, *Der Spiegel* printed results in early July 1992 of the EMNID questionnaire on the standard 'next Sunday' question for voting ("If the *Bundestag* election were to be held next Sunday, for which party would you vote?"). Only 36% of respondents voiced their vote for the CDU, significantly down from 43.8% of the vote received in the 1990 elections. The SPD share of public support rose to 39%, up from 33.5% in 1990, while the FDP stayed relatively constant at 10%. The ruling coalition did not enjoy a majority of support in the populace at the time, and the SPD may have better represented the concerns of the German people.[65]

The Cabinet Decision and Bundestag Debate

In spite of mixed sentiments in the polity, German cabinet leaders met on July 15, 1992, to discuss a potential role in the new NATO and WEU initiatives. Under intense pressure from Conservatives at the meeting, Kinkel changed his position on the deployment decision and agreed to allow limited monitoring participation.[66] Kinkel and Defense Minister Rühe made a joint announcement immediately after the meeting that the government would deploy one destroyer and three reconnaissance planes to the WEU–NATO patrol of the Adriatic. However, they made it clear that German forces were only to monitor commercial traffic while remaining at least fifteen miles from the coast at all times.[67]

Opponents of the government plan were not willing simply to accept the cabinet decision as the final say on foreign policy, and SPD legislators launched an immediate and vocal protest of this government action. They believed that the governing coalition had intentionally tricked them by making an important change in foreign policy just a few days after most legislators had left Bonn for a summer vacation. Critics also charged that the policy change was a "violation of the literal interpretation of the Basic Law and a blatant misuse of power by the cabinet."[68]

On July 22, the Social Democrats forced a special session of the *Bundestag* (a rare parliamentary action in German history) to provide the legislature with an opportunity to debate the government move. At the session, Kinkel presented the coalition's position that Germany should "drop its shirker role in foreign policy . . . and should quit behaving like an impotent dwarf in world politics."[69] In response, the leader of the SPD *Fraktion* in the legislature, Hans-Ulrich Klose, argued that this decision was part of a German government effort to skirt the issue of a constitutional amendment to permit out-of-area military operations, and he charged that the coalition was moving "too far, too fast." Klose stated that the Social Democrats would "not permit a sneaking movement toward combat missions around the world." Ironically, SPD leaders also argued against the government plan by citing the results of the *Süddeutsche Zeitung* poll, which showed that an overwhelming majority of Germans opposed this action.[70]

At the end of the debates, the *Bundestag* passed a resolution supporting the government's position on the question by a comfortable majority.

Some experts interpreted this action as the first major deployment of conscripts in a potential combat zone well outside the NATO area in the history of the Federal Republic.[71] The German government did deploy the troops and conduct support operations for the embargo monitoring mission in the Adriatic, but the situation in Bosnia continued to deteriorate.[72]

AWACS PATROLS AND OPERATION DENY FLIGHT

The period between January 1993 and July 1994 represented a third, significant stage in the evolution of German foreign policy in response to external strategic dilemmas and opportunities. It began with a NATO request for German soldiers to participate in overflights of Bosnia and was to end with a dramatic Constitutional Court ruling that Germany could participate in future peacekeeping operations outside the traditional NATO area.

The AWACS Challenge

The military situation in Bosnia continued to deteriorate in the winter months of 1992–1993, in spite of diplomatic efforts, economic sanctions, and humanitarian relief operations carried out by Western nations. By January 1993, Serbian irregulars had gained control of about 48% of Bosnian territory and threatened to overrun several UN "protected areas" in Bihac, Sarajevo, Tuzla, and elsewhere. At the same time, reports of human rights violations were increasing in the Western media. Information filtering out of Bosnia suggested that Serbs were practicing "ethnic cleansing" against Muslim and Croat villages in the mountains of Bosnia and were refusing to abide by Geneva Convention standards for the treatment of prisoners of war.

Consistent with earlier developments, NATO allies and high-ranking United Nations officials increased the pressure on Germany to provide a more focused commitment to the Western response to the crisis in the Balkans. The foundation for these new efforts was UN Security Council Resolution 781 (October 9, 1992), which created a no-fly zone over Bosnia. This zone would require regular airborne patrols over the region, and NATO aircraft were responsible for implementing the resolution. NATO leaders planned to deploy Airborne Warning and Control Systems (AWACS) aircraft to provide blanket radar coverage of regional airspace. This presented a problem for the German government, however, because *Luftwaffe* officers made up about one third of all AWACS crews. In essence, NATO allies were calling on the German government to commit troops to potential combat areas outside of Western Europe—a direct contradiction to the standing German government interpretation of the Basic Law. Nevertheless, NATO Secretary General Willy Claes made it clear that German participation would be "integral to the successful air-borne monitoring operations."[73]

NATO requests for German assistance in regional operations coincided with a visit by UN Secretary General Boutros-Ghali to Bonn. The Secretary General met with high-ranking German officials in January 1993, and reportedly pressured them to provide a stronger show of support for international efforts to respond to the crisis. Boutros-Ghali then issued a series of focused public statements. He argued on television networks that Germany was "the third most important country in the world," and said that the world needed "the full participation of Germany in peace-keeping, peace-making, peace-enforcement, and peace-building operations if we want a strong United Nations."[74] At a joint public appearance, Foreign Minister Kinkel agreed with Boutros-Ghali and warned that domestic squabbles over the constitutionality of participation in peace missions abroad might jeopardize Germany's international credibility.[75]

Key allies also attempted to pressure Germany to become more engaged in quasi-military responses to the Bosnia crisis. The Clinton administration announced that the United States would lead "Operation Deny Flight" over Bosnia, but U.S. officials also sought support from friends and allies in the region.[76] Secretary of State Warren Christopher publicly called on the German government to provide greater support for NATO initiatives and to increase German commitment of Transall transport planes for an airlift of humanitarian relief supplies to key pockets of isolated peoples in eastern Bosnia. The French government also increased pressure on Germany to provide a strong response to the crisis in the Balkans. After extensive consultations on the crisis, France and Germany issued a joint Declaration on Former Yugoslavia in which they asserted that solving the conflict was their "top foreign policy priority."[77]

Domestic Conditions and the AWACS Request

External pressures presented government leaders with an opportunity to construct a legitimating coalition for action, but they were well aware that it would be an uphill battle. A number of officials expressed concern that this type of troop commitment to a combat area would be unconstitutional, and opposition leaders warned that such action would extend the government's foreign policy powers beyond their legal foundation. The AWACS challenge led to a three-month-long debate inside the government and, ultimately, to a decisive July 1994 Constitutional Court ruling on the question.

At the elite level, Kohl, Rühe, and Kinkel were all forced to reassess their base of domestic support for a further expansion of Germany's involvement in the civil war in the former Yugoslavia. Kohl responded to the proposal for AWACS participation with muted optimism, but (characteristically) authorized other Conservatives to take the lead on the matter. Defense Minister Rühe became the point man in the government campaign to build public support for this action. In an interview on December 28, 1992, Rühe made it clear that the government intended to allow German crews to fly on AWACS missions. In public statements, the Defense Minister repeatedly articulated the Conservative line that this type of German support for multilateral peace operations was perfectly legal and mandated in Article 24 of the Basic Law. No constitutional change would be necessary prior to a deployment of this nature, cabinet officials argued.

The record shows that, on a personal level, Foreign Minister Kinkel was sympathetic to the government line on the AWACS challenge. However, he was well aware of the need to build support inside his own party for such an action, and he entered into a delicate series of maneuvers to secure it. Thus, the Foreign Minister repeatedly rode the fence on the question. He made several statements in support of German participation in international peace operations during Boutros-Ghali's visit, and he agreed with the Secretary General that an extended German role in such operations was necessary to support its "international credibility" on such matters.[78] On January 12, 1993, however, Kinkel said that the FDP could not abide by this commitment in light of the current "constitutional situation," and warned that his party would attempt to force the government to withdraw German crews from the AWACS.[79]

Disagreements inside the cabinet on the AWACS question spilled over to the party level. CDU/CSU leaders argued strongly that this type of military commitment was appropriate as a responsible partner and perfectly legal. Chairman of the CDU/CSU Foreign Policy Committee Hornhues argued that Germany should be prepared to respond more forcefully to the situation. This, he contended, was clearly mandated in Article 24 of the Basic Law, and furthermore was necessary for Germany to remain a reliable partner in NATO.[80] Rupert Scholz, a former defense minister, also shared this position. At the time, he coyly suggested that any opposition challenge to such a commitment could not possibly be addressed by the Constitutional Court because the Court faced an "extraordinarily heavy workload" of other pressing matters. Wolfgang Schäuble, Chairman of the CDU/CSU *Fraktion*, also discounted the matter as insignificant and argued that an amendment to the Basic Law was not an urgent issue. In a January 1993 public statement on the matter, he said that Germany simply would "not be able to refrain from participating in the long run. . . . We cannot always stand aside. We will make an independent and responsible decision in every individual case."[81]

Conservative leaders in the CSU supported the AWACS deployment and made it clear that they resented FDP resistance on the issue. In fact,

CSU Chairman Theo Waigel publicly attacked coalition Liberals over this matter. Referring to a suggestion by FDP *Fraktion* members that they would seek an injunction to block the cabinet's decision on AWACS, he argued that the FDP pursued intensely contradictory policies that constantly undermined government policy. In a fit of rage, Waigel declared that the Liberals were "whiners," and this was to be expected because "the FDP is always like that!"[82]

In spite of criticism from Conservatives, the Free Democrats went forward with their plan to challenge the CDU/CSU position on the AWACS deployment. FDP leaders clearly perceived the AWACS request as a strategic dilemma with long-term legal, political, and social implications that had to be addressed. The first FDP approach to the question was to attempt to pressure Conservatives into considering an amendment to the Basic Law that would cover this type of deployment and others.[83] FDP Construction Minister Irmgard Schwaetzer criticized government plans for the deployment and called for such an amendment, saying that "everybody must be ready for a compromise and move toward each other." FDP Justice Minister Leutheusser-Schnarrenberger was also quite vocal in her critique of the AWACS matter and demanded that the Conservatives first consider constitutional changes.[84]

Faced with junior party resistance and calls to amend the Basic Law, CDU/CSU leaders agreed to a special party conference to be held on January 13, 1993, to discuss the types of change in the constitution that would be needed to allow *Bundeswehr* participation in peace operations abroad. The first day of the meeting was surprisingly harmonious, and Conservatives and Liberals agreed to an acceptable modification of the Basic Law. Leaders agreed to amend Article 24 of the Basic Law by adding a new third clause. The article would be modified to read:

Federal Armed Forces, notwithstanding Article 87a, may be deployed:

1. For peacekeeping measures, in accordance with a Security Council resolution or within the framework of the regional agreements, as defined in the UN Charter, as far as the Federal Republic of Germany is party to them;
2. For peacemaking measures, based on Chapters 7 and 8 of the UN Charter, in accordance with a Security Council resolution;
3. *For the assistance of states allied to the Federal Republic of Germany, in accordance with alliance treaties;*
4. For the assistance of other states in the execution of the right to collective self defense, in accordance with Article 51 of the UN Charter, in conjunction with partners within the framework of alliances or regional agreements as defined in the UN Charter, to which the FRG is party.

In the case of items 1 and 2, these deployments require the agreement of the majority of members, and in the case of number 4, the agreement of two thirds of the members of the Bundestag.[85]

Coalition members were pleased with the outcome of the talks and the proposed amendment to the Basic Law. Hornhues declared that the amendment wording "resolved in precise terms the interpretational arguments about Articles 24 and 87a of the Basic Law." Meanwhile, Foreign Minister Kinkel called the agreement a "dramatic breakthrough," and he noted the importance of seeking parliamentary approval prior to any deployment of *Bundeswehr* troops abroad.[86] Several critical voices to the agreement remained inside the FDP, however, and these concerns were soon to play out in a different manner.

The Social Democrats and Green/Alliance '90 parties were opposed to the AWACS deployments and were not pleased with the coalition's attempt to amend the Basic Law to allow wider deployments of German troops in future operations.[87] Hans-Ulrich Klose declared the amendment proposal "dead on arrival" for consideration by the *Bundestag* and said that the plan went much too far.[88] The SPD and Greens opted to attempt to join with opponents in the Free Democratic Party to challenge the government plan to commit German crews to AWACS missions.[89] Meanwhile the SPD opposed any government plan that would allow the expansion of German military use without sharp constraints. SPD representative Günter Verheugen gave a speech in plenary debate at the *Bundestag* in which he warned that the cabinet was on the way to "einem Rückfall zur Denkweise der Kanonenbootdiplomatie des Wilhelminismus."[90]

This new security policy question came at a time when public sentiments remained quite mixed about major foreign policy action. In a public opinion poll conducted in February 1993, 62% of respondents stated that they believed Germany should assume a more active role in international affairs, but only 53% believed that Germany should participate in peacekeeping operations.[91]

The Government Acts

The AWACS issue came to a head in early April 1993. Conservative leaders had surveyed the domestic scene and calculated that they could garner support for the *Bundeswehr* commitment to NATO. On Friday, April 2, 1993, Conservative cabinet members forced through an initiative declaring the government's intention to deploy German crews on AWACS over Bosnia in coming months. At the same time, the SPD, FDP, and Greens/Alliance '90 parties sponsored an official challenge to the plan in the Constitutional Court. One press report of the standoff called April 2, 1993, the ultimate political showdown: "High noon in Bonn."[92]

Constitutional Court proceedings began several days later, placing Klaus Kinkel in an extremely awkward political position. Kinkel, the leader of the FDP, had to argue for the government in court and against his own membership's petition against the AWACS deployment. In spite of the irony, the Foreign Minister effectively presented the government's case on the AWACS mission and argued that the planned operation could not be equated with a direct combat mission in any way. He said that the AWACS planes would monitor the air exclusion zone over Bosnia while flying patterned routes hundreds of kilometers from the front line of combat. Ultimately, Kinkel pled the case that Germany should be viewed as a reliable partner. He argued that *Bundeswehr* soldiers should be in a position to "take part in peacekeeping blue-helmet missions and in exceptional circumstances in peace-making measures."[93]

On April 12, 1993, the Constitutional Court ruled in favor of the government and authorized the deployment of German crews on AWACS missions over the Balkans. NATO operations began later that day, but the ruling did not end the controversy inside the German government. A small protest erupted in the *Bundestag* immediately after the announcement of the decision. Once again, FDP Justice Minister Leutheusser-Schnarrenberger criticized the ruling and warned that it did not mean that additional *Bundeswehr* deployments could continue unchecked.[94] SPD leaders including Klose, Gansel, and parliamentary manager Günter Verheugen demanded that the parliament have the ultimate right to decide on this "anti-constitutional deployment of German soldiers." The floor of the *Bundestag* was crowded with critics from the left, but no serious legislative challenge was mounted at the time.[95]

The situation in the former Yugoslavia continued to deteriorate between April 1993 and April 1994, in spite of the establishment of the no-fly zone over Bosnia. A tone of quiet desperation crept into German discourse on the question of Bosnia. According to a Foreign and Defense Ministry report on the situation released in 1994, NATO's Operation Deny Flight had become "both successful and insignificant" in changing the course of events in the Balkans.[96] The report determined that the Serbs were emerging as the victors of the war in terms of territorial gain. Thus, ministry officials argued that little could be done to change the reality of the military situation and suggested that "final talks" would end the war in favor of Serbia. By September 1993, the government essentially concluded that the game was over in Bosnia and that the coming diplomatic settlement was no longer politically reversible under the present international conditions. Inside Germany, a virtual public malaise had arisen regarding foreign policy direction for the future.[97]

From Bad to Worse

German responses to the civil war in the former Yugoslavia reflected both the grim prognosis of the situation in the Balkans and a deep uncertainty of the proper course of government action back at home.[98] In a

Bundestag speech in September 1993, Foreign Minister Kinkel seemed to articulate international and domestic uncertainty on the proper response to the civil war in the Balkans. Kinkel spoke out against a German military commitment to the former Yugoslavia, given historical factors and the complexity of the conflict. At the same time, he urged "moderation in the demands made of others"—a response to increased criticism of French, British, and U.S. foreign policy responses to the crisis. The foreign minister emphasized that the Federal Republic should not criticize other states' responses to the civil war in the former Yugoslavia, given its own reluctance to carry a heavier burden of responsibility in the region. He suggested that the German polity should self-consciously consider its own willingness to bear risks and burdens in responding to crises like the Yugoslav civil war, and review its stand on humanitarian aid commitments around the world.

Kinkel's complicated message reflected the uncertainty that had crept into the German cabinet by the fall of 1993.[99] In a more general sense, developments in Germany were a result of debate on the proper course of action, active opposition in the *Bundestag* to any major initiative on foreign policy, the loss of control of the majority in the *Bundesrat*, and mixed public sentiments.[100] At the same time, criticism of German inactivity rose to a fever pitch. One editorial in the *Frankfurter Rundschau* captured the mood of the time, characterizing German security policy as "half-hearted . . . and complicated by doubts."[101]

In a last-ditch effort to develop a stronger stand on the conflict, Klaus Kinkel and Alain Juppé, the French Foreign Minister, announced the "Kinkel-Juppé Initiative" in November 1993. This joint announcement signalled a willingness among key Contact Group players to stand firm on certain conditions for containing the conflict. The Kinkel-Juppe' initiative called for an increase in European humanitarian aid to Bosnia. The German and French governments demanded that the warring factions in Bosnia maintain supply corridors for international humanitarian aid convoys to the Dalmatian coast and an air corridor to Tuzla, the embattled UN-protected area. The initiative also identified two major problems foreseen by the Contact Group—an insecure situation in Bosnia while territorial questions were being settled, and the difficult "Krajina question" between Serbia and Croatia.[102]

In late November, the EU sponsored a special peace conference in Geneva with the hopes of implementing the Kinkel-Juppe' plan as part of a final solution. The conference proved unsuccessful, however, as representatives of the factions could not agree on the details of a post-conflict settlement plan for aid corridors or a settlement of the Krajina question. At a meeting of the OSCE Council of Ministers in Rome, Kinkel vented his frustration at the lack of progress in the peace negotiations. Kinkel lamented the sense of helplessness the international community had in dealing with this conflict, saying "there is the concept of preventive diplomacy," but in practice, "we still see too little of it and then often too late."[103]

Despair Brings a Ray of Hope

Germany and the world looked on as a series of tragic events unfolded in Bosnia in early 1994. On February 7, a Serbian artillery unit fired on Bosnian Muslim civilians shopping in a central marketplace of Sarajevo, killing dozens of people and creating a firestorm of controversy in the West about how to respond.[104] NATO allies immediately condemned the brutal attack and emphasized the possibility of a military response to such violations of human rights and decency.[105] Two days later, the North Atlantic Council decided on a new course of action, demanding that Serb forces pull back their heavy weapons from the hills surrounding Sarajevo and honor a 20-kilometer weapons-exclusion zone. The Council threatened air attacks against artillery and tanks that were not removed from the zone quickly.[106]

The attack on the Sarajevo marketplace also seemed to energize the German domestic debate about the proper response to the civil war in the former Yugoslavia. Chancellor Kohl condemned the attack, and even suggested the need for NATO to conduct airstrikes against Serb artillery positions. Ironically, however, this statement was later retracted by one of the chancellor's press spokesmen. Foreign Minister Kinkel publicly condemned the attack and supported the NATO declaration of the weapons-exclusion zone. He suggested that the alliance consider the expansion of such zones to other embattled UN safe havens including Tuzla, Bihac, and Mostar.[107] Defense Minister Rühe joined in the public statements of support for stronger NATO action in the region.

The government stand on the NATO response to the Serb attack on civilians in Sarajevo gained support inside the German polity. In a significant political move, SPD leader Rudolf Scharping condemned the attack and stated his resolve to support government efforts to stand up to such terrible violations of human rights. Scharping even claimed that, at the time, there were "no serious differences on foreign policy between the Social Democrats and the Kohl government."[108] German leaders were also aware of public support for some sort of combined international response to this situation. A crowd of 25,000 people held a peace demonstration in Bonn's Munster Square to call attention to the plight of the Bosnian Muslims and to commemorate the 250,000 dead in Bosnia. This vigil drew a significant amount of press coverage in Germany and suggested a growing grassroots concern about the social and humanitarian tragedies of the civil war.

In the face of Western resolve, Bosnian Serb forces pulled their artillery and tanks back from the declared weapons-exclusion zone around Sarajevo before the NATO deadline, galvanizing alliance support for a more assertive role in the region. On February 28, 1994, two NATO F-16s shot down four Bosnian–Serb fighters that were violating the no-fly zone over Banja Luka. In response to continued aggression against UN safe havens in Gorazde and Mostar, NATO warplanes executed airstrikes over Serb positions outside Gorazde on April 6, 1994.[109]

German leaders of all political persuasions voiced support for the NATO airstrikes and retaliation against attacks on civilians in Sarajevo. Cabinet leaders spoke proudly of the effectiveness of NATO action, and characterized these airstrikes as "justified, necessary and right." Ironically, even SPD parliamentary leader Hans-Ulrich Klose characterized the airstrikes as the "correct step" in these circumstances.[110] As spring gained momentum, so too did optimism about a potential solution to the crisis in the former Yugoslavia. German leaders seized three major opportunities to resolve internal disputes about foreign policy behavior and define a solid foreign policy construct based on a strong political and legal foundation. These developments were to have a lasting impact on German foreign policy development during the post-Cold War era.

NOTES

1. Helmut Kohl, "Ziele und Prioritäten der Innen- und Außenpolitik," in Presse- und Informationsamt der Bundesregierung, *Bulletin*, no. 84, 25 July 1992, pp. 809.

2. Confidential Interview, Bundeshaus (Bundestag Legislative Offices), Bonn, 22 June 1996.

3. Klaus Kinkel, "Peacekeeping Missions: Germany Can Now Play Its Part," *NATO Review*, vol. 5, no. 3, 1994, p. 3.

4. See John G. Stoessinger, *Why Nations Go to War* (New York: St. Martin's Press, 1998), pp. 185–195.

5. Christopher Bennett, *Yugoslavia's Bloody Collapse: Causes, Course and Consequences* (London: Hurst, 1995); see also Laura Silber and Alan Little, *The Death of Yugoslavia* (London: Penguin, 1997).

6. Stoessinger, *Why Nations Go to War*, 1998, p. 191.

7. Noel Malcolm, *Bosnia: A Short History* (New York: New York University Press, 1994), pp. 54–55.

8. See Warren Zimmerman, "The Last Ambassador: A Memoir of the Collapse of Yugoslavia," *Foreign Affairs*, vol. 74, no. 2, March–April 1995, pp. 2–20.

9. For more information on the origins of the conflict in the former Yugoslavia, see Bogdan Denitch, *Ethnic Nationalism: The Tragic Death of Yugoslavia* (Minneapolis, MN: University of Minnesota Press, 1994); James Gow, *The Triumph of the Lack of Will: International Diplomacy and the Yugoslav War* (New York: Columbia University Press, 1997); David Gompert, "How to Defeat Serbia," *Foreign Affairs*, vol. 73, no. 4, July–August 1994, pp. 30–42.

10. See Branka Magas, *The Destruction of Yugoslavia: Tracking the Breakup 1980–92* (New York: Verso Publishing, 1993).

11. See Susan L. Woodward, *Balkan Tragedy: Chaos and Dissolution After the Cold War* (Washington, DC: Brookings Institution Press, 1995).

12. Misha Glenny, *The Fall of Yugoslavia: The Third Balkan War* (New York: Penguin Books, 1992), p. 86.

13. Magas, *The Destruction of Yugoslavia*, 1993, p. 71.

14. "The Wars Have Just Begun," *New Statesman*, vol. 6, December 1994, pp. 16–17.

15. Magas, *The Destruction of Yugoslavia*, 1993, p. 97.

16. See Sabrina Petra Ramet, "War in the Balkans," *Foreign Affairs*, vol. 71, no. 4, 1992, pp. 174–181.

17. John Newhouse, "No Exit, No Entrance," *The New Yorker*, 28 June 1993, p. 44.

18. Hans Stercken, "Jugoslawien und die Europaeische Gemeinschaft: Nationalismus und Separatismus bringen keine Loesung," in *Deutschland-Union-Dienst*, 20 November 1990, p. 2.

19. "Statement of Chancellor Helmut Kohl on the Results of the European Council Meeting in Luxembourg, June 28–29, 1991," *Bulletin*, no. 78, 9 July 1991, p. 635.

20. "Kommunique des KSZE-Krisenmechanismus über eine Mission nach Jugoslawien, Prag, 3 July 1991," *Europa Archiv*, no. 21, 1991, pp. D534–536.

21. William Drozdiak, "Pressure Rising in Europe for Action on Balkan War," *Washington Post*, 25 June 1991, p. A3; see also John Zametica, "The Yugoslav Conflict," *Adelphi Paper*, no. 270, Summer 1992, pp. 58–74.

22. "Erklärung von Rom über Frieden und Zusammenarbeit," reprinted in *Bulletin*, no. 128, 13 November 1991, pp. 1033–1037.

23. Cabinet leaders also authorized an airlift of relief supplies for Bosnia that began in July 1992; *Deutschland Nachrichten*, 29 May 1992, p. 1; *International Herald Tribune*, 5 July 1992, p. 1; see also John Tagliabue, "Kohl Threatens Serbia Over Cease-fire Violations," *New York Times*, 8 August 1991, p. A8.

24. See statement of Kohl on the Situation and Developments in the Soviet Union and Yugoslavia, *Bulletin*, no. 94, 5 September 1991, p. 752; a very clear statement on the matter was given by Chancellor Kohl in a speech in Berkeley, California, reprinted in *Bulletin*, no. 102, 20 September 1991, p. 813.

25. Hans-Dietrich Genscher, "Für Recht auf Selbstbestimmung," *Das Parlament*, 15–22 November 1991, p. 7; "Drei Tage Lang am Telefon," *Der Spiegel*, 8 July 1991, p. 128.

26. "Verkehrsabkommen außer Kraft: Flugverkehr mit Jugoslawien gestoppt," *Süddesutsche Zeitung*, 10 December 1991, p. 2.

27. Heinz-Jürgen Axt, "Hat Genscher Jugoslawien entzweit? Mythen und Fakten zur Außenpolitik des vereinten Deutschlands," *Europa-Archiv*, vol. 12, 1993, pp. 351–361.

28. "Drei Tage Lang am Telefon," *Der Spiegel*, 8 July 1991, p. 128.

29. Genscher, "Die EG sollte Koraten und Slowenien Assoziierung anbieten," *Die Welt am Sonntag*, 1 December 1991, p. 9.

30. Hans-Dietrich Genscher, *Erinnerungen*; see also *Der Spiegel*, 11 September 1995, pp. 67–70.

31. Horst Teltschik, *329 Tage: Innenansichtender Einigung*, (Berlin: Siedler Verlag, 1990), pp. 347–348.

32. Deutsche Presse Agentur, 18 February 1991.

33. "Mehr beobachter nach Jugoslawien," *Frankfurter Allgemeine Zeitung*, 30 July 1991, p. 2; see also "Bonn dringt auf Sanktionen gegen Serbian nach dem Scheitern des EG Vermittlungs-versuchs," *Frankfurter Allgemeine Zeitung*, 7 August 1991, p. 1.

34. Interview with Author, 29 April 1993; see also "Genscher: Beobachter nach Slowenien," *Frankfurter Allgemeine Zeitung*, 1 July 1991, p. 2.

35. See, for example, a statement by Alfred Dregger, Chair of the CDU/CSU Bundestagsfraktion, *Deutschland Union Dienst*, vol. 45, no. 120, 27 June 1991, p. 31.

36. Rühe, as quoted in William Drozdiak, "Germany Critizes European Community Policy on Yugoslavia," *Washington Post*, 2 July 1991, p. A16.

37. *Frankfurter Allgemeine Zeitung*, 25 May 1991, p. 4.

38. INFAS Meinungsreport, BPA Nachrichtenabteilung/Ref.II A5, July 1991.

39. Forsa-Institut/Deutsche Presse Agentur Survey, no. 251, 29 July 1992.

40. Robin Knight with Srdjan Trifkovic, David Lawday, and Douglas Stanglin, "Their Neighbor's Keepers?" *U.S. News and World Report*, 19 August 1991, p. 27.

41. "Beschlüsse der EG-Außenminister—Erklärung zu Jugoslawien," reprinted in *Bulletin*, no. 144, 16 December 1991, pp. 1173–1175; see also "EC to Recognize Breakaway Yugoslav Republics," *Facts on File—World News Digest*, 19 December 1991, p. 957 F1.

42. "Drei Tage Lang am Telefon," *Der Spiegel*, 8 July 1991, p. 128.

43. Flora Lewis, "Bavarian TV and the Balkan War: Diplomacy and the Image," *New Perspectives Quarterly*, 22 June 1994, p. 12.

44. *Deutsche Presse Agentur*, 5 May 1991.

45. "Wir bleiben nicht bei Mördern," *Der Spiegel*, 20 June 1991, pp. 118–125.

46. "Discussion between Chancellor Helmut Kohl and the President of Croatia," reprinted in *Bulletin*, no. 140, 10 December 1991, p. 1144.

47. "Friedensmission in Kroatian praktisch gescheitert," and "EG-Beobachter fordern gewalsames Vorgehen gegen jugoslawische Armee," *Süddeutsche Zeitung*, 4 December 1991, p. 1; see also "Zur Unterstützung für Kroatien und Slowenien: Bonn hat Anerkennung beschlossen," *Süddeutsche Zeitung*, 16 December 1991, p. 2.

48. "Die Mitgliedstaaten der EG einigen sich auf Richlinien zur Anerkennung neurer Staaten: Beschluß der Außenminister," *Frankfurter Allgemeine Zeitung*, 18 December 1991, p. 3.

49. See the Bundestag debates, "NATO-Debatte im Bundestag," *Das Parlament*, 15–22 November 1991, p. 5; for general public attitudes about action, see Johann Georg Reißmüller, "Absurditäten statt Politik," *Frankfurter Allgemeine Zeitung*, 18 December 1991, p. 1.

50. *Deutschland Nachrichten*, 20 December 1991, p. 1.

51. BBC Summary of World Broadcasts, Yugoslav Telegraph Service, 11 October 1993.

52. Trevor Salmon, "Testing Times for European Political Cooperation: The Gulf and Yugoslavia, 1990–1992," *International Affairs*, vol. 68, no. 2, 1992, pp. 233–254.

53. James Gow, *The Triumph of the Lack of Will: International Diplomacy and the Yugoslav War*, (New York: Columbia University Press, 1997), pp. 129–141.

54. *International Herald Tribune*, 16 July 1992, p. 1.

55. Confidential interview, Mershon Center, The Ohio State University, Columbus, Ohio, 29 April 1993.

56. "Genscher, Bonn's Foreign Minister 18 Years, Resigns," *New York Times*, 28 April 1992, p. A3.

57. *Defense News*, 11–17 May 1992, p. 12.

58. CDU/CSU Pressedienst, Bonn, 21 January 1992.

59. CDU/CSU Pressedienst, "Zum Appell von UNO-Generalsekretär Butros Ghali, deutsche Soldaten für die UN-Eingrifftruppe zu stellen," Erklärung von der Stellvertretetende Vorsitzende der CDU/CSU Bundestagsfraktion, Bonn, 12 July 1992.

60. Author's confidential interview #5, June 1996.

61. *Deutschland Nachrichten*, 3 July 1992, p. 1.

62. "Hin und Her in der SPD über den Einsatz der Marine," *Die Welt*, 19 July 1997, p. 3.

63. *Der Spiegel*, 24 August 1992, p. 44.

64. "Bundestag Billigt Adria-Einsatz der Marine Kluft zwischen Koalition und SPD," *Süddeutsche Zeitung*, 23 July 1992, p. 1. Additional information taken from author's notes and personal observation of the *Bundestag* debate.

65. *Der Spiegel*, 22 June 1992, pp. 40–47.

66. "Einsatz ohne Grenzen," *Der Spiegel*, 20 July 1992, p. 22.

67. "Einsatz der Marine in der Adria beschlossen," *Süddeutsche Zeitung*, 16 July 1992, p. 7.

68. Confidential interview #2, June 1996.

69. "Regierungserklärung, abgegeben von Außenminister Kinkel," reprinted in *Bulletin*, no. 83, 23 July 1992, pp. 805–808; see also Deutscher Bundestag, *Stemographischer Bericht*, 101. Sitzung, Bonn, 22 July 1992, pp. 8608–8660.

70. "Bundestag Billigt Adria-Einsatz der Marine Kluft zwischen Koalition und SPD," *Süddeutsche Zeitung*, 23 July 1992, p. 1.

71. Meanwhile, diplomats continued their efforts to broker a peace plan through shuttle diplomacy. In October 1992, the Vance–Owen Plan called for the division of Bosnia into ten cantons. Unfortunately, this plan received support only from the Croats, while Serb and Muslim leaders rejected the power-sharing plan.

72. See "Dokumente zum Konflikt im früheren Jugoslawien II: Der Vance-Owen Plan und der Sicherheitsrat bis Juni 1993," *Europa-Archiv*, vol. 18, 1993, pp. D357–D368.

73. "Dokumente zum Konflikt im ehemaligen Jugoslawien," *Europa-Archiv*, vol. 7, 1993, pp. D143–D161.

74. *Der Spiegel*, 15 January 1993, p. 132.

75. Craig R. Whitney, "U.N. Asks Bonn to Send Troops as Peacekeepers," *New York Times*, 12 January 1993, p. A9.

76. "Resolution 781 (1992) des Sicherheitsrats der Vereinten Nationene über ein Verbot militärischer Flüge im Luftraum über Bosnien-Herzegowina, verabshiedet am 9 Oktober 1992 in New York," transcript reprinted in *Europa-Archiv*, vol. 7, 1993.

77. "Bundesminister des Auswärtigen Dr. Klaus Kinkel, Deutlandfunk, 16 December 1992, Transcript recorded in *Stichworte zur Sicherheitspolitik*, Presse- und Informationsamt der Bundesregierung, Bonn, 16 December 1992.

78. The Court ruled that German troops could be deployed in AWACS flights over the former Yugoslavia, but emphasized the responsibility of the *Bundestag* in deciding such issues. Subsequently, the legislators voted 338 to 208 to support German participation in the overflights; *Deutschland Nachrichten*, 23 April 1993, p. 1.

79. German Information Center, "Coalition in Conflict over Military Intervention; Proposed Constitutional Change Fails in First Vote," *This Week in Germany*, 28 January 1993, p. 1.

80. CDU/CSU Pressedienst, "Hornues: Kein neues Nein Deutschlans zur Beteiligung an UNO-Militärmissionen," no. 5145, 16 December 1992; see also CDU/CSU Pressedienst, "Hornhues: AWACS-Beteiligung Testfall für deutsche Verläßlichkeit in UNO und NATO," no. 6029, 22 March 1993.

81. "AWACS-Streigt: FDP Politiker für Koalisitions Ausstieg," *Das Bild*, 5 April 1993, p. 1.

82. Ibid., p. 1.

83. Confidential Interview, Mershon Center, The Ohio State University, Columbus, Ohio, 29 April 1993.

84. This criticism from the Liberals did not please key Conservative leaders. One CSU critic called FDP Justice Minister Leutheusser-Schnarrenberger a "political lightweight who does not meet the required challenges," and "the type of political nuisance which results if one appoints people as ministers who do not have sufficient political experience." Quoted in "AWACS-Streit: FDP Politiker für Koalisitions Ausstieg," *Das Bild*, 5 April 1993, p. 1.

85. "Government Offers Proposal on Bundeswehr NATO Operations,"*Foreign Broadcast Information Service—Western Europe*, 1993, vol. 41, p. 12.

86. *New York Times*, 14 January 1993, p. A4.

87. Confidential interview, Bundeshaus—Hochhaus Tulpenfeld (Bundestag Legislative Offices), Bonn, 5 July 1996.

88. One of the events that shaped opponents' views on the question of intensifying German involvement in the region was a February 7, 1993, attack on a German Transall transport plane on an aid flight from Zagreb to Sarajevo. The German Transall aircraft was forced to abandon the flight when it was fired on over Bosnia. Defense Minister Volker Rühe condemned the attack as "an act of criminal aggression" and a "treacherous attack that was a terrible violation of international law and an offense against humanity." Aid flights were temporarily suspended, and critics of German involvement viewed the deterioriating situation with great concern; see FBIS-WEU-93-024, 8 February 1993, p. 12.

89. German Information Center, "Coalition in Conflict over Military Intervention; Proposed Constitutional Change Fails in First Vote," *This Week in Germany*, 28 January 1993, p. 1.

90. *Frankfurter Allgemeine Zeitung*, 16 January 1993, p. 4.

91. Poll results recorded in Ronald D. Asmus, *Germany's Geopolitical Maturation*, RAND Issue Paper (Santa Monica, CA: RAND, 1993).

92. "Kohl und Kinkel vor Gericht," *Der Spiegel* 14, 1993, pp. 18–22, vol. 47; see also "Erklarung der Bundesregierung in der Sitzung des Bundeskabinetts am 2 April 1993," Pressemitteilunng, Bonn, 2 April 1993, no. 116/9.

93. "Kinkel Says Bosnia AWACS Flights Not Combat Missions," in FBIS-WEU-065, 7 April 1993.

94. "Bundestag to Keep Crews in NATO AWACS Over Bosnia," in FBIS-WEU-93-076, 10 April 1993, p. 13.

95. *Frankfurter Allgemeine Zeitung*, 13 April 1993, pp. 1–2.

96. Lothar Rühl, "Bonn Analysis Views Serbs as Winners," *Die Welt*, 24 September 1993; reprinted in FBIS-WEU-93-186, p. 17.

97. See William Horsley, "United Germany's Seven Cardinal Sins: A Critique of German Foreign Policy," *Millenium: Journal of International Studies*, vol. 21, no. 2, Summer 1992; see also Wolfgang F. Schlör, *German Security Policy: An Examination of the Trends in German Security Policy in a New European and Global Context*, Adelphi Paper #277, June 1993.

98. For a summary of German foreign policy challenges in 1993, see Ole Diehl, "UN-Einsätze der Bundeswehr: Außenpolitische Handlungszwänge und innenpolitischer Konsensbedarf," *Europa-Archiv*, vol. 8, 1993, pp. 219–227.

99. "Bundestag Discusses Solution for Bosnia," FBIS-WEU-93-184, 24 September 1993, p. 126.

100. Holger H. Mey, "Germany, NATO, and the War in the former Yugoslavia," *Comparative Strategy*, vol. 12, 1993, pp. 239–245.

101. The *Frankfurter Allgemeine Zeitung* stated that "Europeans, and now the United Nations, are running the risk of doing themselves out of their credibility through their shameful wait-and-see behavior and devastating leniency towards the Serbian aggressors." See the *Frankfurter Allgemeine Zeitung*, 18 April 1994, p. 1.

102. "Erklärung des deutschen Außenministers, Klaus Kinkel, zur Juppe'-Kinkel Inititiative für den Bosnien-Konflikt," 18 November 1993; see also transcript of "Resolution 48/88 der Generalversammlung der Vereinten Nationen zum Krieg in Bosnien-Herzegowina, am 20 December 1993 in New York," reprinted in *Europa-Archiv*, 7 Folge 1998, pp. D222–D223.

103. "Kinkel Hopes for Bosnia Agreement," *Deutsche Presse Agentur*, 30 November 1993; reprinted in FBIS-WEU-92-339, 1 December 1993, p. 1.

104. "Der Konflikt im ehemaligen Jugoslawien vom Juli 1993 bis Anfang März 1994," *Europa-Archiv*, vol. 7, 1994, pp. D211–D238.

105. "Erklärung der Wueropäischen Union zur Lage in Sarajewo, berabshiedet am 7 Februar 1994 in Brüssel," *Europa-Archiv*, vol. 7, 1994, pp. D361–D362.

106. "Beschluß des Nordatlantikrats vom 9 Februar 1994 über Ultimatum zum Abzug aller schweren Waffen von Sarajewo," reprinted in FBIS-WEU-92-036, pp. 41–42.

107. "Interview des deutschen Außenministers, Klaus Kinkel, mit dem *Rheinischen Merkur*, vom 24 February 1994 zur Lage in Bosnien-Herzegowina," reprinted in *Europa-Archiv*, vol. 7, 1994, pp. D234–D237.

108. Josef Joffe, "Abandoning Megalomia Reminiscent of Emperor William," reprinted in FBIS-WEU-92-028, p. 24.

109. "Entscheidung des NATO-Rates vom 22 April 1994 in Brüssel zu Gorazde," *Bulletin*, no. 39, 2 May 1994; see also the United Nations "Resolution 913 (1994) des Sicherheitrats über die Entwicklung des Krieges in Bosnien-Herzegowina, verabschiedet am 22 April 1994 in New York," *Europa-Archiv*, vol. 21, 1994, pp. D629–D630.

110. "Erklärung des Bundesministers des Auswärtigen, Klaus Kinkel, vor dem Deutschen Bundestag am 14 April 1994 in Bonn zur Lage im ehemaligen Jugoslawien," *Europa-Archiv*, vol. 21, 1994, pp. D621–D631.

5

Action and Engagement: The Bosnia Crisis, 1994—1999

I have never wanted to give the Federal Republic of Germany a militaristic role. However, we now have the situation where we like
other countries can freely decide in each individual case whether we
will use the *Bundeswehr* outside NATO area. . . . The brake that was
holding us back is gone.
                                        —Klaus Kinkel, 1994[1]

We have encountered such a high degree of consensus for IFOR among
the population and in the *Bundestag* . . . but the danger [of German military action] is there, of course. You have to weigh it up against the
hundreds of thousands who died in the war in Yugoslavia, all the civilians who lost their lives. The French have lost 50 soldiers there over
the past few years. In the final reckoning, they died for Europe.
                                        —Volker Rühe, 1995[2]

1994 was a watershed year in the restructuring of German foreign policy
regarding the war in Bosnia, and German officials were able to build a
surprisingly strong political consensus for action in the region during the
next four years. This chapter describes the evolution of German

Figure 5.1
Strategic Dilemmas in the Bosnia War

Stages/Dates	Strategic Dilemma	Foreign Policy Response
IV. 1994–1995	NATO Request for Aircraft/ ECR-Tornado Deployment	Slow Commitment of Aircraft With Limits
V. 1995	Serbian Advances and UN Crisis/ Rapid Reaction Force	Commitment of Troops and Assets to the RRF
VI. 1996–present	Dayton Peace Accord/ IFOR, SFOR, and DFOR	Deployment of Ground Troops and Assets

responses to three major strategic dilemmas from 1994 to 1996, and how such crises, in turn, shaped domestic political orientations at several levels (Figure 5.1). Once again, a pattern of evidence demonstrates how German leaders recognized both needs and opportunities to negotiate around domestic constraints and reshape their commitment to global security in the post-Cold War era.[3]

AN HISTORIC RULING BY THE FEDERAL CONSTITUTIONAL COURT

After years of uncertainty about its approach to foreign policy, the German government reached an important milestone in April 1994 when the Federal Constitutional Court in Karlsruhe began to consider the out-of-area troop deployment issue. This review and hearing cycle was designed to weigh the constitutionality of troop deployments and political requirements for such actions in the future, with the objective of establishing a definitive ruling on the question. Some government leaders also viewed this as a unique opportunity to establish legal foundation for foreign policy normalization.

Three past petitions to the Court regarding the use of force in the post-Cold War era served as the foundation for the 1994 review: the July 1992 challenge by Social Democratic Party representatives to the commitment of troops to the NATO–WEU naval embargo in the Adriatic; the SPD case against the deployment of *Bundeswehr* soldiers in Somalia in December 1992; and the SPD–FDP challenge in February 1993 of the constitutionality of German participation in the AWACS monitoring mission over the Balkans.[4] Until the 1994 combined hearing, each of these petitions had raised tough questions about the criteria for the use of force and constitutional interpretation. These petitions had received Court attention in the form of interim evaluations, but in all cases the justices ruled in favor of the coalition government.

Formal hearings before the Constitutional Court justices began in early April 1994. Government leaders including Kohl and Kinkel appeared before the Court to argue that Article 24 of the Basic Law allowed involvement in a "system of mutual collective security" (and that no constitutional change would be necessary for future *Bundeswehr* deployments in that context). Kinkel argued that in the future, Germany must be involved without reservation in UN operations to secure world peace. Despite setbacks, he said, the United Nations was becoming "the central guardian of peace for the human race. . . . Germany has to come down from the spectator's gallery" of international security.[5] Experts on military affairs testified that the government was well within its rights to deploy force in carefully controlled circumstances. On behalf of the government, they contended that NATO and UN forces had every right to use force to protect declared safe havens.[6] Meanwhile, opposition SPD and Green Party leaders countered in Court that participation in out-of-area operations was specifically forbidden by articles of the Basic Law and represented a dangerous expansion of German foreign policy parameters.

On July 12, 1994, the Constitutional Court announced its ruling in favor of the government. The judges declared that Article 24 of the Basic Law offered the best guidance on the out-of-area question and that German participation in international military operations outside the territory of NATO would not violate the constitution. Specifically, they concluded that Basic Law allowed the participation of German armed forces in UNOSOM II, the deployment of naval forces for NATO and WEU missions in the Adriatic for the monitoring of UN-imposed embargoes against the Federal Republic of Yugoslavia, and the AWACS enforcement operation of the UN-imposed no-fly zone over Bosnia–Herzegovina.[7] They said that the Basic Law offered "a constitutional foundation for an assumption of responsibilities that are typically associated with membership of such a system of collective security." They ruled that the *Bundeswehr* could be deployed in potential combat environments, so long as the government secured a simple majority of support in the *Bundestag* for ratification of troop deployment plans.[8]

Reactions to the Court Ruling

The July 1994 Court decision truly represented a landmark ruling in favor of the German government and its strategy for foreign policy development in the 1990s. The ruling was met with widespread enthusiasm outside and inside the country. The decision announcement coincided with a special visit to Bonn and Berlin by U.S. President Bill Clinton. On July 12, Clinton presided over a ceremonial deactivation of the last U.S. military unit stationed in Berlin—fifty years after the end of World War II. When asked how he felt about the ruling and German troops operating abroad again, Clinton stressed the importance of the German–American partnership in the post-Cold War era and said that he was completely comfortable with Germany's foreign policy normalization. Saying that he did not want to meddle in internal German affairs, Clinton added rather diplomatically, "I think anything that can be done to enable Germany to fulfill the leadership responsibilities that it is plainly capable of fulfilling is a positive thing." Meanwhile, UN Secretary General Boutros-Ghali, who had been less diplomatic and more adamant in his call for an expansion of German foreign policy responsibilities (and specifically, contributions to UN peace operations around the world), said that the decision was "necessary as a prelude to a more active German role within international security structures."[9] At the same time, NATO officials in Brussels welcomed Germany's new role and expressed optimism about more intense security cooperation in the region and beyond.[10]

The response among key German leaders was one of high praise and optimism. Kohl, Kinkel, and other government officials attended the reading of the Court decision and appeared to relish the announcement. In the aftermath of the ruling, Kohl praised the Court's decision, saying that "Germany was eager to work with its European partners and the United States in guaranteeing peace throughout Europe and the world."[11] In response to President Clinton's encouragement for foreign policy activism, Kohl said:

The special relationship between Germany and America is intensifying, and Germany is ready to assume a more assertive foreign policy posture. The excuse that Germany had for the past forty years was that as a divided country we were unable to take certain decisions. . . . That is no longer valid. One cannot be a reunified country with 80 million people with the kind of economic strength we have, with the kind of prestige we claim for ourselves, if we do not fully assume our responsibilities and fulfill our obligations.[12]

Foreign Minister Kinkel provided extensive comments on his interpretation of the ruling in a series of high-profile interviews. When asked whether his call for Germany to stop acting like "an impotent dwarf" in the 1992 debate over the Adriatic deployment had been answered by the July 1994 decision, he said:

We want to be neither a dwarf nor a giant. From 1945 to reunification, Germany deliberately exercised restraint in security and military policy . . . we must not become presumptuous after the Karlsruhe ruling, the policy of restraint will be continued. I have said [that] in the future, we will have to say no more often than yes. I have never wanted to give the Federal Republic of Germany a militaristic role. However . . . we now have the situation that we like other countries can freely decide in each individual case whether we will use the *Bundeswehr* outside NATO area.[13]

The foreign minister also elaborated on what he saw as a new German foreign policy driven by specific "German interests" whereby they would respond to challenges around the world on a case-by-case basis. Kinkel admitted that German military participation in a Gulf War scenario would now be possible from a legal point of view, and he added:

When I think of Rwanda, for instance, I would say that German interests were touched upon when the sixteen members of *Deutsche Welle* were trapped in their transmitter and we had to ask the Belgian paratroopers for assistance to help them. Apart from that, the terrible events in Rwanda require help. The international community must not look away while genocide is committed there. . . . In the conflict between Iraq and Kuwait we had an obligation to our American friends and also because of our German interests, an obligation that we were unable to fulfill because of our constitutional situation. We then provided financial aid.[14]

When asked about the implications of the ruling for the German response to the crisis in the Balkans, however, his response took a different tone. Kinkel concluded: "I think that a mission of German soldiers in the former Yugoslavia will not find a majority because of the historical situation. . . . German soldiers would probably be in greater danger in the former Yugoslavia than others."[15] He concluded that henceforth, Germany "need not hide our light under a bushel, but we should keep our feet on the ground. . . . In the future, we will say no to missions more often than yes."[16]

In a statement that reflected the German government's commitment to a new, more active foreign policy profile in the wake of the Karlsruhe ruling, Defense Minister Rühe said:

Today, the *Bundeswehr* is still best prepared for the most unlikely case—an aggression against NATO. It is least prepared for the most likely case—the new tasks associated with international crisis management. For this reason, the German government has initiated a fundamental reform of the German armed forces that will give them the necessary shape to master the challenges of today and tomorrow. . . . The main emphasis of the reform will be the build-up of highly professional reaction forces with a high degree of readiness and availability, and able to cover the entire spectrum of crisis management tasks.[17]

On the Bosnia question, however, Rühe offered a conditional statement that "Wir wollen nicht ein Teil des Problems, sondern ein Teil der Problemlösung sein," and he effectively ruled out troop deployment to the Balkans.[18]

Finally, it is important to note how the German public reacted to the Court ruling. An editorial in the *Süddeutsche Zeitung* labeled the Court hearings as "the most consequential struggle since the 1955 debate over rearmament," and the decision as one that "changes Germany's entire foreign and military policy."[19] The polity's broad welcome of the decision stood in contrast to the mood of the past year. Government leaders had been quite concerned about the general public's dissatisfaction with the Conservative–Liberal coalition. Public opinion polls showed that the Union party had lost 10% of its popular support base between 1990 and 1994.[20] According to an Institut für Demoskopie survey conducted in the aftermath of the Constitutional Court ruling, the coalition enjoyed the strongest level of public support. In the standard "next Sunday" question, 41% of Germans indicated their support for the CDU/CSU, 35.5% favored the SPD, and the FDP garnered 7.5% of public support.[21] Kohl and other officials interpreted diffuse public support in the wake of the ruling as a sign of consensus.

Another opportunity to gauge public support for government policy came in federal- and state-level elections in October 1994. The election results carried a mixed message. The coalition suffered a loss of electoral support, but was able to hold on to a narrow majority for control of the legislature. The coalition garnered 48.4% of the popular vote and received 341 seats in the Bundestag (which narrowed its previous margin of 134 Bundestag seats to ten). The FDP garnered 6.9% of the vote, or 47 seats; Rudolf Scharping and the SPD won 36.4% of the vote (or 252 seats in the Bundestag); and the Alliance '90/Grüne and PDS parties won smaller percentages of the popular vote.[22] Despite the narrowness of the victory, Kohl voiced confidence that his coalition's ten-seat majority in the Bundestag would be "more than adequate" for the government to carry out its domestic and international agenda.

Overall, these legal and political developments in the first ten months of 1994 laid the foundation for a major sea-change in German foreign policy. A new level of elite consensus and legal latitude on foreign policy was soon put to the test, however, by alliance pressures for an intensified German commitment to security in the Balkans.[23]

TORNADO DEPLOYMENT AND AIR STRIKES IN BOSNIA

The Tornado Controversy

If 1994 was a watershed year for the evolution of German foreign policy, 1995 produced some of the most intense external challenges yet experienced. The fourth strategic dilemma for foreign policy restructuring actually began in November 1994, when NATO's Supreme Allied Commander (SACEUR), General George Joulwan, approached the German government with a series of requests to use German ECR-Tornado aircraft for NATO operations. The SACEUR sought a general commitment from the German government to support United Nations Protection Force (UNPROFOR) peacekeepers from Yugoslavia. Specifically, NATO leaders wanted the support of the German ECR-Tornadoes, because they offered optimal low-level attack, radar suppression, and reconnaissance capabilities that might be needed in air strikes against Bosnian Serb installations.

The Tornado requests highlighted both the significant progress that the German government had made in redefining its foreign policy, and some lingering debates about the proper scope of foreign policy in the wake of the Karlsruhe ruling. General Joulwan communicated his first request to the German government in November 1994, asking for a commitment of fighter jets for a potential NATO operation to extract UNPROFOR soldiers from the Balkans. The record suggests that key German leaders had not carefully considered new boundaries for roles and missions in the months immediately following the Karlsruhe ruling. Officials in the MOD were clearly the most prepared domestic political actors for such a request, but the chancellor, defense minister, and foreign minister simply had not conferred on the details of such future operations. Even Wolfgang Schäuble, leader of the CDU/CSU parliamentary group, went on record saying that he saw no need for the *Bundestag* to make an immediate decision, considering the UN did not "envisage an immediate military mission for the German Tornadoes."[24] This led to an interesting maneuver on the part of the German leadership—they opted not to respond to the original request. One high-ranking government official rationalized the decision with the reasoning that the SACEUR had not sent the request through official channels; therefore, it could not be considered for a formal action by the government.[25]

In December 1994, however, General Joulwan repeated the request for a German commitment through more formal and official channels, making it clear that this was a NATO request that could not be ignored. Kohl and other cabinet officials recognized this as well, and the request prompted a new round of private (and sometimes public) debate about the proper German response. Publicly, Kohl seemed to hesitate in the articulation of a German response. When questioned about the NATO request at a press conference, for example, he stated that because of historical reasons, the German government should send "only as few troops as possible to the Balkans."[26] Asked if the German government was prepared to protect NATO allies from the Serbian air defense, Kohl answered with a vague "no." Quite cautious in tone and words at the press conference, the chancellor repeatedly emphasized that "the first German military operation should take place on the basis of a consensus."[27] Ultimately, Kohl was determined to prevent the *Bundeswehr's* first potential combat mission outside the NATO area from becoming its first post-Cold War military defeat.[28]

Other cabinet officials, however, were more willing to consider the deployment of German troops as a logical extension of foreign policy normalization in the post-Cold War era. CDU/CSU *Fraktion* chairman Wolfgang Schäuble claimed to represent the coalition parliamentarians when he stated that they would fight for a *Bundestag* majority, so that the deployment of Tornadoes could occur should the need arise.[29] In mid-December, Defense Minister Volker Rühe stated that Germany would be capable of providing six to eight Tornadoes, but that this was ultimately a political decision for the government. He said:

I think we have to consider the NATO request for Tornado combat aircraft very openly and be basically ready to show more solidarity. . . . Since we continue to rule out using ground forces in Bosnia—German soldiers would really be part of the problem there—I think that one has to consider this very openly . . . it is a political decision whether we demonstrate increased solidarity with NATO, which is fulfilling an important assignment there.[30]

Ever cautious, the Defense Minister added that "we are not overlooking at all the fact that this will not bring about a solution to the Yugoslav problem."[31] *Bundeswehr* Inspector General Naumann spoke in favor of a positive German response to the NATO request, arguing that the alliance was simply acting in support of the UN operation in Bosnia and should not be interpreted as such an extreme commitment.[32]

Other leaders disagreed. Foreign Minister Kinkel led a quiet but consistent opposition to the NATO request inside the cabinet. In a public statement, Kinkel said that the request "would be examined," but warned that a deployment of German soldiers to the Balkans under any circumstances would be problematic and "should be avoided."[33] Kinkel believed that the 1994 Constitutional Court decision did not provide the type of blank check interpreted by Conservatives, and he felt that this operation would potentially be quite dangerous for German troops. Once again, however, Kinkel found himself pressured from both sides—cabinet leaders strongly suggested that this request be honored in the spirit of upholding international commitments, while members of his own party in the coalition government resisted such a move.[34]

Opposition leaders outside the cabinet were split on the issue. SPD Chairman Rudolf Scharping offered his support for the use of German combat aircraft in Bosnia. Again, this was indicative of a progressive shift by Scharping and others in the top echelons of the SPD to accept a more active German foreign policy posture in light of post-Cold War era alliance obligations within the framework of the United Nations and NATO.[35] However, this was not a sign that the SPD was united in support for dramatic changes in German foreign policy. SPD leader Günther Verheugen argued strongly that Germany should reject any such request from NATO as a violation of the Basic Law. He warned that "any distinction made by the government between ground troops and combat planes was unrealistic," and any German involvement in combat missions in the Balkans ran the risk of escalating the conflict and violated the constitution.[36] Deputy Chairman of the SPD, Oskar Lafontaine, and another prominent SPD politician, Heidemarie Wiezorek-Zeul, publicly challenged Scharping's support for the government.[37] At a January 1995 meeting of the SPD board of directors, Lafontaine reportedly warned that "if Germany enters the war in Yugoslavia, there will be a rebellion within the party."[38] In fact, Scharping's decision to support the government deployment left deep scars in the SPD over foreign policy matters—wounds that were slowly healed by time and several twists of fate.

Public attitudes on the Tornado request were mixed. In response to general surveys on German willingness to support military operations abroad, a significant percentage of respondents supported participation in UN peacekeeping operations. A poll by Infratest Burke Berlin found that as many as 75% of Germans supported the use of military force for humanitarian purposes and traditional peacekeeping missions, but the support declined when specific scenarios including combat missions were described.[39] In one such survey in December 1994, 62% of respondents opposed German provision of Tornadoes to satisfy the NATO request.[40]

The Government Acts

Given disagreements inside the cabinet and party organizations, Conservative leaders resolved that they must convince the FDP to negotiate concessions in their position. Kohl and others communicated their concerns about the implications of a German non-response to junior party officials and scheduled a cabinet meeting for December 20, 1994, at which the deployment issue would be on the agenda. After weeks of public and private debate, the cabinet decided to commit German aircraft to the operation in the Balkans.[41]

In an exclusive interview after the decision, Kinkel described his rationale for the seeming reversal of the FDP position on the question. After consultations with top leaders of the FDP, Kinkel said, the party was determined not to concede on the military utility of the operations. Instead, they would support the deployment purely as a humanitarian response to the crisis in the region. Instead, Kinkel argued:

The people concerned are facing another terrible winter . . . if relief flights can only be carried out under cover of fighter aircraft with special anti-missile defense systems and this is what our Tornadoes have—I would personally say that we cannot dodge our responsibility. After all, human life must be protected.[42]

This humanitarian rationale also appealed to the opposition. Shortly after the announcement of the cabinet decision, Scharping said that his party would also support the deployment on the same principle protection of humanitarian relief flights. He said that "if protection is required in order to do so [conduct relief operations in the skies over Bosnia], we will have to give such protection."[43] Ironically, as conditions worsened in Bosnia, German resolve to deploy forces to the region strengthened.

A *Bundestag* debate and vote regarding the deployment decision were held on December 20, 1994. In the vote, an oversized majority favored deployment. Parliamentarians from the CDU/CSU and the FDP voted overwhelmingly to authorize this deployment, but the big surprise was the number of Social Democrats who also voted in favor of this initiative. Not all Social Democrats supported the measure, however, and some launched a vocal opposition in parliament to government actions. Green Party spokesman Jürgen Trittin warned that this troop commitment to the region would inevitably lead to an escalation of the conflict.[44]

The decision to authorize the deployment of ECR-Tornadoes was an important step in the broadening of German commitments to the Balkan crisis. Unfortunately, it did not end disagreements inside Germany about the best foreign policy course to use in response to the escalating civil war in Bosnia.

THE RAPID REACTION FORCE CONTINGENCY

The crisis in the Balkans took on a new dimension in 1995 when Western leaders began to consider the deployment of ground troops to the Balkans to galvanize a diplomatic, political, economic, and military endgame in the conflict. The changed situation prompted two important initiatives that would require Germany to deploy *Bundeswehr* troops to the former Yugoslavia: the Rapid Reaction Force plan of spring 1995 and the NATO Implementation Force mandated by the Dayton Peace Accords of November 1995.

Background on the Rapid Reaction Force

The winter thaw in early 1995 enabled Serbian military advances and brought about a major change in the strategic situation on the ground in Bosnia. By April, Muslim troops and Croat forces in Bosnia were on the verge of total defeat at the hands of the Bosnian Serbs and the JNA. For the next four months, the world witnessed some of the worst violence of the war in the Balkans. Bosnian Serbs assaulted the UN safe havens of Tuzla, Srebrenica, and Sarajevo, and actually captured UN peacekeeping troops for use as human shields for strategic targets in Serb-controlled territory. In late May, more than 300 UN peacekeepers were taken hostage by Serb forces after a series of NATO air strikes, and Serb forces were advancing on British peacekeepers near Gorazde, Ukrainians in Zepa, and Dutch forces in Srebrenica. In early June, an American pilot was shot down over Bosnia (and later recovered in a secret rescue operation), increasing Western concerns about the severity of the conflict. The spring of 1995 also saw mass displacements and systematic genocide conducted against Bosnian Muslim men of fighting age outside Srebenica after the town's surrender to Serb forces. The challenges and crises in Bosnia in 1995 demanded a response by the international community.

Conditions were so bad in Bosnia in May 1995 that NATO and United Nations officials ordered preparations for the deployment of a new, multinational Rapid Reaction Force (RRF) to save the UN mission in Bosnia. The NATO North Atlantic Council met in late May in the Netherlands, and leaders sent out a strong warning to the Bosnian Serbs to stop further aggression. Council members argued that attacks on UN-protected areas and the imprisonment of UN peacekeepers were unacceptable, and they claimed that NATO forces stood ready to respond to such provocations with force if necessary.[45] The Clinton administration subsequently announced the forward deployment of 3,500 U.S. troops and attack helicopters from Germany to Italy for a possible military action in the Balkans.[46] At the same time, the SACEUR began contacting NATO member governments to request their support for an RRF contingency. General Joulwan made a point of personally contacting top German leaders to request their support for an RRF contingency, once again presenting the government with a strategic dilemma.[47]

It should be noted that the RRF contingency reflected the alliance's new mindset as the organization began to shift its focus to peace operations and conflict management, to dramatically widen its membership through the Partnership for Peace program, and to consider more flexible force structures to better respond to various crisis contingencies. The NATO Council Summit meetings in June 1994, 1995, and 1996 saw the passage of plans to implement a Combined Joint Task Force arrangement (CJTF) that would permit NATO to carry out its mission more flexibly and efficiently. Based on a "coalition of the willing," the CJTF would create new "separable, but not separated" military units for specific operations. The RRF plan was to be the first implementation of that contingency, and it would invite willing European governments to supply troops for the operation.[48]

Some critics in the United Nations, NATO governments, and inside Germany voiced concern that the UN might cross the "Mogadishu Line," and fundamentally alter the nature of the peacekeeping operations in the region. A reference to the debacle of the American-led intervention in Somalia, this concept suggested that the United Nations must carefully avoid a transformation from peacekeepers to combatants. An RRF contingency would provide needed heavy weaponry and air support, but might also unconsciously promote combat preparations and mission creep, which many viewed as the downfall of UN operations in Somalia. Lord Owen, the European Union mediator in the Balkans, announced in June 1995 that he would resign his position, taking the opportunity to warn that "impartiality and the perception of impartiality was the quickest and only sure way to gain the release of the United Nations soldiers being held hostage by the Bosnian Serbs and to unblock relief convoys and re-open negotiations."[49]

German foreign policy decision makers faced a series of external challenges and demands for action by June 1995. First, European and American leaders discussed the deteriorating situation in Bosnia at the Group of Seven (G-7) economic summit in Halifax, Nova Scotia. Prior to the summit, British Prime Minister John Major had already announced his decision to deploy 1,500 troops to Bosnia and put 5,000 more on alert to rescue the UN mission. Members of the British parliament cheered when Major called the taking of hostages "a despicable act that would guarantee the Bosnian Serbs unremitting hostility and a pariah status."[50] At the G-7 summit, U.S. officials pressured allies for some sort of firm diplomatic statement. President Clinton said that if UN troops were forced to withdraw from the Balkans, he would favor lifting the weapons embargo to allow the Bosnian government to better arm itself. This stand effectively forced the Europeans to develop the RRF contingency plan.[51] After some debate, all G-7 leaders agreed to a compromise resolution that demanded an end to Serbian aggression and warned of impending Western military action. Helmut Kohl supported the G-7 resolution, well aware of its implications for German troops.

Not long after the Halifax Summit, the French government called for an emergency meeting of the UN Security Council to discuss the creation of an RRF to save UN operations in the Balkans. On June 16, 1995, the UN Security Council joined forces with NATO leaders in passing a resolution that called for troop protection and support for the UNPROFOR peacekeepers in the region. The resolution passed as fighting was spreading around Sarajevo, raising the possibility that UN troops would have to withdraw if they could not fulfill their mandate of protecting civilians and delivering relief supplies. The new RRF contingency was designed to augment the 40,000 UNPROFOR troops in the region with an additional 12,500 soldiers to be supplied primarily by Britain, France, and the Netherlands. Secretary General Boutros-Ghali claimed that the RRF would provide "well armed and mobile forces to respond to threats to UN personnel."[52]

This action came as no surprise to the German government—in fact, planning for this contingency was already underway. Civilian and military strategists in the Defense Ministry had developed operational plans for such missions in the wake of NATO meetings on CJTF. As early as January 1995, Klaus Rose, CSU Chairman of the *Bundestag* Defense Committee, had confirmed news reports that the *Bundeswehr* was preparing to lend support to a possible withdrawal operation for UNPROFOR. He claimed that Germany was prepared to offer NATO 2,000 German soldiers, twenty-eight aircraft, fourteen warships and one field hospital for deployment to specified sites.[53] At the same time, however, the Foreign Ministry was working on a contingency that would involve only 1,000 German soldiers, eight new ECR-Tornado aircraft, medical assistance, air transport, and additional staff for the international headquarters.[54] The Foreign Ministry claimed that this force would be responsible for responding to crises in the region, including the defense of UN safe havens and support for other humanitarian and peacekeeping operations in the region.[55]

Domestic Conditions and the RRF Contingency

German government leaders chose to interpret the request for a troop commitment for a possible RRF deployment as a strategic opportunity. Ironically, the external strategic dilemma posed by the rapidly deteriorating situation in Bosnia seemed to create a situation in which German leaders faced less internal opposition to action. In these circumstances, it was Foreign Minister Kinkel who stated that since Germany had supported all decisions by the UN Security Council and NATO during the establishment of the RRF, there was only one possible response: "we want to and have to show responsibility."[56] In a series of press statements throughout June 1995, Kinkel referred to the overriding need for the German government to show solidarity with the UN and NATO forces.

While Kinkel maintained a firm line of support for German participation in allied military action in the Balkans, the FDP organization was sharply divided. At a special party conference held in Mainz in mid-June 1995, FDP delegates elected Wolfgang Gerhardt as the new party leader to succeed Kinkel, who had been at the helm during a two-year run of bad luck for the Liberals in regional elections. In fact, the FDP had failed to clear the 5% hurdle in representation for eleven state parliaments during the past two years as well as in the June 1994 European Parliament election. In his farewell speech to the party, Kinkel worried openly that the power of the FDP had waned because it was a more functional coalition maker than a party with a clear identity, and further commented that the FDP had too rarely asserted itself against its partners during the past thirteen years. Gerhardt, too, emphasized this theme in his keynote address, arguing that "the FDP must strengthen its identity and make clear its differences with the Christian Democrats. . . . We are first and foremost Free Democrats, and coalition partners secondly."[57]

Defense Minister Rühe and key planners at the Ministry of Defense (MoD) approached the RRF contingency somewhat differently than did Kinkel. In statements to the press at the time, Rühe again sounded a note of caution in his emphasis that German ECR-Tornadoes would only be used defensively and in extreme contingencies. Kinkel seemed intent to keep the mission of any German troops deployed in the region carefully bounded.[58] Rühe also repeated his concerns that NATO should not have to pick up the slack for failures in UN operations.[59] In press statements during June of 1995, Kinkel consistently would refer to the overriding need for the German government to show solidarity with the UN and NATO forces.

There were, however, degrees of difference between Kinkel's position in June 1995 and that of Defense Minister Rühe and key civilian and military planners at the MoD. Volker Rühe said in early June 1995 that "we are preparing our troops for a withdrawal or partial withdrawal [of UNPROFOR]. . . . If we are asked, we must be open to such a request. This is now the government's position. In the parliamentary groups of the government coalition, there is also widespread agreement emerging for our international solidarity. I hope that the majority of the SPD will also agree." However, he went on to say that he envisioned this mainly involving aircraft, ships, and paramedics—not ground troops.[60] The defense minister seemed intent to keep the mission of any German troops deployed in the region carefully bounded.[61]

The most interesting developments in party positions regarding the RRF deployment issue actually occurred in the opposition parties. As noted earlier, Rudolf Scharping had led a faction of the SPD to support the December 1994 parliamentary decision to authorize the deployment of ECR-Tornadoes to the region, in spite of internal disagreements on the question. Karsten Voigt, a foreign policy spokesman of the SPD parliamentary group, later explained that his party saw serious problems with German plans for intervention at two levels. First, he said that government statements indicated a serious difference of opinion between Kinkel and Rühe, and warned that this might undermine German foreign policy. Second, he emphasized that his party supported United Nations peacekeeping efforts in the region, but opposed combat operations.[62]

The RRF debate clearly highlighted division inside the SPD. Scharping carefully articulated the SPD line that any deployment of troops should be confined to medical or logistical support operations, but this was simply too much for liberals in the party. In the fall of 1995, however, Scharping was ousted as party chairman, in a move quite reminiscent of the political demise of Chancellor Helmut Schmidt (and more recently, of Kinkel's loss of power in the FDP). Like Scharping in 1995, Schmidt had supported a conservative foreign policy cause in 1982, namely the NATO modernization of intermediate-range nuclear forces. Like Scharping, Schmidt had lost his chancellorship due to extreme internal party opposition from the liberal wing. While less severe, Scharping's losses were indicative of continued ideological polarization in the SPD.[63]

The story of division and strife in opposition parties extended to the Green Party organization. The traditional "Green line" on use of force questions was that any deployment of *Bundeswehr* troops for anything other than humanitarian operations was out of the question. For years, the Greens were vocal proponents of pacifism in all government policy, but the acute crisis in the Balkans in mid-1995 presented the Green party leadership with a real dilemma. Here was a very serious humanitarian crisis reminiscent of the horrors of World War II, just a few hundred kilometers from German soil, that essentially demanded a Western response.

The strategic dilemma created a small storm of controversy inside the Green Party organization in the late spring of 1995 when Joschka Fischer, a member of the party's board of directors, circulated a policy paper in which he called for a redefinition of party principles on foreign policy. Fischer called for a more active German government role in promoting UN humanitarian and peace operations in the Balkans. The dilemma continued to provoke internal debate in the weeks leading up to the *Bundestag* debate on the RRF question. Ultimately, the Greens decided that they would call for "massive German support by nongovernmental organizations for humanitarian aid shipments" instead of voting for the government plan to commit to the RRF. Three members of the Green Party, however, later admitted to voting with the government.[64]

The strategic opportunity created by the NATO request also fit with government efforts to ensure strong public support for this potential RRF action. Polls at the time showed that Germans strongly supported an active contribution to NATO missions. From unification to 1995, public support for the alliance had increased steadily. Public support for NATO was 57% in 1991, but by 1995 it had increased to 71% (consistent with higher ratings of the 1980s). One Institut für Demoskopie survey found that 74% of all German respondents indicated that they would support "NATO involvement in new crises on Europe's periphery."[65] Experts suggest that Germans were all too aware of the instability in nearby regions like the former Soviet republics and the Balkans, leading them to seek stability in the Western alliance. When faced with more specific questions about support for German participation in the RRF deployment, however, the public demonstrated mixed sentiments. In July 1995, 48% of Germans said that the *Bundeswehr* should participate in the operation, while 46% opposed the deployment.[66]

Editorials in prominent newspapers also suggested that the public had mixed feelings about the RRF deployment. An interesting opinion was offered up in the *Frankfurter Rundschau*:

For the first time since the end of the Second World War, German soldiers are preparing for a combat mission. Simply accusing the government of warmongering would be unfair. That is not Bonn's intention, but still, everything points to it. This chancellor, infused with the idea of Europe, and his coalition colleagues believe that they cannot do otherwise than to deploy soldiers. They believe this despite evidence to the contrary about the wisdom of the decision made by the British and French to send a multinational rapid reaction force, which is a provocation for the Serbs.

Another editorial in the *Mitteldeutsche Zeitung*, captured the spirit of uncertainty about the implications of the RRF:

Agreement with the government's decision to deploy troops is guarded, but so is opposition to the decision. Reflective tones predominate on both sides. *Bundestag* deputies are facing a question of conscience. The history of the 20th century has shown again and again that politicians direct their soldiers into battle for seemingly plausible reasons, but that they don't know how to get them safely out again. Responsibility for the well being of every single German soldier lies not with the UN and not with allied forces in Bosnia. It lies with the *Bundestag*.

In spite of broad and indirect critiques in the mass media, leaders believed that there was a growing consensus in the summer for military action. One editorial in a Berlin newspaper, *Der Tagesspiel*, summed up the atmosphere of inevitability in the government's response to the latest crisis in June 1995: "The government's decision has been made and it holds no surprises. Germany will participate in protecting the UN Blue Helmets in the former Yugoslavia. Although it sounds like a routine decision, in reality it marks the close of a chapter of German security policy."

Germany Commits to the RRF

Given their base of domestic support, government leaders moved ahead with plans for a German commitment to the Rapid Reaction Force. On June 26, 1995, the cabinet agreed on a support plan and forwarded the matter to the *Bundestag* for review.[67] This proposal called for the participation of approximately 1,500 *Bundeswehr* members, including medical groups for a joint German–French field hospital to be set up in Split, Croatia, security personnel, and crews and maintenance staff for Tornadoes and transport aircraft. The cabinet plan would cost Germany an estimated $240 million.[68] After the cabinet meeting, Kinkel, Rühe and Naumann held a joint press conference to discuss their support for the decision and build a strong case for the impending *Bundestag* debate and vote on the initiative. Toward the end of the press conference, Kinkel and Rühe confidently reminded the public that only a simple majority would be needed for parliamentary approval of the deployment, consistent with the 1994 Constitutional Court ruling.[69]

Parliamentary debate on the RRF contingency ran from June 28-30, 1995. On the evening of June 28, members of the *Bundestag* committees on defense and foreign affairs met to consider the government proposal and later voted to approve it.[70] During the climax of the debate on June

30, Kinkel argued the importance of the 1994 Constitutional Court ruling. He said:

The Federal government is asking the German *Bundestag* for its consent to this
decision. In the post-war era, Germany has experienced consistent and unwa-
vering protection on security concerns from allies and friends. But today, not only
is German solidarity with allies in question, but also new definitions of German
interests and the implications of current policies. . . . We have a political and
moral obligation to help in Yugoslavia, especially in consideration of our past. . . .
Therefore, today's vote of the German Bundestag has great significance. Namely,
the creation of a common European foreign and security policy as well as the
credibility and prestige of Germany to the outside world. We are not allowed to
just talk about foreign and security policy, we must also practice it![71]

The coalition government was able to garner more support for this
action by stipulating tight boundaries on the mission. In fact, the *Bundestag* resolution restricted the scope of the military mission in several
ways. First, the government promised that deployment of ECR-Tornadoes would be confined strictly "to protect and assist NATO warplanes by
flying close air support for the UN Reaction Force." The Defense Ministry
pledged that this restriction would be enforced by the presence of German Air Force General Walter Jertz at the air base in Italy, who became
the government watchdog on operational restrictions by ensuring that
German troops did not participate in wider operations.[72] Second, the
Bundestag stipulated that German planes could only "protect and assist
the UN Rapid Reaction Force when attacked" and not in offensive operations. In an important speech on the day of the *Bundestag* vote, Defense
Minister Rühe pledged that the German Tornadoes would "only be used
if there is an aggression on the ground, namely an attack against the
blue-helmet troops."[73]

The government plan to deploy German troops in the RRF received an
oversized majority of support in the *Bundestag* (386–258) on June 30,
1995.[74] Chancellor Kohl hailed the *Bundestag* vote as a "major turning
point in foreign and defense policy." Kinkel and Rühe both welcomed the
outcome and their ministries continued preparations to coordinate an
RRF deployment with allies. Even Green Party leader Joschka Fischer
acknowledged that it was an historic decision. Leaders agreed that this
commitment by the German government to deploy ground troops to
potential combat operations was to be the first of its kind in the history
of the Federal Republic of Germany.[75]

Deployment and Combat Operations

While the Rapid Reaction Force plan was never fully implemented,
Germany did provide increased support for air operations in the theater.
NATO leaders held a special conference in London in July 1995 to review

the status of military operations in Bosnia. NATO Secretary General Willy Claes issued a formal statement at the end of the conference warning that any attack by Bosnian Serb forces on UN-protected areas (including Gorazde, Tuzla, Bihac, or Sarajevo) would be met by a "substantial and decisive response." At the same time, the North Atlantic Council directed military planning authorities to prepare plans for retaliatory strikes.[76]

The German cabinet authorized the deployment of a dozen ECR-Tornadoes and eight Transall transport aircraft, with ground crews, to the NATO operation in the Balkans in August 1995. They also extended offers for further logistical support and coordination with NATO and UN forces in the region.[77] These deployments were considered partial implementation of the RRF force structure agreements authorized by the *Bundestag* on June 30, and the actual movement of forces drew little attention from the German domestic arena.

Based in Piacenza, Italy, the German planes were incorporated quickly into regular NATO air operations monitoring the no-fly zone over Bosnia and conducting ground reconnaissance. For several weeks, they were deployed primarily to take low-level flight reconnaissance photographs of the locations and troop movements of Bosnian Serb factions in the war.[78] Many of the reconnaissance missions were designed to familiarize the pilots with the terrain, as well as gain vital information of Serbian troops. On September 1, 1995, however, German ECR-Tornadoes participated in their first air strikes on Bosnian Serb military positions as part of a NATO operation. NATO planes struck Serb artillery positions and ammunition depots in the hills of Bosnia with German support, and military observers recorded more than 300 detonations.[79] German soldiers saw combat for the first time since World War II.[80]

THE DAYTON PEACE ACCORD AND IFOR TROOP DEPLOYMENT IN THE BALKANS

A final strategic challenge and opportunity was presented to the German government in the NATO Implementation Force plan. Developments between 1991 and 1995 had enabled the coalition leadership to gradually consolidate support for an entirely new security policy construct, one which permitted out-of-area operations and even allowed German soldiers to engage in combat within collective security arrangements. The readiness of the German polity to commit to the RRF was evidence of this change in perspective.

The Dayton Peace Agreement was completed on November 21, 1995, at Wright–Patterson Air Force Base in Ohio. Leaders of the warring groups in Bosnia committed to a peaceful settlement of the conflict, and to working toward long-term resolution of differences. According to the agreement, Bosnia–Herzegovina would remain intact with its 1992 international borders legitimized. Successor state relationships after the war would be governed by standards established in the UN Charter and the Helsinki Final Accords that called for the confirmation of sovereignty, territorial integrity, political autonomy, and peaceful relations. Sarajevo would be reunified and all sides would pledge the universal guarantee of human rights augmented by an Organization for Security and Cooperation in Europe (OSCE) monitoring program. All parties to the conflict would also provide for the safe and secure return of refugees to their respective home regions. Furthermore, the agreement would establish a collective parliament, central bank, a presidency, and bureaucracies for the combined states. An international tribunal for the investigation and prosecution of war criminals would be based in The Hague, Netherlands.[81]

The Dayton Accords represented the culmination of years of violence and diplomatic maneuvering by members of the Contact Group. These agreements called for all sides to support the reconstruction of the region, the repatriation of refugees, and the promotion of democratic and human rights statutes through a collective effort. Contact Group members and other Western powers joined the leaders of the warring factions in Yugoslavia in pledges of strong humanitarian relief efforts. In December 1995, the World Bank offered to provide $3 to 4 billion for reconstruction, and the EU Commission followed up with a significant aid package as well.[82]

While the cornerstones of the Dayton Peace Agreement included a new political system, reconstruction, and the repatriation of refugees, the superstructure of this arrangement would be supported by a massive international peace enforcement operation. The NATO Implementation Force (IFOR) would be a buffer zone-type peace implementation force, comprised of some 60,000 troops from NATO member countries including France, Great Britain, Belgium, Denmark, and the Netherlands, as well as non-NATO countries, including Russia.[83] Officials claimed that the international peace mission would help to restore order to the region and pave the way for free and fair democratic elections to be held in all zones of Bosnia in September 1996.[84] Ultimately, officials believed that the elections and Dayton agreements would establish a foundation for peace by the end of the IFOR deployment in December 1996.

German government officials were involved with the Dayton Accord blueprint pre-negotiation, and cabinet leaders called for an active German role in the NATO Implementation Force (IFOR) even before the historic Wright–Patterson talks. German military officers had, in fact, participated in the force structure planning process in Brussels for just such a contingency throughout the fall of 1995. On October 12, 1995, the NATO Supreme Allied Commander had formally requested a German pledge of support for the IFOR plan and publicly outlined plans for a

potential contribution of 4,000 soldiers for a variety of duties in the operation (the fourth-largest contingent of troops in the operation).[85] The
contingency plan called for only one year of service, and the preliminary
estimates of the cost of German participation were around DM 700 million.[86] Key allies of Germany would also provide significant troop commitments to the operation: the United States pledged to send 20,000
soldiers to Bosnia, the United Kingdom 13,000, and France 11,000.

Accordingly, German leaders joined other Contact Group and Western
leaders for an IFOR Implementation Conference in London on December
8, 1995, where they pledged German resources to support the post-war
order in Bosnia. On December 14, 1995, leaders met again in Paris to sign
a formal peace treaty to end the civil war in the former Yugoslavia.[87]

Domestic Conditions and IFOR

German leaders had already committed the government to support the
implementation of a peace settlement in the former Yugoslavia (through
the RRF contingency) in the summer of 1995. In the fall, Defense Minister Rühe attempted to prepare the German public for a potential troop
deployment to a peace implementation force in theater. Rühe had actually provided the first glimpse of a government plan to deploy *Bundeswehr*
soldiers in the new contingency in an October interview in *Der Spiegel*.
Rühe made it clear that German foreign policy responsibilities had
changed in the post-Cold War era, and that the government might have
to commit troops to this peace enforcement operation. In an interesting
set of comparisons and contrasts, the defense minister contended: that
German foreign policy responsibilities had changed. If the government
were to be confronted by another Gulf War scenario, it would be forced
to act in a manner consistent with international commitments; but there
was a clear distinction between the Somalia operation and plans for a
Balkans peace enforcement operation. The IFOR deployment would be
nothing like the Somalia debacle. Finally, Rühe openly denied the criticism that Conservatives in government were practicing "salami tactics"
by consciously using strategic opportunities for force to create a greater
military profile in the post-Cold War era.[88]

Foreign Minister Kinkel also provided support for government plans to
deploy troops in the IFOR Operation. In a preliminary parliamentary
debate on the initiative, Kinkel argued that peace in Bosnia related
directly to stability in Europe. He put forward a very powerful and persuasive argument for how the German contribution to the new force in
the region would provide guarantees for human rights, end the instability in the region, address problems of refugees, and provide strong support. Kinkel stated publicly that the IFOR contingency was an important
multilateral operation and that Germany must be prepared to "do its

part" to keep the peace in the post-Cold War era. Like Rühe, the Foreign Minister also challenged opponents of the government plan by saying that they should stand up for German responsibility for peace and human rights in Europe. He said, "we must all together work to promote full-hearted European and transatlantic partnership."[89]

Once again, some of the most interesting political maneuvering on the IFOR question occurred in the opposition parties. Social Democratic Party representatives met to review the organization and its platform at a special party conference held in November of 1995. Party Chairman Scharping had pledged that he would support a deployment of German soldiers to IFOR and that he would encourage his party colleagues to vote in favor of the operation. However, in a rousing speech before the assembly, Saarland Minister President Oskar Lafontaine stated his opposition to the deployment of German aircraft in Bosnia and to any participation in combat operations.[90] Scharping and Lafontaine also differed in their attitudes toward ongoing domestic problems, such as unemployment and the question of full support for European monetary integration. By an overwhelming majority of 321 to 190, conference delegates boldly voted to replace Scharping with Lafontaine. Scharping was reelected to his post of head of the party *Fraktion* in the *Bundestag*, but the party conference certainly suggested a shift in control of the organization.[91]

Social Democrats were able to agree to confront the IFOR contingency head on, in spite of political wrangling at the party conference. They agreed to carefully consider the implications of the operation for the *Bundeswehr* and recognized that plans were consistent with successful peace operations in the recent past. Accordingly, a resolution was passed at the party congress that underscored the differences of opinion inside the party, and essentially freed delegates to vote their conscience on the plan. The resolution ruled out "the dispatch of units with a combat mission and the use of German fighter jets," but left the party's deputies with the option of parliamentary approval of the use of ECR-Tornadoes as part of an overall peacekeeping package.[92] Scharping later represented the SPD by providing broad-based support for IFOR in the *Bundestag*.[93]

The Greens and Alliance '90 parties also sponsored a series of special conferences at which they considered their foreign policy orientations in light of the new strategic opportunities. At a conference on peacekeeping operations and German responsibilities in a changing international security environment, held in Bonn in the fall 1995, the Greens engaged in a very open and interesting discussion on the question of how and when they might support the deployment of German troops for peace operations. Some leaders of the Green foreign policy group urged the party to develop a consistent list of criteria for peace operations, while others feared that this would be the beginning of a resurgence of militarism in German politics.[94]

The presidium of the Green Party, chaired by Jürgen Trittin and led by party foreign policy spokesman Ludger Volmer, continued to argue the strict pacifistic platform, and they opposed attempts by *Fraktion* leader Joschka Fischer to move the party to a more centrist foreign policy stance. Once again, Fischer called for moderation of the government's foreign policy stance by arguing that the Greens should now join the opposition SPD in supporting the government. In fact, several days before the meeting, he had submitted an open letter to party delegates in which he argued that Germany should take part in this humanitarian peace-keeping operation. He contended that the Greens must "hold firm to nonviolence in all other cases and say 'yes' to peacekeeping blue-helmet missions." Fischer argued that Germany should support operations that opposed genocide and were consistent with the UN Charter, but this position was challenged by leftists on the Green governing committee.[95]

One critical assessment of this rift in the Green Party related it to the larger political war in Germany. If the Greens were to adopt the more centrist foreign policy position advocated by Fischer, this move could open the way for coalitions with the Social Democrats at the state and national levels. An editorial in the *Frankfurter Rundschau* during this period notes that Fischer faced a serious uphill battle to "make the Greens suitable national coalition partners for the SPD at a level where they need to do more than just fight against automobiles or obstruct nuclear power projects."[96]

In an interesting Green Party conference summary document, the "Schlußfolgerungen der Abgeordneten," party members articulated a two-tiered response to such challenges.[97] First, party members reiterated their commitment to nonviolence in foreign policy, with an emphasis on conflict prevention and moderation. They made it clear that the party still was reluctant to consider peacekeeping in the post-Cold War era, and that Germany should never participate in combat missions.[98] However, the Greens also admitted that there were some circumstances of severe human rights violations and instability that would compel them to support the deployment of German troops abroad. Leaders accepted the fact that the party should support German participation in UN blue-helmet operations under certain bounded conditions.[99] Finally, the party leadership requested that *Bundestag* delegates reject participation in IFOR, but they agreed to allow some latitude for votes of conscience.

To the general public, the IFOR contingency seemed a foregone conclusion once the Dayton Agreement had been finalized. In fact, the Conservative–Liberal coalition deserved credit for their foresight to begin to build public consensus for the peace enforcement deployment in the fall months of 1995. The announcement of the Dayton Accords thus triggered a seemingly automatic response by European governments and signaled to the German public that a deployment was in the offing. An editorial in the *Frankfurter Rundschau* of November 29, 1995, captured the public mood of inevitability in the period:

Once again, the government arouses suspicion that it is misusing a peacekeeping mission for its own purposes. Domestically, in order to put the opposition under moral pressure and force them to decide between accepting combat units or looking like they are refusing peace . . . it forces the *Bundestag* to vote on a foregone conclusion, thus degrading parliamentary approval to a matter of form.[100]

The Government Acts Quickly on IFOR

Cabinet leaders met on November 28, 1995, and agreed on an initiative to support the IFOR deployment.[101] In fact, key government officials had openly designed and refined contingency plans for the deployment well in advance of the meeting. Kinkel and Rühe already had indicated the government's interest in complying with NATO's request for troops as early as October. Thus, the November cabinet meeting was not much more than a rubber stamp of the government contingency plan for IFOR. The cabinet produced a document describing the plan, with an impressive title: *Tischvorlage: Deutsche Beteiligung an den militärischen Maßnahmen zur Absicherung des Friedensvertrages für Bosnien-Herzegowina; Gemeinsame Kabinettsache des Bundesministers der Verteidigung und des Bundesministers des Auswärtigen.*[102] In a press conference following the meeting, Kohl and Kinkel outlined the government plan to send 4,000 troops, transport planes, and other supplies to the Implementation Force as early as January 1996; the projected German cost of the operation would be DM 700 million.[103] Finally, they made clear that the initiative would be submitted to the *Bundestag* for a vote in its final session of 1995.

The *Bundestag* debate concerning the IFOR initiative was both serious and symbolic. Foreign Minister Kinkel presented the government plans to the *Bundestag*, and gave a powerful speech in favor of the deployment. Kinkel made the case for the operation on several levels. First, he said that Germany should be committed to end the long civil war in the former Yugoslavia, and he argued that the government should be prepared to demonstrate that commitment strongly. He made an important point that peace in the former Yugoslavia was directly related to stability in Europe. Second, Kinkel contended that Germany should provide responsible support on the side of its EU and NATO partners. He argued that IFOR would be a sign of transatlantic partnership, including significant commitments of troops from the United States, United Kingdom, and France. Third, the foreign minister made the very powerful and persuasive argument that the German contribution to the new force in the region would provide guarantees for human rights, end the instability in the region, and address problems of refugees. Kinkel effectively argued that it was time for the German government to "stand up for German responsibility for peace and human rights in Europe."[104]

While the Foreign Minister's speech set the tone for the government in the IFOR debate, key conservative leaders also voiced their support for the deployment. Chairs of the *Fraktion* Defense Policy Committees and the Foreign Affairs Committees, Klause Rose and Karl-Heinz Hornhues (respectively), argued that Germany had a very serious responsibility to allies—and indeed to the world—to support this peace mission.[105] In a speech shortly before the final vote, Kohl himself argued that "the international community's expectations of unified Germany are different from those placed upon the old Federal Republic." In the past, the Federal Republic might have been able to leave military missions to its allies, but "today it must stand alongside them in preserving peace." He concluded that Germany "must not and can not withdraw from such a mission."[106]

The IFOR contingency also received a great deal of attention from traditional skeptics and opponents in the *Bundestag*. The legislation was potentially fractious because it presented some rather difficult issues for the SPD and Greens. In addition to "necessary self-defense" of the soldiers in the deployment, it also contained some references to combat situations. Nevertheless, Scharping and *Fraktion* leaders offered quiet support for the NATO IFOR mission, not as a "matter of war and fighting but of defense and implementing the peace." In the end, about 80% of SPD delegates voted with Scharping to support the government plan.[107] Delegates from the Greens/Alliance '90 and the Party of Democratic Socialism maintained their skepticism about the contingency. In the wake of their party conferences on the question, Green *Fraktion* members opted to split their votes relatively evenly on IFOR.[108] The presidium of the Green party, chaired by Jürgen Trittin, continued to oppose attempts by Joschka Fischer to move the party to a more centrist foreign policy stance (which could clear the way for coalitions with the SPD at the state and national levels). Gregor Gysi and the parliamentarians representing the PDS stood in firm opposition to the plan, however. Gysi warned that IFOR would escalate the conflict in the former Yugoslavia, and he expressed his concern that NATO member states were promoting a militarization of German foreign policy in the post-Cold War era.

The government plan to contribute German troops to the Implementation Force mission passed by an overwhelming margin: 543 to 107. Opponents of the plan included about fifty SPD deputies who broke ranks with the leadership to vote against committing the *Bundeswehr*, half of the Greens/Alliance '90 delegates, and the PDS.[109] The minimal opposition provided the government with its largest mandate ever for the deployment of *Bundeswehr* troops abroad, and this represented another significant turnaround in the German foreign policy profile.

Some government leaders celebrated this landmark change. Defense Minister Rühe spoke out publicly on his views that this was the right and proper decision. In one interview in the wake of the vote, he noted that, "unlike previous Bundeswehr deployments, the troops nor the public are boastful or sulking," and he contended that this decision represented a watershed in German foreign policy resolve. In another high profile address to commanding officers of the *Bundeswehr*, Rühe described the mandate of the mission:

NATO and the *Bundeswehr* are facing the greatest missions of their history. With the full support of the parliament and the people, our soldiers will help to secure peace in the former Yugoslavia. While making the preparatory decisions we received [so] much encouragement and support that we can speak of a new consensus. Germany is meeting its obligations and can be proud of its soldiers.

Enforcing the Peace in the Former Yugoslavia, 1996–1999

Bundestag approval allowed German troops to begin deploying to the Balkans in conjunction with other NATO IFOR contingents. One day after the vote, the first two *Bundeswehr* officers flew into Sarajevo for advance reconnaissance for the coming operation. General Georg Kerl and Lieutenant-Colonel Hermann Beckmann met with NATO and UN officials on the ground to set the stage for a forward deployment of German staff officers to Sarajevo. General Kerl joked with members of the German media on hand, saying that he was surprised that two soldiers could cause such a media frenzy.[110] Several days later, media attention shifted to the deployment of 180 more *Bundeswehr* officers in Sarajevo to coordinate command and control structures for NATO mission. The first NATO troop contingents arrived in Croatia on December 20, 1995, and the main body of troops followed in January. German deployments began in earnest in January 1996, and progressively built through March.

In total, 3,000 German soldiers were based in Piacenza, Italy, and another 1,000 deployed directly to Croatia for the IFOR operation. According to government declarations, the Defense Ministry maintained that German forces would only be stationed in the western region of the Balkans and serve the NATO mission in a supporting role.[111] Their primary missions were to include police protection of non-governmental organization programs (ranging from refugee assistance to medical care), engineering and reconstruction projects for infrastructure (including bridges, water lines, and roads), and rehabilitating housing in the region.[112] However, it should be noted that German soldiers did serve in several areas of potential tension and even combat. Government sources confirmed in December 1995, that some eighty elite German troops would be deployed to the Srebrenica region of Bosnia to provide security for British and French supply lines. Officials claimed that this battalion was the only German group that might possibly have to contend with fighting as part of their mission.[113]

From January to December 1996, German soldiers contributed to the regional peace enforcement effort and helped with rebuilding and infrastructure projects in Croatia and Bosnia. Somewhat remarkably, the basic outlines of the Dayton Peace Accords and the rules of engagement for the Implementation Force held throughout 1996. There were very few casualties among IFOR troops during the first year of deployment, and they made significant progress in civil reconstruction projects. NATO leaders soon realized, however, that the mandate for a peace enforcement operation in the former Yugoslavia would have to continue beyond the original planned termination date of December 1996. In the summer of 1996, European leaders acknowledged that an extension of the commitment might be necessary, but Clinton administration officials remained strangely silent on the extension question. As fate would have it, 1996 was a presidential election year in the United States, and Clinton would have had to face tough questions about the purpose, progress, and duration of the U.S. troop presence in IFOR had he embraced extension prior to November.

As early as the summer of 1996, German officials supported the extension of the peace enforcement mission in the Balkans. Kohl, Rühe, and Kinkel were all convinced of the need to maintain a longer-term presence as encouragement and support for the consolidation of democracy in the region. These assumptions were confirmed by a series of problems related to the September 1996 elections in Bosnia, which had originally been mandated by the Dayton Agreements and which (it was hoped) would pave the way for a peaceful democratic transition in the Balkans. Instead, the elections were fraught with charges of local and regional political corruption, tarnished by threats of serious election-related violence, and basically institutionalized the polarization of ethnic national identities in post-war occupation zones of Bosnia.

German officials began to consider what more they could do to promote a peaceful transition in the region in the wake of these elections in Bosnia. Defense Minister Rühe traveled to Sarajevo two days after the vote to meet with military leaders of the IFOR peace mission and his British counterpart, Michael Portillo. Following consultative meetings, Rühe took the opportunity to speak out in favor of an extension of the operational mandate. He admitted, "I think everyone knows we can't leave here, but a renewed mandate must of course be strictly limited." Rühe suggested that the extended mission would last at least another year, and he even speculated that German troops could be stationed in Bosnia and nearer to the front lines of the operation.[114]

One week later, German leaders and their NATO partners gathered in Norway for an official conference that included two important issues on the agenda: a review of the status of IFOR with an eye toward the future, and the question of NATO enlargement. Citing the need to stabilize the political situation in Bosnia, the ministers voted unanimously in favor of continuing the mission after its current mandate expired in late December 1996. NATO leaders later refined the operational plan for the mission to be termed the "Stabilization Force" or SFOR. This deployment would pare down the overall troop commitment in the region to 34,000, and the mandate for the operation would extend to June 1998. This time, Defense Minister Rühe was able to announce the official government position that 2,000 to 3,000 *Bundeswehr* troops would be committed to SFOR.[115]

In a speech before the UN General Assembly on September 25, 1996, Foreign Minister Kinkel also expressed his opinions about the deployment and the overall evolution of German foreign policy responsibilities. Reaffirming Germany's commitment to multilateralism, Kinkel called on the member states of the UN to take decisive action to bolster the organization's effectiveness and efficiency. Kinkel used the opportunity to assert that Germany would support an extension of the mandate for the IFOR mission beyond its planned expiration in December, and would maintain its commitment to the preservation of peace in Bosnia. Kinkel chose to interpret Germany's contribution to the IFOR operation as altruistic multilateralism, noting that, "no country, no region, and no group of states can bear all of the world's burdens and troubles alone." Kinkel ended his speech with a call for a significant restructuring of the UN Security Council, including assigning a permanent seat on the Council to the Federal Republic of Germany.[116]

Perhaps the most interesting postscript to the IFOR story is the way that opposition parties jumped on the bandwagon in support of the German role in peace enforcement in the Balkans. By late 1996, it became clear that the success of the IFOR operation in keeping the peace presented government opponents with a real challenge. In the fall months, SPD leader Rudolph Scharping told reporters that his party had supported the mission in the past—including the *Bundestag* vote of December 1995—and that his party would continue to do so. In fact, Scharping made it clear that fall that the SPD would not even oppose a deployment of German soldiers to the front lines of the peace enforcement operation in Bosnia. He argued very clearly that it would not be a question of sending German troops off to Bosnia to fight; Scharping explained the point of the mission would be to "realize a peace agreement in the civil realm and to guarantee it militarily."[117]

On December 17, 1997, NATO foreign ministers endorsed plans to keep peacekeeping troops in Bosnia through the year 2000. Under the new plans, Russia and NATO forces would maintain deployments in a new "Deterrence Force," or DFOR, that would consist of 22,000 troops (some 14,000 fewer than the SFOR operation). Once again, the German government pledged to contribute 3,000 troops for the mission and maintain a steady forward presence to promote a peaceful, democratic transition in the mission. In mid-June 1998, Bundestag deputies voted 528 to 37 to continue participation in the operation.[118] Troops continued their reconstruction efforts and monitored the peace largely without incident.[119]

CONCLUSION

This chapter has demonstrated how the crisis in the former Yugoslavia became a major catalyst for the normalization of German foreign policy. Strategic dilemmas in 1994 and 1995 dramatically accelerated the debate about foreign policy responsibilities that was underway in the domestic political arena, and prompted radical political strategy in the decision to deploy ground troops. Key government officials have privately confessed that while it was a terrible humanitarian crisis, Bosnia was critical to German foreign policy restructuring. By 1996, domestic opposition to the deployment of German troops in foreign countries—outside the NATO area and even in potential combat areas—had virtually faded away. As of this writing, German soldiers continue their peace enforcement mission in the former Yugoslavia.

NOTES

1. "Kinkel Views Bundeswehr Out-of-Area Missions," in *Süddeutsche Zeitung*, 16 July 1994, pp. 1, 5.
2. "Rühe Discusses NATO Mission in Bosnia," interview transcript from *Stern*, 14 December 1995, pp. 181–183; reprinted in FBIS-WEU-95-240, 14 December 1995.
3. Klaus Kinkel, "Peacekeeping Missions: Germany Can Now Play Its Part," *NATO Review*, 5 October 1994, p. 3.
4. *Deutschland Nachrichten*, 15 July 1994, p. 1.
5. "Kinkel Calls for Participation in UN Operations," quoted in news report on Berlin DDP/ADN on 13 April 1994; reprinted in FBIS-WEU-94-071, 13 April 1994, p. 12.
6. Rüdiger Moniac, "Rühe—NATO Air Strikes in Bosnia Absolutely Necessary," *Die Welt*, 12 April 1994; reprinted in FBIS-WEU-94-071, 13 April 1994, p. 12.
7. "Urteil des Bundesverfassungsgerichts über Verfassungsbeschwerden gegen internationale Einsätze der Bundeswehr, verkündet in Karlsruhe am 12 Juli 1994," *Europa-Archiv*, 15 Folge 1994, pp. D427–D431; see also *Frankfurter Allgemeine Zeitung*, 13 July 1994, pp. 1, 3.
8. Craig R. Whitney, "Court Permits German Troops a Foreign Role," *New York Times*, 13 July 1994, p. A1.

9. *Deutschland Nachrichten*, 15 July 1994, p. 1.

10. Craig R. Whitney, "Court Permits German Troops a Foreign Role," 1994, p. A1.

11. This position was clearly popular in the Konrad Adenauer Stiftung; see confidential interview, Konrad Adenauer Stiftung, Sankt Augustin, 9 June 1996.

12. Thomas L. Friedman, "Clinton Calls on Germany to Be Partner," *New York Times*, 12 July 1994, p. A4.

13. "Kinkel Views Bundeswehr Out-of-Area Missions," 1994, p. 1.

14. FBIS-WEU-94-137, 18 July 1994, p. 15–16.

15. Ibid., pp. 15–16.

16. Karl-Ludwig Guensche, "Kinkel Warns Against National Solo Actions," *Die Welt*, 11 July 1994, p. 2.

17. Rühe Address, 24 August 1994 , speech to Aspen Institute Research Group.

18. "Bundesminister der Vertiedigung Volker Rühe in einem Gespräch mit dem Wallstreet Journal Europe und dem Handelsblatt," 26 August 1994; reprinted in *Stichworte zur Sicherheitspolitik*, September 1994.

19. *Süddeutsche Zeitung*, 13 July 1994, p. 1; another editorial appeared on the same day in the *Frankfurter Allgemeine Zeitung*, which stated " . . . to be sure, the Federal Constitutional Court's decision on sending *Bundeswehr* troops outside the territory of NATO does not give the government—any government, a free hand in using the *Bundeswehr*. The decision adheres closely to the instances at hand: the Adriatic, AWACs, Somalia. But the decision also says, and this points to the future, that the collective security systems the Federal Republic has joined—the United Nations foremost, but also NATO and the Western European Union—can change in character, as we have seen since 1989."

20. Allensbach Institüt für Demoskopie survey, "Am Sonntag wird ein neuer Bundestag gewählt," *Frankfurter Allgemeine Zeitung*, 15 October 1994, p. 5; declining public support for the Conservative–Liberal coalition was a reflection of several factors including economic and social problems in Germany and *Politikverdrossenheit*. The economy was in recession, unemployment was high, and public indebtedness had topped $1.3 trillion. Widespread disillusionment with political leadership in the post-unification era, coupled with intra- and inter-pary disagreements, threatened the ruling coalition's hold on power. For example, the Free Democrats suffered almost a year of steady defeat in state parliamentary elections in 1993–1994 and were faced with the real possibility of losing their role in the government completely. The FDP slogan for the elections reflected leaders' concerns: "*Diesmal, geht es um alles*" (this time, everything's at stake). Predictably, the central theme of the SPD campaign was "social justice" and focused on job programs and economic stimuli to re-energize the German economy; see "Die Union mit deutlichem Vorsprung vorn," *Frankfurter Allgemeine Zeitung*, 17 October 1994, p. 1; *Deutschland Nachrichten*, 9 September 1994.

21. "Die Stärke der Parteien," *Frankfurter Allgemeine Zeitung*, 15 October 1994, p. 5.

22. "Die Union mit deutlichem Vorsprung vorn," *Frankfurter Allgemeine Zeitung*, p. 1; see also Craig R. Whitney, "Kohl's Slate Slips as Germans Vote: Keeps Small Edge," *New York Times*, 17 October 1994, p. 1.

23. Presse- und Informationsamt der Bundesregierung, "Einsätze der Bundeswehr im Rahmen der UNO, Vergassungsrechtliche Aspekte, Urteile (Auszüge)

zu AWACS, UNOSOM II, sowie des Bundesverfassungsgerichts vom 12.07.1994, Auszüge aus Gesetzes- und Vertragstexten Bundespresseamt," July 1994.

24. "Weitere Einsätze der NATO Luftstreitkräfte im Bosnien-Konflikt," *Stichworte zur Sicherheitspolitik*, December 1994; see also Franz-Josef Meiers, "Germany: The Reluctant Power," *Survival*, Autumn 1995, p. 86.

25. Udo Bergdoll, "Aus Bonn ein vernebeltes Nein," *Suddeutsche Zeitung*, 8 December 1994, p. 1; "Bonner Versteckspiel im Tornado-Dilemma," *Neue Zürcher Zeitung*, 9 December 1994, p. 1.

26. "Luft und Wasser," *Der Spiegel*, 12 December 1994, pp. 22–24.

27. Jurgen Gottschlich, "Germans to the Front," *Die Tageszeitung*, 3 December 1994, p. 10.

28. Martin Lambeck, "Tornados as Yardstick," *Die Welt*, 5 December 1994, pp. 43–44.

29. "Wie im Somalia," *Der Spiegel*, 5 December 1994, pp. 18–21.

30. Munich ARD Television Network interview, 1 December 1994; transcript reprinted in FBIS-WEU-94-232, 2 December 1994.

31. FBIS-WEU-94-232, 3 December 1994, p. 66.

32. Katja Gloger and Jochen Schildt, "Facts must first be put on the table," *Stern*, 4 December 1994, pp. 170–172.

33. FBIS-WEU-94-232, 3 December 1994, p. 21.

34. F. Weckbach-Mara, "German Tornados for Sarajevo Before the End of This Year," *Bild am Sonntag*, 18 December 1994, pp. 4–5.

35. *Vienna Kurier*, 15 January 1995, p. 3.

36. "Kein Hurra geschreien," *Der Spiegel*, 19 December 1994, pp. 18–21; see also "SPD Warns Bonn Against Bosnia Combat Missions," interview transcript from Berlin DDP, 1 December 1994; reprinted in FBIS-WEU-94-232, 2 December 1994.

37. Meiers, "Germany: The Reluctant Power," 1995, p. 91.

38. "Party Positions," FBIS-WEU-95-126, 30 June 1995, p. 13.

39. "Wie in Somalia," *Der Spiegel* 49, 1994, pp. 18–19.

40. "Ganz verbindlich," *Der Spiegel* 50, 1994, pp. 22–26.

41. "Bundeskabinett beschließt Stritkräfteaufenthaltsgesetz," Pressvermittlung, BMVG, 21 December 1994; reprinted in *Stichworte zur Sicherhetispolitik*.

42. "Interview with Foreign Minister Klaus Kinkel (FDP)," *Bild am Sonntag*, 19 December 1994; reprinted in FBIS-WEU-94-243, pp. 23–24.

43. Ibid., pp. 23–24..

44. FBIS-WEU-94-247, 22 December 1994, p. 5.

45. "Erklärung zur Lage im ehemaligen Jugoslawien," from the North Atlantic Council meeting on 30 May 1995 in the Netherlands, *Bulletin*, no. 48, 12 June 1995, p. 429.

46. R. W. Apple, Jr., "Allies Seem Near Accord to Bolster Bosnia Force," *New York Times*, 2 June 1995, p. A10.

47. "Kommunique der Ministertagung des Nordatlantikrats," transcript of agreement communique by the NATO North Atlantic Council in the Netherlands on 30 May 1995, *Bulletin*, no. 48, 12 June 1995, pp. 425–429.

48. Ibid., pp. 425–429; this is supported by information drawn from confidential interview, Mershon Center, The Ohio State University, Columbus, Ohio, 1 June 1995.

49. John Darnton, "U.N. Buildup in Bosnia Eyes 'Mogadishu Line'," *New York Times*, 7 June 1995, p. A18.

50. John Darnton, "Britain and France to Send More Troops," *New York Times*, 1 June 1995, p. A11.

51. Barbara Crossette, "Security Council Approves Sending Reinforcements to Bosnia," *New York Times*, 17 June 1995, p. A7.

52. Ibid., p. A7; see also "Selbs geleimt," *Der Spiegel* 25, 1995, pp. 37–38; Eric Schmitt, "U.S. Force May help U.N. Troops to Regroup," *New York Times*, 1 June 1995, p. A10; see also "A Balkan Quagmire Beckons," *Economist*, 3 June 1995, pp. 41–42.

53. FBIS-WEU-95-010, 17 January 1995, p. 11.

54. "Dabeisein ist alles," *Der Spiegel*, 6 June 1995, pp. 22–27.

55. "Press Statement on Safe Areas by the Secretary General Following North Atlantic Council Meeting on 1 August 1995," reprinted in *NATO Review*, September 1995, p. 7.

56. Speech by Foreign Minister Klaus Kinkel at the Bundestag, Bonn, 30 June 1995, pp. 15–17; reprinted in FBIS-WEU-95-126.

57. "Wolfgang Gerhardt Succeeds Kinkel as National Chair of the Free Democrats," *Deutschland Nachrichten*, 16 June 1995, p. 1.

58. "Letzter Versuch," *Der Spiegel*, 3 July 1995, p. 26–28.

59. See, for example, radio interview with Karsten Voigt, the foreign policy spokeman of the SPD parliamentary group, Cologne Deutschland Rundfunk Network in German; FBIS Translation Excerpt, FBIS-WEU-95-108, 6 June 1995, pp. 5–6.

60. Interview with Defense Minister Volker Rühe, Stefan Kornelius and Martin E. Sueskind, "You Do Everything that You Say You are Going to Do," *Süddeutsche Zeitung*, 3 June 1995, p. 7.

61. "Letzter Versuch," *Der Spiegel*, 3 July 1995, p. 26–28.

62. Translation Excerpt, FBIS-WEU-95-108, 1995, pp. 5–6.

63. Confidential interview, Bundeshaus (Bundestag Legislative Offices), Bonn, 19 June 1996; Support for this came from confidential interview, Friedrich Ebert Stiftung, Bonn, 19 June 1996.

64. Confidential interview, Bundeshaus—Hochhaus Tulpenfeld (Bundestag Legislative Offices), Bonn, 5 July 1996.

65. Dr. Renate Koecher, "Unerwartete Wende," *Frankfurther Allgemeine Zeitung*, 14 June 1995, p. 5.

66. "Bosnieneinsatz—die Bürgermeinung," Forschungsgruppe Wahlen; reprinted in *Stichworte zur Sicherheitspolitik*, 10 July 1995.

67. "Antrag der Bundesregierung, Kabinettsbeschluß vom 26 June 1995, "Deutsche Beteiligung an den Maßnahemn zum Schutz und zur Unterstützung des schnellen Einsatzverbands im früheren Jugoslawien einschließlich der Unterstützung eines eventuellen Abzugs der UN-Friedenstruppen."

68. "Kabinett über Bosnien-Einsatz einig," *Süddetusche Zeitung*, 22 June 1995, p. 1; "Bundeskabinett entschedidet am Montag," *Frankfurter Allgemeine Zeitung*, 22 June 1995, p. 2; "Kabinett stimmt Einsatz deutscher soldaten in Bosnien zu," *Frankfurter Allgemeine Zeitung*, 27 June 1995, p. 1.

69. Press conference transcript with Rühe, General Inspector Naumann, and Kinkel on 26 June 1995; reprinted in Presse- und Informationsamt der Bundesregierung Referat Außen-, Sicherheits- und Europapolitik, Stand July 1995.

70. *Deutschland Nachrichten*, 30 June 1995, pp. 1–2.

71. Deutscher Bundestag, *Stenographischer Bericht*, 13. Wahlperiode—48. Sitzung, Plenarprotokoll 13/48, Bonn, Freitag, den 30 Juni 1995, pp. 3955–4019.

72. Stefan Kornelius, "Medienwirbel um deutsche Tornados," *Süddeutsche Zeitung*, 20 July 1995, p. 1.

73. Rühe quoted in Deutscher Bundestag, *Stenographischer Bericht*, 48th Session, Bonn, 30 June 1995, p. 4000; for more analysis of these restrictions, see Franz-Josef Meiers, "NATO's Peacekeeping Dilemma," *Arbeitspapiere zur Internationalen Politik*, no. 94 (Bonn: Forschungsinstitut der Deutschen Gesellschaft für Auswärtige Politik, May 1996).

74. "Der Bundestag mit deutlicher Mehrheit für den Bosnien-Einsatz der Bundeswehr," *Frankfurter Allgemeinze Zeitung*, 1 July 1995, p. 1.

75. "Dabeisein ist Alles," *Der Spiegel*, no. 26, 6 June 1995, pp. 22–25.

76. "Press Statement on Gorazde by NATO Secretary General Willy Claes," issued statement following North Atlantic Countil Meeting on 25 July 1995; transcript in *NATO Review*, September 1995, p. 7.

77. "Pressekonferenz zum Kabinettbeschluß vom BM des Auswärtigen Dr. Kinkel, BM der Verteidigung Rühe und des Generalinspekteurs der Bundeswehr Naumann"; transcript reprinted in *Stichworte zur Sicherheitspolitik*, August 1995.

78. "Deutsche Kampfflugzeuge seit Anfang Agust über Bonien im Einsatz," *German News*, 2 September 1995.

79. "Erster Einsatz für deutsche Tornados in Bosnien," Deutsche Welle Report, 1 September 1995; see also interview with Defense Minister Volker Rühe, in *Der Welt am Sonntag*, 3 September 1995, p. 1; confirmation in confidential interview, Deutsche Gesellschaft für Auswärtige Politik, Bonn, 19 June 1996.

80. "Peitsche und Zuckerbrot," *Der Spiegel*, no. 36, September 1995, pp. 22–26; "Erster Einsatz für deutsche Tornados in Bosnien," *Deutsche Welle Report*, 1 September 1995; see also interview with Defense Minister Volker Rühe, in *Der Welt am Sonntag*, 3 September 1995, p. 1; "Germans Fly Combat Sortie," *International Herald Tribune*, 2 September 1995, p. 1; "Ertsmals Kapmfeinzatz der deutschen Tornados," *Süddeutsche Zeitung*, 3 September 1995, p. 1; "Bundestag voll informiert über Tornado-Einsatz," *Süddeutscher Zeitung*, 4 September 1995, p. 1.

81. Klaus Kinkel, "Erklärung der Bundesregierung zur Friedensvereinbarung für Bosnien," presented to the Bundestag on 30 November 1995, reprinted in *Bulletin*, no. 100, 4 December 1995, p. 973; see also Bundesministerium der Verteidigung Presse- und Informationsstab Referat Öffentlichkeitarbeit, "Maßnahmen zur Absicherung des Friedensvertrages für Bosnien-Herzegowina," Reihe Stichworte für die Öffentlichkeitsarbeit und Truppeninformation, December 1995.

82. Klaus Kinkel, "Erklärung der Bundesregierung zur Friedensvereinbarung für Bosnien," 1995, p. 973.

83. Bundesministerium der Verteidigung Presse- und Informationsstab Referat Öffentlichkeitarbeit, "Maßnahmen zur Absicherung des Friedensvertrages für Bosnien-Herzegowina," December 1995.

84. "Allgemeines Rahmenübereinkommen für den Frieden in Bosnien-Herzegowina, paraphiert am 21 November 1995 in Dayton, Ohio (Auszüge)," treaty reprinted in *Internationale Politik*, January 1996.

85. For more details on the Dayton Peace Accords, see "Allgemeines Rahmenübereinkommen für den Frieden in Bosnien-Herzegowina, paraphiert am 21 November 1995 in Dayton, Ohio (Auszüge)," January 1996; see also confidential interview, Mershon Center, The Ohio State University, Columbus, Ohio, 1 June 1995.

86. German Information Center, "Cabinet Approves German Participation in NATO's Bosnia Peacekeeping Force; Bundestag Confirmation Expected," *The Week in Germany*, 1 December 1995, p. 1.

87. "Maßnahmen zur Absicherung des Friedensvertrages für Bosnien-Herzegowina," Reihe Stichworte für die Öffentlichkeitsarbeit und Truppeninformation, Bundesministerium der Verteidigung Presse- und Informationsstab Referat Öffentlichkeitarbeit, December 1995.

88. "BM der Verteidigung Rühe zum Bosnien-Einsatz der Bundeswehr," *Der Spiegel*, 16 October 1995; other key Conservative leaders including Karl-Heinz Hornhues came out in support of the deployment, given Germany's commitments to peace in the Balkans and existing alliance arrangements. For that matter, Hornhues had stressed that German participation in an international peace operation was consistent with Article 24 of the Constitution throughout the post-Cold War era; author's interview, #4, Bonn, Germany, 1996.

89. Der Bundesminister des Auswärtigen, Dr. Klaus Kinkel, gab in der 74. Sitzung des Deutschen Bundestages am 30 November 1995 zur Friedensvereinbarung für Bosnien folgende Erklärung der Bundestregierung ab.

90. "In Mannheim Jubel und eine Unterschriftensammlung für Lafontaine," *Frankfurter Allgemeine Zeitung*, 16 November 1995, p. 1.

91. *Deutschland Nachrichten*, 17 November 1995, p. 1.

92. "Im SPD Strit über Bundeswehreinsätze setzt sich Lafontaine durch," *Frankfurter Allgemeine Zeitung*, 18 November 1995; "Die SPD wird mit zwei Zungen reden," *Süddeutsche Zeitung*, 18 November 1995, p. 6.

93. See also "Vorlage für die Sitzung der Fraktion am 28.11.1995," Bundeshaus, Document from the Vorsitzender der SPD-Bundestagsfraktion.

94. *Peace-Keeping als Bestandteil von Konfliktschlichtung im Rahmen einer kooperativen europäischen Sicherheitsordnung*, Dokumentation veranstaltet von der Bundestagsfraktion Bündnis 90/Die Grünen, Referat Öffentlichkeitsarbeit, Bundeshaus Hochhaus Tulpenfeld, 11 November 1995.

95. Bündnis 90, Die Grünen, "Beschluß der 6. Ordentlichen Bundesversammlung Bremen, 1.-3. 12.1995, in "Unsere Kontroverse um Dayton," Bundestagfraktion Publication, Lang und Schlüssig 13.27, pp. 1–6.

96. *Frankfurter Rundschau*, 29 November 1995, p. 5.

97. *Peace-Keeping als Bestandteil von Konfliktschlichtung im Rahmen einer kooperativen europäischen Sicherheitsordnung*, 11 November 1995.

98. Ibid.

99. Bündnis 90, Die Grünen, "Unsere Kontroverse um Dayton," Bundestagfraktion Publication, Lang und Schlüssig 13.27; see also Bündnis 90, Die Grünen, "Beschluß der 6. Ordentlichen Bundesversammlung Bremen, 1.-3. 12.1995, in "Unsere Kontroverse um Dayton," (Bonn: Bundestagfraktion Publication, Lang und Schlüssig 13.27), pp. 1–6.

100. *Frankfurter Rundschau,* 29 November 1995, p. 6.

101. "Beschluß der Bundesregierung zur deutschen Beteiligung zur Absicering des Friedens-vertrages für Bosnien-Herzegowin und Beschlußvorschlag für den Deutschen bundestag, Presse-mitteilung, Bundespresse agentur, 28 November 1995; reprinted in *Presse- und Informationsmat der Bundesregierung Referat Außen, Sicherheits- und Europapolitik* (Bonn, December 1995).

102. Ibid.

103. "Tischvorlage: Deutsche Beteiligung an den militärischen Maßnahmen zur Absicherung des Friedensvertrages für Bosnien-Herzegowina; Gemeinsame Kabinettsache des Bundesministers der Verteidigung und des Bundesministers des Auswärtigen," *Datenblatt,* no. 13, p. 4006.

104. Der Bundesminister des Auswärtigen, Dr. Klaus Kinkel, 74. Sitzung des Deutschen Bundestages am 30. November 1995 zur Friedensvereinbarung für Bosnien folgende Erklärung der Bundesregierung; "Erklärung der Bundesregierung zur Friedensvereinbarung für Bosnien," presented by Foreign Minister Kinkel to the German Bundestag; reprinted in *Bulletin* 100, S973–S976, 4 December 1995.

105. "Erklärung der Bundesregierung zur Friedensvereinbarung für Bosnien," *Bulletin,* S973–S976.

106. Plenarprotokoll 13/76 des Deutschen Bundestages vom 6. Dezember 1995; *Deutschland Nachrichten,* 8 December 1995, p. 1.

107. Ibid.

108. "Entwurf zu einem Änderungsantrag/Entschließungsantrag der Fraktion Bündnis 90/Die Grünen im Deutschen Bundestag—zum Beteiligung an der Umsetzung des Friedensvertrages für Bosnien-Herzegowina" in "Unsere Kontroverse um Dayton," Bundestagfraktion Publication, Lang und Schlüssig 13.27, pp. 16–17.

109. Plenarprotokoll 13/76 des Deutschen Bundestages vom 6. Dezember 1995; see also FBIS-WEU-95-128; "Vote called inevitable step in foreign policy," *Die Welt,* 1 July 1995, p. 12.

110. Kerl, as quoted on the Deutsche Press Agentur, German News Listerv, 8 December 1995, at: germnews@model2an.physik.uni-ulm.de.

111. German Information Center, "Cabinet Approves German Participation in NATO's Bosnia Peacekeeping Force; Bundestag Confirmation Expected," *The Week in Germany,* 1 December 1995, p. 1

112. "Gemeinsam drinnen," *Der Spiegel,* no. 28, 9 July 1996, pp. 28–29.

113. "Gebirgsjäger nach Bosnien unterwegs," *German News,* 19 December 1995, p. 1.

114. "Germany Takes Stock after Bosnian Elections," *Deutschland Nachrichten,* 20 September 1996, p. 2.

115. "NATO in Favor of Continuing Its Peacekeeping Mission in Bosnia," *Deutschland Nachrichten,* 27 September 1996, p. 1.

116. Ibid., p. 1; see also "Maßnahmen zur Absicherung des Friedensvertrages für Bosnien-Herzegowina," Reihe Stichworte für die Öffentlichkeitsarbeit und Truppeninformation, Bundesministerium der Verteidigung Presse- und Informationsstab Referat Öffe tlichkeitarbeit," December 1995.

117. "Germany Takes Stock after Bosnian Elections," *Deutschland Nachrichten,* 20 September 1996, p. 2.

118. *Deutschland Nachrichten,* 26 June 1998, p. 2.

119. "NATO Signs Expansion Agreement, Approves New Bosnian Mission," *Deutschland Nachrichten,* 19 December 1997, pp. 1–2.

6

Coercive Diplomacy and the Crisis in Kosovo

For the first time in the Federal Republic's history the electorate have with their direct votes brought about a change of government. They have authorized the Social Democrats and Alliance 90/Greens to lead Germany into the next millennium. . . . The European Union and NATO will remain the twin pillars of German foreign and defense policy [and] Germany will uphold its responsibilities and commitments to the international community. In Europe and the world, we remain a reliable partner.

—Gerhard Schröder, 1998[1]

The dramatic federal election victory by the parties of the left in September 1998 set the tone for change in Germany. Led by Chancellor Gerhard Schröder (SPD) and Foreign Minister Joschka Fischer (Green Party), the SPD–Green coalition government took office with a domestic agenda focused on tackling economic woes such as unemployment. The Kosovo crisis of 1998–1999 presented the German government with a foreign policy challenge that demanded immediate attention, however. Faced with evidence of Serb paramilitary assaults on ethnic Albanians in Kosovo, Germans were confronted with the dilemma of how to balance

Figure 6.1
Strategic Dilemmas in the Kosovo Crisis, 1989–1999

Stages/Dates	Strategic Dilemma	Foreign Policy Response
I. 1989–1999	Serb Crackdown on Kosovo/ KLA Insurgency	Coercive Diplomacy, NATO Air War, German Troops Participate
II. 1999	Operation Allied Force/ Preparations for Ground War	Oppose Ground War, Seek Diplomatic Solution, Peacekeeping

the now contending lessons of history, "never again war" and "never again Auschwitz." At first, their solution was to conduct coercive diplomacy—pressuring Yugoslav President Slobodan Milosevic to negotiate a limited autonomy deal for Kosovo while at the same time threatening the use of military force to stop the killings. When negotiations broke down in March 1999, the German government decided to participate in NATO's "Operation Allied Force," a massive air war against Serbia and the largest military assault in Europe since World War II. A new stage of the crisis began in April 1999 when NATO began secretly planning for a ground war against Serbia, but the contingency led to serious disagreements inside Germany and threatened to bring down the coalition government. This chapter analyzes major foreign policy decisions taken by German leaders during the crisis in Kosovo.

THE FEDERAL ELECTIONS OF 1998

On September 27, 1998, Gerhard Schröder and the Social Democratic Party won the German federal elections with 40.9% of the popular vote (translating to 298 seats in the *Bundestag*). The SPD dramatically outpaced the incumbent CDU/CSU, which garnered only 28.4% of the vote (245 seats). The Greens/Alliance '90 earned 6.7% of the popular vote (47 seats), and the FDP received 6.2% of the vote (44 seats). The SPD and Greens quickly established a new coalition government with an oversized majority in the *Bundestag*.

The election placed Gerhard Schröder in an important role as leader of German foreign policy development for the twenty-first century. His new coalition cabinet included Foreign Minister Joschka Fischer and Defense Minister Rudolf Scharping (SPD). Both had led their respective parties in the mid-1990s toward the acceptance of a stronger German foreign policy profile. In 1995, Fischer had issued the controversial position paper calling for support of the deployment of German troops abroad, and even the potential use of force in defined circumstances. In 1994, Scharping was the SPD candidate for chancellor and chairman of the party. Scharping eventually lost both positions of power, and was condemned at the time by the left wing of the party for supporting the normalization of German foreign policy, for cooperating with Conservative–Liberal coalition on major issues, and in Oskar Lafontaine's words, for "lacking necessary charisma" to lead the party. Nevertheless, both Fischer and Scharping became key players in the federal election campaign of 1998.[2]

Once in office, Foreign Minister Fischer quickly distinguished himself as a prominent and assertive foreign policy actor. During a visit to the United States in November 1998, for example, Fischer spoke out on the importance of continuity in German foreign relations, and demonstrated a clear commitment to security policy coordination with the United States. The foreign minister made it clear that the new German government would support NATO policy concerning the growing crisis in Kosovo. In an effort to banish doubts about the influence of Green pacifism on the coalition, Fischer said unequivocally that there would be "no Green Party foreign policy, but rather only German foreign policy."[3]

THE KOSOVO CRISIS

Historical Background

Like other challenges in the Balkans, the modern crisis in Kosovo was deeply rooted in history. Kosovo, a small southern province of Serbia (Yugoslavia), had a population of about two million in the early 1990s. Of the population of Kosovo, 90% were ethnic Albanian, or "Kosovars," who followed Islamic religious practices. The remaining 10% were Serbs, adherents of Orthodox Christianity. The demographics of the province belied the tremendous religious and historical significance of Kosovo for Serbia, however. Kosovo was the site of several Serbian Orthodox shrines that had been established in the Dark and Middle ages, and Serbs viewed the province as the heart of their centuries-old religious traditions. In 1389, southern Slavs lost a major battle with the Ottoman Empire in Kosovo at the "Field of Blackbirds," beginning a 500-year period of Turkish rule of the Balkans. The Serbs did not succeed in fully conquering Kosovo until the Balkan wars of 1912–1913, when they destroyed all vestiges of Ottoman rule and forcibly expelled tens of thousands of ethnic Albanians from the region.[4]

Kosovo experienced more complex political forces after World War II. In the immediate aftermath of the war, the Kosovars were ruled in "semi-colonial fashion by the Serbian communists, whose discriminatory policies caused an estimated 250,000 Albanians to emigrate from the province."[5] In 1974, Tito recognized limited autonomy for Kosovo and for Vojvodina (both regions that held large, non-Serb populations) in the region as part of his new constitutional arrangement, and this tenuous political status continued for more than a decade.

In the late 1980s, Slobodan Milosevic actually chose Kosovo as a staging ground for his rise to political power in Yugoslavia. In a famous speech given in the region on the occasion of the 600-year anniversary of the Serb defeat at the hands of the Turks at the Field of Blackbirds, Milosevic invoked a memory of the war and proclaimed a glorious Serbian future—one in which the Serbs "no longer humiliated—would do battle for their state, national, and spiritual integrity."[6] Milosevic suspended Kosovo's provincial autonomy and introduced direct rule from Belgrade.

Ethnic Albanians in Kosovo were outraged by the suspension of their political autonomy and deeply resented the Serb crackdown on their province. In 1991, the Kosovo political assembly voted in favor of political independence and set up a shadow government for the region. Civic groups began sponsoring underground educational and cultural programs. In 1996, the Kosovo Liberation Army (KLA, or UCK in Albanian) was formed as a guerrilla movement to fight for independence by targeting Serb paramilitary units and police in the province. The KLA rapidly gained support from younger ethnic Albanians in the region, and they began to receive secret shipments of military supplies from neighboring countries.

From Simmer to Boil

Western governments grew increasingly concerned about Kosovo in the 1990s. From the onset of the breakup of Yugoslavia in 1991, the German government shared the perspective of its allies that a conflict in Kosovo could have far more serious consequences for European security than even the wars in Slovenia, Croatia, or Bosnia. They feared that a crisis in Kosovo might have the potential to ignite a broader war by drawing in Bulgaria, Turkey, and Greece. The Bush administration was so concerned about unrest in Kosovo that the president instructed the U.S. embassy staff to read a one-sentence message to Milosevic on December 24, 1992, which said: "In the event of conflict in Kosovo caused by Serbian action, the United States will be prepared to employ military force against Serbians in Kosovo and in Serbia proper."[7] NATO allies issued similar warnings to Milosevic throughout the decade.

A series of KLA attacks and Serb reprisals brought the simmering crisis to a boil in 1998. Milosevic responded to KLA attacks on Serbs by intensifying the military presence in the province and by ordering sweeps of key villages in the search for the partisans. In one case, Serb police units killed dozens of suspected militants and their families in Drenica. Images of slain Kosovars were televised around the world, and streams of refugees from the region quickly increased in volume. One elderly woman fleeing the fighting on a road northwest of Pristina was interviewed by a Western correspondent in June 1998. She said simply: "It is war. We have become Bosnia."[8]

At a NATO conference in June, U.S. Secretary of Defense William Cohen asked the allies to agree to develop military contingency plans for intervention in Kosovo, but European leaders were quite skeptical of the idea. Opponents, including German Defense Minister Volker Rühe, questioned the level of Western commitment to military intervention and the legitimacy of allied military actions taken without explicit authority from the UN Security Council. There was a great deal of disagreement about such planning for other reasons, as well. First, the situation in Kosovo was rapidly deteriorating, and questions of right and wrong became more ambiguous in the province with the rise of the KLA. Second, the Clinton administration simply did not exert a great deal of leadership in NATO regarding the Kosovo situation because of distractions in the domestic political arena (such as the impending Congressional elections and the Lewinsky scandal). Finally, military planning for Kosovo was affected by broader debates about a new "strategic concept" for the alliance in the post-Cold War era.[9]

Coercive Diplomacy

Serb attacks and KLA reprisals in September 1998—and the televised images of massacres—finally launched the West into action. On September 23, 1998, the UN Security Council passed Resolution 1199, which called for a cease-fire in Kosovo, a withdrawal of Serb forces from the province, and the safe return of refugees. At the same time, NATO allies agreed on a strategy of coercive diplomacy to end the violence in Kosovo. Allied planners considered a range of possibilities for the threat of force against Serbia, including a massive air campaign or an all-out ground war that might lead to military occupation. In September 1998, NATO reported its worst-case scenario that 200,000 troops would be required to stop the killings in Kosovo and to occupy Serbia; 75,000 troops would suffice for a more narrowly defined mission to occupy Kosovo and create safe havens for ethnic Albanians in the province. At the time, ground war contingencies were met with open skepticism from Western leaders, but there was support for a concentrated program of air strikes to achieve Western objectives.[10] On September 24, 1998, NATO leaders agreed to warn Milosevic that an activation order for allied air strikes might be issued in the near future.

NATO leaders also agreed to sponsor diplomatic negotiations to find a peaceful settlement for Yugoslavia short of the use of force. U.S. envoy Richard Holbrooke and his diplomatic team traveled to Belgrade and negotiated directly with Milosevic for nine days. On October 13, 1998,

Holbrooke announced a settlement on Kosovo. Milosevic agreed to withdraw the majority of Serb military forces from the province and ordered the end of paramilitary and police repression of the Kosovars. The Serbian leader further agreed to permit 1,800 unarmed, international inspectors from the Organization for Security and Cooperation in Europe (OSCE) to monitor the peace in Kosovo, and to allow overflights by NATO reconnaissance planes in the province as further verification of Serb compliance with the agreement. Back in Washington, President Clinton hailed the deal as a triumph of coercive diplomacy.[11]

Led by U.S. ambassador William Walker, OSCE observer groups began to patrol Kosovo in November 1998. Unfortunately, the warring factions in the region viewed the October agreement more as a window of opportunity to gain strategic advantage than a pledge for permanent peace. NATO officials claimed that Serbian forces began sending reinforcements and needed equipment to the region under cover of darkness in the late fall. Meanwhile, KLA forces took the opportunity to move troops and resupply. Ethnic Albanians living in other countries, including the United States, actually increased their financial support for the KLA in the winter of 1998–99. Within weeks, both sides were engaged in attacks and counterattacks once more—but this time, OSCE observers were caught in the middle. When William Walker was personally threatened by a belligerent, drunken Serb wielding a gun and a hand grenade, the OSCE stepped up their appeals to government leaders to provide more security for the operation. It became all too clear that the October agreement was not a long-term solution to the crisis.

OPERATION ALLIED FORCE

A Downward Spiral of Events

The crisis in Kosovo intensified in the winter months of 1998–1999. In December 1998, a Serb paramilitary unit killed thirty-six ethnic Albanians who were suspected of being KLA rebels. The Kosovars retaliated in sporadic firefights in northern Kosovo (which OSCE observers duly witnessed and catalogued). Later, KLA guerrillas attacked a café and killed six young Serbs. Experts on the crisis estimated that some 2,500 Kosovars had been killed in the struggle for autonomy by the end of 1998, and more than 200,000 Kosovars had fled their homes in the province in fear of Serb paramilitary assaults.[12]

In January 1999, NATO intelligence officers detected signs of a Serbian military buildup around Kosovo. They learned that the Serbs planned a massive encircling operation against the KLA, code named "Potkova" (Horseshoe), after the spring thaw. The Serbs planned to move tanks and artillery into Kosovo to attack KLA strongholds and drive out hundreds of thousands of ethnic Albanians from key areas. Intercepted messages suggested that military leaders believed that if the operation "only attacked a village a week," the West would tolerate the crackdown in Kosovo.[13]

On January 15, 1999, Serb forces executed forty-five unarmed villagers in Racak. The bodies were discovered by the OSCE monitors, and the massacre received intense media coverage in both Europe and the United States. This tragedy served as a true catalyst for a change in NATO policy. President Clinton telephoned Western leaders to gather support for diplomatic negotiations backed by a more aggressive threat of the use of force. As part of an effort both to allow a last chance for Milosevic and the Kosovars to come to an agreement—and to convince the Europeans that all reasonable efforts had been taken to avoid the use of force—special rounds of diplomatic negotiations were held at Rambouillet, France, in February and March of 1999. Unlike Dayton, however, Milosevic never attended the conference, and the Serb delegation refused to sign any agreement that included the deployment of NATO peacekeeping troops in Kosovo.[14] When the talks broke down in mid-March, Serb military units began "live fire" exercises in Kosovo.[15]

The situation in Kosovo had reached a nadir. A Western intelligence assessment published in March concluded that Milosevic intended to ethnically cleanse all 1.8 million Albanians living in the province within a week.[16] U.S. and NATO estimates indicated that there were 30,000 Serbian forces in Kosovo (twice the allowed limits under the October 1998 agreement), and an additional 40,000 troops with 300 tanks were massing along the Kosovo border.[17]

German Domestic Political Conditions, Spring 1999

The German government deliberated on the proper response to the Kosovo crisis in 1999. From January onward, there was some agreement among elites in Germany that military action would be necessary against Milosevic. Notwithstanding the historical and ethical questions surrounding any consideration of the use of force, cabinet leaders generally agreed on the need to participate in allied operations. In fact, there was a surprising absence of a serious public debate about the possibility of military action—a debate that had been so omnipresent during the Gulf War and Bosnia crisis. Instead, leaders shared the opinion that the humanitarian tragedy in Kosovo must be stopped.

Chancellor Schröder suggested that Germany be prepared to support the NATO alliance in air strikes against Serbia. He publicly argued the case for some participation in alliance operations throughout the winter and spring months of 1999.[18] The chancellor found justification for German action in his belief that the "fundamental values of freedom, democracy, and human rights" were being flouted in Kosovo.[19] As a pledge toward enforcement of a peaceful settlement, Schröder promised in February to send 2,000 troops to help enforce a cease-fire in Kosovo, saying that "Germany is now a full-fledged partner in promoting security in Europe."[20]

Defense Minister Scharping was also outspoken in his support of action in Kosovo. He was actively engaged in NATO planning for one of several military contingencies, including peacekeeping operations in Kosovo and even an air war against Serbia to force a negotiated settlement. In a well-publicized interview with *Der Spiegel*, Scharping stated that Germany remained committed to a peaceful settlement of the Kosovo issue, but that the security and freedom of the Kosovars and the cessation of the humanitarian catastrophe came first. Scharping employed unusually strong language in the interview, saying that NATO was dealing with a Yugoslavian government without scruples, who despised the very essence of humanity, and that the only chance for peace was a credible foreign policy backed up with strong military pressure. He claimed that Germany was in full agreement with its allies on how to respond to the crisis. When asked how he felt about being the first defense minister in Germany to order a military action against a sovereign country since World War II, Scharping said that he believed that Germany simply "had no other choice."[21]

The Kosovo crisis was a particularly serious challenge for Foreign Minister Joschka Fischer. Representing the pacifist Greens, Fischer was forced to balance his commitment to a peaceful solution in Kosovo with the need for serious military threats against Milosevic. Fischer's statements in the spring of 1999 made clear his personal convictions that Germany should be fully committed to participate in NATO contingencies for the use of force in Kosovo. Fischer believed that the conflict in Kosovo was not simply a question of ethics, morals, or human rights, but rather "a direct attack against the security of Europe."[22] In an address to the *Bundestag* on February 25, Fischer stressed the need for a comprehensive plan for the Balkans to be shared with western allies, requiring a long-term commitment by the international community.[23]

Cabinet leaders received support from major political parties for their program of German involvement in NATO operations against Serbia. The record shows very little evidence of the type of soul-searching in *Bundestag* and party conference debates on Kosovo that had been so prevalent throughout the 1990s when it came to questions of possible military action. Cabinet leaders effectively had interpreted the Kosovo crisis as a moral challenge, and parties were hard pressed to counter this description in the wake of media reports of atrocities in the province. The Social Democratic Party generally rallied around Schröder government proposals to support NATO operations in Kosovo. Conservative opposition leaders expressed their support for coercive diplomacy, but they warned the

SPD–Green coalition not to commit any ground troops to Kosovo without a negotiated settlement.[24] Only representatives of the Party of Democratic Socialism (PDS) were outspoken in their criticism of German support for NATO at the time. Party leader Gregor Gysi denounced the government's plans, saying that "after what has happened this century, Germany above all has no right to drop bombs on Belgrade."[25]

In the critical spring months of 1999, members of the Green Party did express some concerns about government support for NATO initiatives. The Greens held a very important party conference in Erfurt in early March, where Fischer defended Germany's plan to support NATO policy. He rejected the notion that the alliance's insistence on sending forces into Kosovo to enforce a peace deal was wrong, and contended that the Kosovars would not sign the Rambouillet Accord without the promised protection of NATO forces.[26] Some leaders of the party supported the cabinet's position on diplomatic negotiations leading to the eventual deployment of peacekeeping troops under a clear mandate from the United Nations.[27] Others expressed real concern about the course of events. Angelika Beer, defense spokesperson for the Greens, predicted that the Kosovo operation might fail—first through negotiations that diminished NATO's credibility, then through an unsuccessful battery of air strikes, and finally through a drawn-out ground war against Serbia.[28]

Support among elites and party organizations for German participation in NATO actions in Kosovo seemed to set the tone for public discourse on the matter. As events built to a crescendo in March 1999, most Germans reacted rather calmly to the possibility of conducting their first offensive military action since World War II, and there was surprisingly little opposition to government decisions. One Infratest survey conducted at the time found that 61% of Germans believed that the NATO air strikes were necessary, and 57% said that they should be maintained until Milosevic accepted the terms set by the allies.[29] An editorial in *Die Welt* said that there was a general "kind of public emptiness" on the Kosovo question at the time.[30] Commenting on this silence, Stephan Speicher wrote in the *Berliner Zeitung* that "the last victim of the fall of the Wall was German pacifism."[31]

German Support for Operation Allied Force

As the crisis deepened in Kosovo, Schröder and Fischer spelled out Germany's position in no uncertain terms: if a political solution could not be found, there would be no alternative to the use of military force to stop further Serb aggression against Kosovo. Cabinet deliberations throughout the week of March 21, 1999, led to a series of *Bundestag* resolutions that authorized the use of German troops and combat aircraft in NATO operations against Yugoslavia.[32] While these resolutions were a very clear expression of support, the parliament retained the authority to review any new proposal for the deployment of ground troops for peace-keeping missions in Kosovo.

On March 24, 1999, four German Tornadoes took off from their base in Piacenza in northern Italy and participated in the first wave of air strikes in Operation Allied Force. Fifteen Tornado jets and hundreds of *Bundeswehr* support troops were actively engaged in NATO operations through June. German deployments in Bosnia and Macedonia were also strengthened and placed on a higher stage of alert at the outset of the air war; *Bundeswehr* troops numbered 2,500 in Bosnia and 3,000 in Macedonia by April 1.

German soldiers were fully engaged in offensive military operations for the first time since World War II. At home, an editorial in *Die Welt* published on the first day of the Kosovo War captured the mood:

The [German] government is standing behind NATO's decision. The message to its alliance partners is: Germany not only enjoys the blessings of the protective shield, it also takes the accompanying responsibilities seriously. Scharping and Fischer are cutting a good figure, and the opposition is avoiding party politics. German soldiers are taking part in the combat operations. This is a symbol of republican maturity; Germany's special role has ended. We have arrived in the European community of states.[33]

THE GROUND TROOPS CONTROVERSY

At the beginning of the Kosovo War, NATO allies portrayed their intervention as a moral imperative. They believed that the bombings would help bring an end to the pattern of ethnic cleansing that had emerged in the province. Furthermore, military action would protect Western interests by preventing the spread of war in that historically volatile region. President Clinton gave a televised address on the first day of the war that outlined the purposes of the campaign:

Our mission is clear: to demonstrate the seriousness of NATO's purpose so that the Serbian leaders understand the imperative of reversing course. To deter an even bloodier offensive against innocent civilians in Kosovo and if necessary to seriously damage the Serbian military's capacity to harm the people of Kosovo. In short, if President Milosevic will not make peace, we will limit his ability to make war.[34]

Operation Allied Force consisted of air strikes against military targets and infrastructure in Kosovo and Serbia carried out by combined NATO forces. Despite bold pronouncements, Western leaders held a secret at the outset of the war—the operation was rather limited and intended only as a short-duration air strike campaign. Rejecting advice from the Pentagon to open the war with a massive and unrestricted barrage to overwhelm the opponent, only ninety-one approved targets, restricted to purely military facilities, were on the bombing list for the first three days.[35] This more limited option was chosen to maintain the unity within NATO, where a number of governments were uncomfortable with any bombing campaign, let alone a massive one. In addition, most civilians in the Clinton administration felt that this moderate air-strike campaign would be sufficient to bring Milosevic back to the negotiating table. General Michael Short, NATO Air Force Commander of Operation Allied Force recalled being told before the war began: "Mike, you're only going to be allowed to bomb two, maybe three nights. . . . That's all some members of the alliance can stand. That's why you've only got ninety targets. This will be over in three nights."[36]

The alliance miscalculated the resolve of Slobodan Milosevic and Serb forces in Kosovo, however. It soon became clear that Milosevic would not politely concede after a few air strikes, and the situation in Kosovo went from bad to worse. NATO leaders ordered the pace of bombing to be escalated, but the alliance did not have enough aircraft in the area to sustain a massive round-the-clock war on Serbian forces and facilities until May 1999.[37]

To further complicate matters, Serb forces took full control of Kosovo in the opening ten days of the bombing and pushed more than 500,000 Kosovars across the border, creating a massive humanitarian crisis in Albania and Macedonia. Within weeks, a total of 860,000 Kosovars had been expelled from the country and another 600,000 were internally displaced. Almost the entire ethnic Albanian population of the province was on the move or in hiding. One senior NATO military official asserted that the alliance always recognized that Milosevic might respond to the air strikes with more aggression, but conceded: "[w]e underestimated the ferocity and velocity of Milosevic's offensive to transform the ethnic balance in Kosovo."[38]

Germany and its allies were forced to continue the air war against Serbia over Kosovo in April and May while at the same time launching major humanitarian relief operations in the theater. On April 1, Schröder announced that Germany would provide DM 25 million in aid for the Kosovar refugees encamped in Macedonia and Albania.[39] An emergency meeting of EU leaders on April 7 in Brussels led to another pledge for DM 24 million in aid. German Interior Minister Otto Schily announced that his government would provide asylum for up to 10,000 Kosovar refugees as needed. On April 8, three airplanes carrying 350 Kosovar refugees arrived in Nuremberg from Macedonia, and thousands of Kosovars were eventually settled in Germany.[40]

Losing the War

By April 1999, many observers of Operation Allied Force around the world began to question whether NATO was actually losing the war. The exploding refugee crisis and humanitarian tragedy, the resilience of the

Serb military and civilian population under the daily pounding of NATO air strikes, and even mistaken attacks on Serb civilian targets all contributed to the perception that things were going badly for the alliance. The accidental bombing of the Chinese embassy on May 7, 1999, the forty-fifth day of air operations, underscored the perception that NATO was on the wrong course.

A secret political struggle was emerging within the NATO alliance about the conduct of the war, and the veneer of rhetoric in support of Operation Allied Force masked a great deal of disagreement among allies in April and May 1999. For example, French President Jacques Chirac told Clinton on day eleven of the operation that he wanted a say in crucial decisions about the war, given France's commitment of sixty aircraft (the second largest contingent of planes in the operation behind the United States). General Clark and military planners began daily consultations with British Prime Minister Tony Blair and French President Jacques Chirac to review and approve targets inside Serbia. Ultimately, officials in Washington, London, and Paris made important choices such as whether to bomb targets that had a largely civilian character, such as the Socialist Party headquarters in Belgrade, television and radio stations, and the electrical systems grid.[41]

Allied discussions about the conduct of the air war became so complicated by early April 1999 that U.S. officials believed General Clark's primary command authority was being undermined. Early in the war, President Clinton told Prime Minister Blair "We need to help Wes Clark because he has to spend half of his time schmoozing with the allies."[42] Their solution to this problem was to create a management committee to smooth over disagreements about the military campaign. The core of the committee included foreign ministers from the United States, Britain, France, Germany, and Italy. They held a five-way conference call almost every day of the war. German involvement in the management committee for the conduct of Operation Allied Force was highly significant. Foreign Minister Joschka Fischer became directly involved in committee deliberations from the outset, and he often served as arbiter in differences among NATO allies over operational objectives.[43]

The Allies Consider Ground Troop Contingencies

In April and May 1999, NATO leaders began to consider the most sensitive question of the war, namely, whether ground troops would be required for an invasion and occupation of Kosovo and Serbia.[44] Most allies agreed on the need for ground troops to participate in some type of peace enforcement operation at the end of the conflict. Deployment of ground troops for an invasion of Kosovo—and perhaps all of Serbia—was another matter entirely. At the outset of Operation Allied Force, NATO leaders had pledged that no ground troops would be deployed for combat operations. In his televised address to the nation on March 24, 1999, President Clinton said U.S. troops could serve as peacekeepers, but declared: "I do not intend to put our troops in Kosovo to fight a war."[45] However, the ground troop option seemed to become more viable as the war dragged on, threatening to become a powder keg that might blow apart the alliance.

On the eve of NATO's fiftieth anniversary summit meeting in Washington, British and French leaders began pressing allies to consider sending ground forces into Kosovo.[46] The Clinton administration viewed this new pressure to consider ground troops as very dangerous for alliance cohesion. Well aware of the difficulties of holding the alliance together even through the air war, Clinton and his cabinet believed that the ground troops contingency might very well bring down governments across Europe. For example, leftists in the Italian government threatened serious political action unless allies would agree to offer a bombing pause as a concession for peace negotiations. The Greek government was deeply opposed to any use of force in the region. The Clinton administration was also well aware of pressure on the German government from the political left and right. Thus, the administration sought a delicate compromise on the issue, to avoid shattering the alliance on the eve of the fiftieth anniversary summit. When Prime Minister Blair met with Clinton in Washington on the evening of April 21 to lobby for ground troops, the president agreed to a deal—Blair would stop talking publicly about an invasion given the serious domestic problems that it caused for allied governments, and Clinton would quietly agree to allow NATO to update old contingency plans for ground operations in the Balkans.[47] NATO officers in Mons, Belgium, and at the U.S. Army's European headquarters in Heidelberg, Germany, started work on top-secret invasion options. Within weeks, they had come up with a preliminary plan for an attack on Kosovo by 175,000 troops—set to begin on September 1, 1999.[48]

The ground troops issue came to a head on May 27, 1999, during a secret meeting of NATO defense ministers held at the German Defense Ministry offices outside Bonn. U.S. Secretary of Defense William Perry, German Defense Minister Rudolf Scharping, British Defense Minister George Robertson, and the defense ministers of France and Italy met for seven intense hours of debate about ground troops.[49] While they did not reach a final decision, the defense ministers were united in their opinions that NATO could not afford to lose the war, and that their five governments needed to reach a consensus on ground troops within the next week. On a very practical level, allied leaders were aware that deployments for a potential ground war were urgently needed; the first snowfall in Kosovo would arrive by the end of October.

German Domestic Political Conditions and the
Ground Troops Contingency

The question of support for ground troop operations in Kosovo became a highly charged issue in the Federal Republic, and threatened to bring down the SPD–Green coalition. While Chancellor Schröder and Defense Minister Scharping were conducting secret negotiations with their counterparts about changing NATO strategy, they were well aware that German participation in a ground war might be politically impossible. The cabinet was highly conscious of the potential collision of two historical lessons—"no more war" and "no more Auschwitz"—that confronted the Federal Republic in the final year of the twentieth century. The Kosovo dilemma tested many assumptions that had guided the normalization of German foreign policy for the previous fifty years. German leaders faced an onslaught of concerns, ranging from remaining a responsible member of the NATO alliance, to German troops going to war in the Balkans, to standing up against ethnic cleansing, to popular concerns about becoming overrun by refugees (who might, in turn, feed tensions at home and contribute to right-wing extremism).

Chancellor Schröder publicly maintained the position that the government should support the air campaign, but not a ground troop contingency. At a meeting of G-7 leaders in early May, Schröder reminded the allies of the historical dilemmas that Germany faced in this conflict, and of popular sensitivities that he believed were affected by participation in the bombing campaign.[50] While Schröder's statements seemed to signal an unwillingness even to consider a ground troop contingency, there is evidence that the *Kanzleramt* was still willing to negotiate the issue with allies throughout May 1999. Michael Steiner, the chief diplomatic adviser to Schröder, said that a minimum of two weeks would be needed to overcome differences between the West and Russia on a ground troops contingency. In that period, the chancellor fervently hoped that the air war would bring Milosevic to agree to a negotiated settlement.

As the war dragged on, Joschka Fischer's support for German involvement in Operation Allied Force drew ever more heated criticism from the political left. In press statements in April and May, Fischer emphasized the continued importance of *Westbindung*. He said that if Germany turned its back on its allies, the Federal Republic's own democratic revolution might be jeopardized. He said, "To me, the West is an indispensable insurance against the return of German nationalism. . . . The more we pursue our interests multilaterally, through Europe, the more we'll get for ourselves."[51] Meanwhile, opponents of government policy reminded Fischer of his own personal history as a leader in the struggle against American imperialism in the 1960s and 1970s, and against NATO modernization of intermediate-range nuclear forces in the early 1980s.

Schröder and Scharping began floating trial balloons for a ground troop contingency in May 1999 during a series of party group meetings, but there were numerous internal disagreements about such an initiative. The Conservative opposition also began vocal challenges to any shift in the mission of Operation Allied Force. On repeated occasions, former Defense Minister Rühe reminded the government that the only mandate given by parliament was to achieve limited strategic objectives and peace for Kosovo, not to wage war in the Balkans. Karl Lamers, foreign policy spokesman of the CDU, also warned that transferring troops to a combat mission against Serbia in Kosovo was not covered in the *Bundestag* mandate. Lamers said: "nobody wants this [ground war], and it is absolutely certain that none of our partners would want this."[52]

The Kosovo crisis of 1999 actually made the Green Party the pivotal forum for elite efforts to build consensus in support of government action. Green leaders were well aware of the erosion of popular support for involvement, and they began to challenge the air strike operation and call for a pause in air strikes.[53] In April, Green Party Environmental Minister Jürgen Trittin declared that the bombings were a "mistake," but later qualified his remark.[54] Staatssekretärin Gila Altmann signed a special paper for the party, urging other Greens to end their support for what she called "abenteuerliche NATO-Politik."[55] In late April, one party conference group voted that the organization could never support the use of ground troops in a war against Serbia. Party leaders also agreed to hold an emergency party conference meeting involving all federal delegates— some 800 representatives of the Greens—to decide on the future of party support for cabinet initiatives on Kosovo.

The special Green Party conference, held in Bielefeld on May 13, 1999, was a defining moment in the short history of post-Cold War German foreign policy normalization. Delegates to the meeting were presented with two competing resolutions. *Fundis* put forward a resolution calling for an immediate and unconditional halt to NATO air strikes. Experts warned at the time that this resolution was intended to undermine government policy and might lead to a collapse in the SPD–Green coalition if it were passed. The other resolution subject to debate urged a temporary cease-fire, and was backed by the party's governing committee as a compromise allowing the Greens to express their views on the war without bringing down the government. One report on the conference summarized the controversy as follows:

At the special party conference in Bielefeld, a compromise formulation is supposed to patch the tears: fundamentally a call for an end to the air strikes and, nonetheless, enough room for maneuver for Fischer so that the bombing can continue until the return of the Kosovar expellees. Realos and Fundis were always two camps within the party. NATO's bombs have deepened the gap between them. . . . It is not the fate of Kosovo that will be decided in Kosovo, but the fate of the Greens.[56]

Joschka Fischer approached the Bielefeld conference as the fight of his political life. He made it known that he would not support the left wing resolution because it would send "the absolutely wrong signal" to Milosevic.[57] In a now famous political speech, Fischer appealed to delegates to "help me, to support me; not to cut the ground from under my feet" by supporting the *Fundis'* resolution. He stated that "[p]eace means that men aren't murdered, women aren't raped and people aren't driven from their homes. If you pass this resolution, I will not act on it!"[58] He forged ahead in his speech in spite of a paint bomb attack on the podium by one protester (which splattered Fischer with red paint and punctured his eardrum) and an interruption by an anti-war streaker. Outside the meeting hall, protesters clashed with police. After extensive debate, the governing committee's resolution out-polled the left wing by a vote of 444–318.[59] Fischer had his victory, and the coalition government received an endorsement by the Greens to continue the air war against Serbia.

Public support for Operation Allied Force was eroding in Germany in April and May of 1999. In fact, the German polity seemed to be engaged in more soul-searching about the war than ever before. Press reports began to appear in early April of the scale of the humanitarian tragedy in and near Kosovo, and there was growing concern that new tactics, including the possibility of sending ground troops, might be necessary to end the war. In one editorial in the prominent newspaper *Die Zeit*, Wolfgang Prosinger wrote that many Germans believed that NATO might lose the war. Given the dilemmas presented by the conflict in Kosovo, he warned that the public would have to confront the ground troops contingency soon, and that it presented a deep moral and political challenge to the German polity.[60]

The media gave greater attention to cost–benefit calculations of German and NATO involvement in the war. *Die Zeit* estimated that Operation Allied Force cost the NATO alliance about DM 120 million per day, of which the United States paid DM 80 million and the Federal Republic of Germany paid DM 5 million. In sum, the war from March 24 to April 15 had cost an estimated DM 3 billion.[61] On a deeper level, Germans wrestled with the question of how much humanitarian relief they could provide for Kosovar refugees. While most Germans believed that they should help ethnic Albanians, they also felt that their government had already sacrificed a great deal to provide asylum and assistance for the 300,000 Bosnian Muslims that fled the violence in the Balkans in the mid-1990s. These feelings of sympathy, coupled with a reluctance to go further, were characterized as a kind of "double morality" by members of the media at the time.[62]

By April 1999, public opinion polls showed mixed sentiments about German involvement in Operation Allied Force. One survey found that 37% of respondents were calling for an immediate end to the air attacks.[63] An EMNID survey conducted in late April charted a precipitous decline in popular support. Only 41% of Germans favored a continuation of the air strikes, while 34% supported a suspension of the bombing to allow diplomatic negotiations. When asked about sending German ground troops to Kosovo, 80% said they opposed such a move and 17% said they favored it.[64]

In April and May of 1999, some Germans took to the streets to protest the war. Opponents sponsored protest marches during the Easter holiday that drew several hundred people, and twenty-five protesters briefly occupied a Green Party office in April. The Green Party conference in Bielefeld on May 13 represented a good example of leftist opposition to the war. While Joschka Fischer spoke to 800 party delegates inside the conference hall, roughly the same number of protesters clashed with police around the city. Some 500 police officers were mobilized to keep the peace in Bielefeld during the conference, prompting Fischer to comment that he never believed that a meeting of the Greens would require police protection.[65]

Drawing a Line in the Air

Cabinet leaders surveyed the domestic political climate on the question of ground troops and determined by late May that there was little support for intensifying German involvement in the war. They realized that they had taken Germany to the end of its domestic political tether, and that continuing the air war and pressing for a diplomatic solution were the only viable paths to achieve NATO goals. Schröder recognized that it was quite possible that open consideration of sending ground troops to the Balkans would topple the coalition government and return the SPD and Green parties to the opposition. Fischer was well aware of the volatility of Green Party sentiment on the matter and felt lucky to have maintained a majority at Bielefeld. One adviser to the cabinet said at the time that "[b]y German standards, the change of policy has already been extensive and radical. We have come a huge distance in a short time, and managed to bring public opinion along. But for the government, ground troops would be too much at this stage."[66]

Schröder became more vocal about German support for the continuation of the air campaign as the path to achieve NATO objectives—and also more critical of a ground troops contingency. At the May 19 NATO summit, Schröder sharply rebuked the ground war option after a day of negotiations and pressure from British leaders. He argued that continued support for air operations was "first and foremost a German position. . . .

[T]he strategy of the alliance can only be changed if all the parties involved agree on it. I am against any change of NATO strategy." In a direct reference to the deliberations, he said, "I will not participate in this specifically British debate on war theories." Later, the chancellor reiterated his position in an interview with a German television station, saying: "It is my view that we will not deploy ground troops in Yugoslavia."[67]

As an alternative to the ground troops option, Schröder and Fischer initiated a major diplomatic campaign to bring the Kosovo War to a close. Fischer developed a six-point peace plan that incorporated NATO's official war goals but added a German diplomatic twist. Germany called for an end to all Serb military and police action in Kosovo, the withdrawal of all military forces from the province, unconditional return of refugees, guarantees of Serbia's willingness to establish a political framework in Kosovo on the basis of Rambouillet, and the deployment of an international military force in the province after the war. The Germans also added several provisions granting stronger roles for Russia and the United Nations in diplomatic negotiations to end the war. Fischer called for the suspension of NATO bombing as soon as a Serb troop withdrawal began, the disarmament of the KLA, and for a major UN role in the administration of Kosovo. After the war, Kosovo would also receive a significant amount of international aid for reconstruction through a stability pact, which Fischer likened to a "Marshall Plan of sorts for the Balkans."[68]

Russia was the key to new German diplomatic initiatives. One top political adviser to Schröder said that he believed it was essential to extend a hand to Russia as a path toward support for a Kosovo resolution in the UN Security Council, and as a way to cut off Russian support for Milosevic. On April 7, German officials announced that they supported a more active Russian role in international negotiations to end the war. Russian President Boris Yeltsin appointed Viktor Chernomyrdin as a special envoy to the Balkans one week later. Chernomyrdin was quickly invited to Bonn, where he exhibited a willingness to work with the West on the Kosovo situation.

Bonn became the hub for diplomatic negotiations on the Kosovo crisis in May and June 1999. At the G-8 summit in Bonn, Russia agreed to join Western leaders in issuing the first, common great power statement on Kosovo. Schröder then began a program of shuttle diplomacy to negotiate a solution for Kosovo. On May 12, the chancellor travelled to Beijing for a prearranged summit (but took on the additional challenge of offering an official apology for NATO's accidental bombing on May 7 of the Chinese embassy in Belgrade). Schröder then traveled to Helsinki to consult with Finland's President Ahtisaari, who had been tapped by Kofi Annan to serve as an intermediary on the Kosovo conflict. From Helsinki, the chancellor continued on to Italy for talks with Prime Minister D'Alema to discuss Italian reservations about continuing the war.

At that meeting, Schröder made it very clear that the use of German ground troops "would not come under consideration." Instead, he believed that there were "encouraging signs for a political solution."[69]

On May 30, 1999, U.S. Deputy Secretary of State Strobe Talbot held talks in Bonn with Schröder, Fischer, President Ahtisaari, and Russian envoy Viktor Chernomyrdin, as the international diplomats prepared for the final shuttle mission to Belgrade the next day. Schröder was optimistic about the prospects for peace, and he told reporters that the world was "on the way to a political solution of the problem and substantial progress has been made."[70] He was right. On June 2, 1999, Ahtisaari and Chernomyrdin negotiated a final settlement with Slobodan Milosevic to end the Kosovo War.[71]

Post-War Settlement and Peacekeeping Operations

The peace deal for Kosovo offered key conditions including the safe return of the Kosovar refugees, the withdrawal of Serb security forces from Kosovo, and a program for civic reconstruction in Kosovo. The plan would be implemented by a NATO peacekeeping force (KFOR) of 50,000 troops.[72] While NATO officials were notified of the deal on June 3, 1999, they remained skeptical until there was clear evidence of Serb compliance. NATO continued air strikes during the five days of technical negotiations that followed, and only ceased air operations against Serbia on June 10, 1999, once evidence of compliance was clear. Up to the last minute, General Clark and other military commanders worried about settling the conflict with deadlines for starting the deployment of invasion forces looming.

On June 11, 1999, U.S. and European troops began moving into Kosovo as Serb forces withdrew. Allied forces established five sectors, each led by a major NATO power including the United States, France, Britain, Italy, and Germany. The initial wave of German peacekeepers moved into Kosovo from Macedonia and established perimeters in their deployment area.[73] As troops entered Kosovo, they found grim reminders of the eleven-week war, including the bodies of some 10,000 Albanian civilians who had been killed during the conflict. Entire villages had been ransacked and destroyed by Serb forces during the war. Troops began preparations for the gradual return of more than 800,000 Kosovars that had been housed in camps in Albania and Macedonia, and of the tens of thousands who had sought asylum in Western countries. Government officials estimated that the war had caused $4 billion worth of damage to industrial plants and infrastructure in the rest of Yugoslavia, and another $23 billion in lost production.[74]

CONCLUSION

Germany celebrated the news of victory in the Kosovo War, and government leaders took credit for maintaining the delicate balance of coercive diplomacy to achieve peace. In private, they breathed a sigh of relief that they had not been forced to confront much more serious challenges during the Kosovo War. The *Bundestag* approved a rotating deployment of 8,500 soldiers to participate in KFOR, up from the 2,500 troops originally planned for peacekeeping duties. German soldiers would be deployed in potentially dangerous regions that were home to KLA strongpoints, but parliamentarians offered overwhelming support for the mission (505–24).[75] On June 19, 1999, G-7 leaders agreed to provide $1.5 billion over three years for the reconstruction of Kosovo.[76]

NOTES

1. "Transcript of Policy Statement by Gerhard Schröder, Chancellor of the Federal Republic of Germany, in the Bundestag on 10 November 1998," German Information Center, Press Release from 10 November 1998.

2. Confidential Interview, Deutsche Gesellschaft für Auswärtige Politik, Bonn, 14 September 1998.

3. Leon Mangasarian, "New Accents in German Foreign Policy," *Deutsche Presse-Agentur*, 6 November 1998.

4. William Hagen, "Kosovo: The History Behind It all," *Foreign Affairs*, vol. 74, no. 4, 1999, p. 57.

5. Ibid., p. 58.

6. Roger Cohen, "Crisis in the Balkans: Kosovo Notebook," *New York Times*, 2 July 1999, p. A1.

7. Barton Gellman, "The Path to Crisis: How the United States and Its Allies Went to War," *Washington Post*, 18 April 1999, p. A1.

8. Chris Hedges, "Serb Forces Open a Major Assault on Kosovo Rebels," *New York Times*, 30 June 1998, p. A1.

9. Roger Cohen, "A Policy Struggle Stirs within NATO," *New York Times*, 28 November 1998, p. A1.

10. According to secondary accounts, the White House believed that a major military operation in Kosovo was completely out of the question. In high level deliberations, President Clinton himself drew parallels between such an operation, the war in Vietnam, and the debacle in Somalia. Key advisers expressed similar skepticism, warning that the general public knew little of the region or its problems, and joking that most Americans could not locate Kosovo on a map. Secretary of Defense Cohen and Chairman of the Joint Chiefs Shelton argued that the operational details were not well developed and that such a mission would be vague and open-ended. Without a clear political purpose and focus, they argued, such a plan should never be considered. One high-ranking official said that "The numbers came in high. No one said yes; no one said no. It was taken off the table. . . . It was a complete eye-roller." Gellman, "The Path to Crisis: How the United States and Its Allies Went to War," 18 April 1999, p. A1.

11. Elaine Sciolino and Ethan Bronner, "Crisis in the Balkans: The Road to War," *New York Times*, 18 April 1999, p. A1; see also Jane Perlez, "Milosevic Accepts Kosovo Monitors, Averting Attack," *New York Times*, 14 October 1998, p. A1.

12. Michael Mandelbaum, "A Perfect Failure: NATO's War Against Yugoslavia," *Foreign Affairs*, vol. 78, no. 5, September–October 1999, p. 2.

13. Elaine Sciolino and Ethan Bronner, "Crisis in the Balkans: The Road to War," *New York Times*, 18 April 1999, p. 1.

14. WGBH, *Frontline: War in Europe*, 2000, http://www.pbs.org/wgbh/pages /frontline/shows/kosovo/etc/script1.html.

15. Steven Erlanger, "Serb View: A Victory," *New York Times*, 24 February 1999, p. A10.

16. Craig Whitney and Eric Schmitt, "Crisis in the Balkans: NATO Had Signs Its Strategy Would Fail Kosovars," *New York Times*, 1 April 1999, p. A1.

17. Whitney and Schmitt, "Crisis in the Balkans," 1999, p. A1.

18. AgenceFrance Presse, "US President, German Chancellor Agree on Tough Kosovo Stance," 11 February 1999.

19. Roger Cohen, "Half a Century after Hitler, German Jets Join the Attack," *New York Times*, 26 March 1999, p. A10.

20. "Schröder's Germany has Decided to be German," *Washington Post*, 11 February 1999, p. 8.

21. Olaf Ihlau and Siegesmund von Ilsemann, "Geduld und Zähigkeit," *Der Spiegel*, vol. 4, 25 January 1999, pp. 138–140.

22. Lally Weymouth, "We Have to Win This," *Newsweek*, vol. 133, no. 16, 19 April 1999, p. 30.

23. German Embassy, "Bonn Parliament Approves Use of 5,000 German Soldiers in Kosovo," *Deutsche Presse-Agentur*, 25 February 1999.

24. Michael Schwelien, "Dann fließt viel Blut," p. 2.

25. Ibid., p. 4.

26. "German Foreign Minister Rejects Criticism of NATO's Foreign Policy," British Broadcasting Corporation, 7 March 1999.

27. "Rot-Grün streitet über Militäreinsatz im Kosovo," *Die Welt*, 4 February 1999, p. 1.

28. Schwelien, "Dann fließt viel Blut," 11 February 1999, p. 2.

29. Infratest survey of April 3–5, as quoted in Caroline King, "The New German Government and the Kosovo Conflict: A Painful Awakening," *Politik*, no. 11, Summer 1999, pp. 4–5.

30. *Deutschland Nachrichten*, 12 March 1999, p. 1.

31. Stephan Speicher, *Berliner Zeitung*, 25 March 1999, p. 6.

32. "Schröder Green Light for a German Role in Air Strikes, but New Approval Needed for German Ground Forces in Any Peacekeeping Mission in Kosovo," *Deutsche-Presse Agentur*, 22 March 1999; see also Bonn rüstet sich zum Kosovo-Einsatz," *Die Welt*, 2 February 1999.

33. Excerpt from *Die Welt*, 25 March 1999, p. 6.

34. Transcript of Clinton's speech reprinted in *New York Times*, 25 March 1999, p. A4.

35. See Adam Roberts, "NATO's 'Humanitarian War' over Kosovo," *Survival*, vol. 41, no. 3, Autumn 1999, pp. 99–117; see also Javier Solana, "NATO's Success in Kosovo," *Foreign Affairs*, vol. 78, no. 6, November–December 1999, pp. 114–120.

36. WGBH, "Interview with General Michael Short," *Frontline: War in Europe*, 2000, http:// www.pbs.org/wgbh/pages/frontline/shows/kosovo/etc/script1.html.

37. Rebecca Grant, "Air Power Made It Work," *Air Force Magazine*, November 1999, p. 30.

38. John Harris, "Clinton Saw No Alternative to Air Strikes," *Washington Post*, 1 April 1999, p. A1.

39. "Bonn Demands End to Serbian Aggression in Kosovo, Pledges Humanitarian Aid for Refugees," *This Week in Germany*, 2 April 1999, p. 1.

40. "Refugees from Kosovo Arrive in Germany," *This Week in Germany*, 9 April 1999, p. 1.

41. Dana Priest, "Bombing by Committee: France Balked at NATO Targets," *Washington Post*, 20 September 1999, p. A1.

42. Ibid., p. A1.

43. Fischer was personally engaged in the management of Operation Allied Force. This led to at least one amusing twist in committee deliberations. According to one report, during the management committee call on May 26, German Foreign Minister Joschka Fischer let out a loud shriek. Secretary of State Albright asked whether he was hurt. In a sheepish voice, Fischer admitted that he was watching a championship soccer game between Manchester United and Bayern Munich. The British won the game 2–1, with two goals in the final 30 seconds; Dana Priest, "Bombing by Committee: France Balked at NATO Targets," *Washington Post*, 20 September 1999, p. A8

44. For an overview of the Kosovo War, see Daniel L. Byman and Matthew C. Waxman, "Kosovo and the Great Air Power Debate," *International Security*, vol. 24, no. 4, Spring 2000, pp. 5–38; see also Barry R. Posen, "The War for Kosovo: Serbia's Political-Military Strategy," *International Security*, vol. 24, no. 4, Spring 2000, pp. 39–84.

45. President Clinton, "Statement By the President to the Nation," 24 March 1999, http://www2.whitehouse.gov/WH/Newhtml/19990324-2872.html.

46. Michael R. Gordon and Craig R. Whitney, "Two Allies Press U.S. to Weigh the Use of Ground Forces," *New York Times*, 22 April 1999, p. A1.

47. Dana Priest, "A Decisive Battle That Never Was," *Washington Post*, 19 September 1999, p. A1.

48. Ibid., p. A1.

49. Ibid., p. A1.

50. Caroline King, "The New German Government and the Kosovo Conflict: A Painful Awakening," *Politik*, no. 11, Summer 1999, pp. 4–5.

51. Josef Joffe, "A Peacenik Goes to War," *New York Times Magazine*, 30 May 1999, pp. 31–33.

52. "German Opposition Official Says Troops in Macedonia Not for Combat Mission," British Broadcasting Corporation, 23 March 1999.

53. Roger Cohen, "Schröder's Blunt 'No' to Ground Troops in Kosovo Reflects Depth of German Sensitivities," *New York Times*, 20 May 1999, p. A1.

54. King, "The New German Government and the Kosovo Conflict: A Painful Awakening," 1999, pp. 4–5.

55. "Kosovo-Krise: Die Grünen vor der Zerreissprobe," *Deutschland Nachrichten*, 23 April 1999.

56. *Bild-Zeitung*, 12 May 1999, p. 4. As quoted in *Deutschland Nachrichten*, 14 May 1999, p. 3.

57. When put to a vote, the government committee's resolution out-polled the left wing by 444–318; "Greens Back Fischer on Kosovo, Urge Temporary Cease-Fire," *This Week in Germany*, 14 May 1999, p. 2.

58. As quoted in Josef Joffe, "A Peacenik Goes to War," 1999, pp. 31–33.

59. "Greens Back Fischer on Kosovo, Urge Temporary Cease-Fire," *The Week in Germany*, 14 May 1999, p. 2.

60. Wolfgang Prosinger, "Der verlorene Krieg," *Zeitung zum Sonntag*, no. 22, 30 May 1999, p. 1.

61. Wolfgang Hoffmann, "Offene Rechnungen," *Die Zeit*, 22 April 1999, p. 27.

62. See Wolfgang Prosinger, "Ein Mann sieht rot," *Zeitung zum Sonntag*, no. 20, 16 May 1999, p. 1; see also "Die Unentschlossenen," *Die Zeit*, no. 23, 2 June 1999, p. 1066.

63. As quoted in Caroline King, "The New German Government and the Kosovo Conflict: A Painful Awakening," pp. 4–5.

64. EMNID Survey, conducted for *Der Spiegel* on April 20–21, 1999; published in "Die Spaltung liegt in der Luft," *Der Spiegel*, no. 17, 26 April 1999, p. 22.

65. Josef Joffe, "A Peacenik Goes to War," 1999, pp. 31–33.

66. Roger Cohen, "Schröder's Blunt 'No' to Ground Troops in Kosovo Reflects Depth of German Sensitivities," 1999, p. A1.

67. Ibid., p. A1.

68. "A Sceptre Haunting: Summary of the German Initiative for Kosovo," *Politik*, no. 11, Summer 1999, pp. 1–5; see also www.auswaertiges-amt.de; "Fischer Puts Forward Kosovo Peace Plan; Bundestag Backs Use of Military Force," *The Week in Germany*, 16 April 1999, p. 1; see also Caroline King, "The New German Government and the Kosovo Conflict: A Painful Awakening," 1999, pp. 4–5.

69. Schröder Sees Progress in Efforts to End Kosovo Conflict, Rules out German Ground Troops," *The Week in Germany*, 21 May 1999, p. 1.

70. Roger Cohen, "Milosevic Agrees to U.N. Presence Inside Kosovo," *New York Times*, 2 June 1999, p. A1.

71. Blaine Harden, "Crisis in the Balkans: Doing the Deal," *New York Times*, 6 June 1999, p. A1.

72. Tom Raum, "Cost of Kosovo Conflict Said to Be $4 Billion," *Washington Post*, 8 June 1999, p. A1.

73. Bradley Graham and Dana Priest, "Troops are Ready to Enter Kosovo; Challenges Likely to Exceed Bosnia's," *Washinton Post*, 4 June 1999, p. A29.

74. "Yugoslavia Says Repair Bill Tops $30 Billion," Canadian Broadcasting Corporation, 16 July 1999, http://www.cbc.news.cbc.ca/cgates/view.cgi?/news/1999/07/15/yugo990715.

75. "Bonn schikt 8500 Soldaten," *Süddeutsche Zeitung*, 12 June 1999, p. 1; see also "Deutschland am Ende des Krieges," *Die Zeit*, no. 24, 10 June 1999, p. 3.

76. Roger Cohen, "Europeans Plan $1.5 Billion Aid for Rebuilding," *New York Times*, 20 June 1999, p. A10.

7

German Foreign Policy for the Twenty-First Century

Without operations in Somalia, without the hard work of the sanitation engineering unit in Cambodia, without the planes from the *Luftwaffe* delivering aid to Sarajevo, without the airdrop of humanitarian aid over Bosnia, without the unconditional participation in AWACS missions over the Balkans, without the minesweeping operations in the Persian Gulf and monitoring of the Adriatic embargo, we would have never arrived where we are today. . . . Germany has proven its capabilities to be a responsible member of broader society. We are prepared for growing responsibilities in the world.

—Volker Rühe, 1994[1]

If you know the special history of Germany, you know that the most important change for German foreign policy with the new government is no change. Continuity is the main focus of our policy, because other ways will not produce the desired results. . . . Our primary objective in foreign affairs now is completing European unification.

—Joschka Fischer, 1998[2]

> Active solidarity and responsible action are expected of Germany [in
> the wake of the terrorist attacks of September 11, 2001],—and will
> also be provided. . . . I made it clear to the president of the United
> States that Germany will meet its responsibility in all areas. That
> expressly includes military cooperation and participation. Germany's
> readiness to ensure security also militarily represents an important
> pledge to its alliances and partnerships. But not only that. The readi-
> ness to live up to our greater responsibility for international security
> also means seeing German foreign policy in a new way.
> —Gerhard Schröder, 2001[3]

German foreign policy clearly has evolved in response to a series of strategic dilemmas in the post-Cold War era, and this study has demonstrated
the importance of domestic conditions that shaped foreign policy restructuring over time. The model of external–internal linkages has proven useful for understanding decision making in both the Conservative–Liberal
coalition of the immediate post-Cold War era, as well as more recent
actions by the Social Democrat–Green government. The evolution of
German foreign policy activism from the Gulf War to Kosovo, the war on
terrorism, and beyond, will have a profound impact on the country's
position in the new century. This chapter reviews patterns of evidence
and draws conclusions about the theory and practice of foreign policy
restructuring.

DILEMMAS AND OPPORTUNITIES AS CATALYSTS FOR FOREIGN POLICY RESTRUCTURING

Primat der Außenpolitik?

The assumption that external challenges force governments to consider foreign policy redirection is supported by both traditional structural
realism and literature in the foreign policy analysis subfield, and it serves
as an important conceptual bridge between the study of external and
internal conditions that may affect foreign policy restructuring. Realists
and many foreign policy analysts have adopted the same basic assumption, that changes in the external operating environment are often catalysts for a reorientation of state behavior.[4] In one of the first studies
focusing on the foreign policy making process, Rosenau argued that foreign policy is essentially a mechanism for the state to adapt to changes in
its environment. Changes in foreign policy are most likely to occur, he
claimed, "when developments abroad give rise to potential threats to
their essential structures."[5] Hermann contended that most foreign policy
change results from external shocks, or "dramatic international events
which have great visibility and immediate impact to the recipient."[6]

This study clearly has shown that strategic dilemmas and opportunities prompted significant German foreign policy change in the 1990s. Many relevant examples from the case material support this argument. The Gulf crisis led to the first major foreign policy restructuring for Germany in the post-Cold War era. The Iraqi invasion of Kuwait and Western efforts to assemble a military coalition for Operation Desert Shield clearly were catalysts for a critical dialogue on the future of German foreign policy. The government's reluctance to become directly involved in the conflict gave way within six months to a general acceptance among elites, major party organizations, and the public, of the need to consider involvement in similar contingencies in the future.

The humanitarian crisis in Somalia was yet another catalyst for debates inside Germany about proper foreign policy responses. Televised images of starvation and of innocents caught in a civil war in Somalia in 1992 helped to mobilize the government, political parties, and the public to reconsider the way that the Basic Law limited troop deployments abroad. Mindful of the international imperative for German assistance in Somalia, but sensing an important domestic political opportunity, Foreign Ministers Genscher and Kinkel used their resistance to out-of-area deployments as leverage to force interparty negotiations on amending the Basic Law in January 1993. While talks collapsed because of disagreements between party positions, Somalia became a trigger for two years of negotiations on German foreign policy restructuring that were finally resolved in the Constitutional Court ruling of 1994.

Conflicts in the former Yugoslavia were major catalysts for German security policy restructuring in the post-Cold War era. In the first half of the 1990s, government leaders were confronted with multifaceted diplomatic, economic, social, and political crises in the Balkans from 1991 to 1994. By 1995, events in the Balkans had exceeded everyone's lowest expectations: combat in Bosnia, genocide and ethnic cleansing in Muslim enclaves such as Gorazde and Srebreniça, and attacks on UN peacekeepers and allied forces in the region. These extreme external shocks essentially forced the German government and its allies to respond by supporting the creation of a Rapid Reaction Force contingency in the summer of 1995, and later, by supporting the deployment of German troops in the Balkans to enforce the Dayton Peace Accord. Clearly, the events of the war in 1995 represented the ultimate strategic dilemma for Western governments. Out of this despair emerged a new resolve to deploy troops and prevent genocide.

That resolve was soon tested in Kosovo. Once again, the West stood witness to ethnic cleansing and paramilitary actions against a minority group in Yugoslavia. As the conflict intensified, the German government was surprisingly united in their support for coercive diplomacy. In March 1999, the government and the public supported German participation in

Operation Allied Force, the largest military assault in Europe since World War II. While the government stopped short of endorsing a ground invasion of Kosovo and Serbia, Germany demonstrated its resolve to serve as a responsible partner in NATO. As of this writing, German peacekeepers are patrolling key regions of Kosovo to enforce the post-war settlement.

The strategic dilemmas of the 1990s served as catalysts to initiate critical dialogues on foreign policy restructuring in Germany. In extreme cases, such as the humanitarian crisis of the Kurds, mass starvation in Somalia, and genocide in Bosnia and Kosovo, strategic dilemmas truly were external shocks that led to immediate and strong foreign policy actions on the part of the German government. These developments appear to confirm the predictions of the restructuring literature that international events and crises can act as immediate causes of change, but they also mirror the basic assumptions of the realist literature. Rosenau's description of foreign policy restructuring as governments "always in motion . . . sometimes slipping behind, moving ahead, holding fast, or otherwise adjusting" to deal with changed international circumstances seems borne out in this study.[7]

Primat der Innenpolitik

International pressures alone were not sufficient to explain the scope, direction, or timing of foreign policy restructuring, however. This book has shown that the path from recognition of a strategic dilemma or opportunity to the formulation of a foreign policy response was rarely simple, direct, or immediate. Rather, the story of German foreign policy restructuring is better understood as fits and starts of uncertainty and hesitancy in policy development spanning a period of years.

In chapter 1, it was suggested that a comprehensive study of change must take into account the deep political debate inside Germany about the development of its new foreign policy construct, and its resultant effect on the decision-making process and government actions. This level of inquiry has produced some fascinating accounts of internal debate. In the case of the crisis in the Persian Gulf, for example, German foreign policy restructuring was limited and relatively slow in comparison to that of its Western allies. Germany faced direct pressure from the Bush administration and NATO officials to contribute troops and money to support Operation Desert Shield in 1990, but this was countered by strong resistance inside the German government. While some Conservatives favored German troop deployment, most leaders were preoccupied with the reunification process at home and did not want Germany to become actively involved in the Gulf crisis for historical, financial, social, political, and legal reasons. Their compromise, checkbook diplomacy, was viewed as generous by most Germans, but outside the country it was criticized as falling short of allied expectations of German commitments to the region. Perceived German inactivity in the winter months of 1990–1991 drew broad reprimands (Figure 7.1).

International pressures for a German response to developments in the civil war in the former Yugoslavia did not produce commensurate or proportional foreign policy change. In fact, the initial German response to the crisis—recognizing the independence of Croatia and Slovenia—challenged the standards set by the international community and suggested that Germany would pursue its own interests based on historical and cultural ties to the region. Later, the AWACS deployment question created a major political debate in Bonn that eventually split the ruling coalition. Conservatives were willing to authorize German officers to remain on post on NATO aircraft that were to monitor the no-fly zone over the Balkans; after all, they argued, German officers made up fully one-third of all AWACS crews and were crucial to the success of the NATO mission. However, Free Democrats believed that the deployment represented a direct violation of the Basic Law and demanded that the government postpone a decision until the amendment question could be resolved. Ultimately, the FDP joined with the SPD and the Greens to challenge the deployment decision in the German Constitutional Court.

This same spirit affected the German response to the NATO request for ECR-Tornado aircraft to be deployed to the Balkans to monitor the no-fly zone. When the SACEUR, General Joulwan, made his initial request to the German government for the assets, key officials decided to simply ignore it as an informal inquiry. Only a second, more formal request and high-profile appeals from NATO allies led to government compliance, but once again, the government ensured that these operations were strictly bounded. The cabinet worked with the *Bundestag* to pass a resolution setting specific limits on German participation in air operations (for reconnaissance and defensive actions), and the government event sent a German military officer to the NATO airbase in Piacenza, Italy, to serve as a watchdog to enforce these operational limits.

After seamless German cooperation with the NATO alliance in Operation Allied Force in March 1999, NATO plans for an invasion of Kosovo stirred up a domestic political debate that threatened to bring down the SPD–Green coalition, and perhaps even shatter the alliance. Chancellor Schröder faced increasing pressure from leaders of Britain, France, and the United States to consider German support for a ground invasion of Kosovo and Serbia if the air war did not achieve its objectives. From the beginning, cabinet leaders knew that they faced domestic political constraints on such a move. Parliamentarians from all major parties were unequivocal in their opposition to a ground invasion, and this led to a growing tide of popular resistance to such a move. No leader experienced this challenge more than Joschka Fischer, who endured weeks of personal

Figure 7.1
Strategic Dilemmas and German Foreign Policy Responses

Strategic Dilemma	International Pressure for Action	German Response
The Persian Gulf Crisis, 1990–1991		
Iraqi Invasion of Kuwait/ Operation Desert Shield	Send Troops and Money	Checkbook Diplomacy
Threats to Turkey and Israel/ Operation Desert Storm	Troops, Money, and Logistical Support	Logistical Support, Help in Defense of Turkey and Israel
Iraqi Attack on Kurds/ Refugee Crisis Relief	Troops, Money, and Support for Relief Efforts	Troop Deployment and Logistical Support
Humanitarian Crisis in Somalia, 1992–1994		
Civil War and Famine/ Operation Restore Hope	Send Troops and Logistical Support	Slow Deployment of Troops and Support
Mission Creep/Attacks on UN Peacekeepers	Phased Withdrawal of Troops	Phased Withdrawal of Troops

The Civil War in the Former Yugoslavia, 1991–1995

Croatia and Slovenia Secede/ Seek Diplomatic Recognition	No Recognition, or Delayed Response	Immediate Recognition, Pressure EU to Follow
WEU Enforcement of Embargo/ Adriatic Monitoring	Deploy Navy and Aircraft for Monitoring Mission	Limited Commitment of Navy and Air Force
Operation Deny Flight/ AWACS Deployment over Bosnia	Allow German Aircrews to Participate in Monitoring	Debate and Reluctant Staff Commitment
NATO Request for Aircraft/ ECR-Tornado Deployment	Send Needed Aircraft with German Pilots and Crews	Slow Commitment of Aircraft with Limits
Serbian Advances and UN Crisis/ Rapid Reaction Force	Commit Troops and Assets to Rapid Reaction Force Contingency	Rapid Commitment of Troops and Assets
The Dayton Peace Accord/ NATO Implementation Force	Commit Troops and Logistical Support for Peace Enforcement	Rapid Commitment of Troops and Assets

The Kosovo Crisis, 1989–1999

Serb Crackdown on Kosovo/ KLA Insurgency	Coercive Diplomacy, Commit Aircraft and Support Personnel	Active Participation in NATO Air War
Operation Allied Force/ Preparations for Ground War	Commit Troops for Ground War Against Serbia	Oppose Ground War, Diplomatic Initiatives

and political assaults designed to derail any change in policy. Faced with the reality that their government might fall, German leaders publicly challenged NATO plans for a ground war and instead launched a major diplomatic initiative to end the war.

These cases highlight the importance of domestic political conditions for restructuring. Hanrieder's work on external–internal linkages in the 1960s argued that analysts must examine the linkages between the "internal predispositions" of the country, including value systems and political culture, and conditions in the external environment for a comprehensive understanding of foreign policy.[8] His suggestion that foreign policy development was ultimately a function of compatibility and consensus seems borne out by this case study. As illustrated in Figure 7.1 on pages 170–171, the "degrees of feasibility" of various foreign policy goals and the amount of domestic political consensus shaped the timing and scope of foreign policy restructuring.[9]

DOMESTIC CONSTRAINTS ON FOREIGN POLICY CHANGE

Elites and Foreign Policy Restructuring

In chapter 1, it was suggested that timely and dramatic foreign policy restructuring would be less likely to occur in response to strategic dilemmas and opportunities when government leaders are divided over the issue. Foreign policy analysts have argued that elites are instrumental in defining foreign policy goals and the scope and direction of policy restructuring.[10]

This line of inquiry was strongly supported by evidence from the cases in this study. All major restructuring initiatives benefited from the leadership of elites along the way. Elite attitudes toward German responses to the civil war in the former Yugoslavia (1991–1995) were both instrumental and problematic for foreign policy restructuring. In all six phases, Kohl and Rühe favored the expansion of German responses to the crisis in the Balkans to some degree. Kohl was clearly determined to provide a strong show of German resolve to support key allies and international organizations, and his leadership in this evolution was critical. Rühe often served as the point man for the government in terms of articulating cabinet plans for diplomatic, humanitarian, and military action in the Balkans (even though the record shows that he had expressed some reservations about normalization along the way).

Foreign Ministers Genscher and Kinkel were also instrumental in the normalization of German foreign policy during the war in Bosnia, but they were somewhat less driven than key Conservative leaders. In the Kosovo crisis, Foreign Minister Fischer again played an important role in articulating government support for involvement in Operation Allied

Force. Ironically, case evidence shows that all three foreign ministers often were caught in awkward political positions, between their personal convictions that certain actions were necessary (and in accord with international pressures and commitments) and sometimes serious resistance in their own junior party organizations. Nevertheless, their support was an essential element of elite leadership in these case studies.

Political Parties

This study also suggested that parties and domestic coalition building would have a significant impact on timely and dramatic foreign policy restructuring. In formulating a German response to the Gulf crisis, for example, CDU/CSU leaders publicly stated their support for direct German participation in Operations Desert Shield and Desert Storm. Key leaders, including the chair of the *Bundestag* foreign affairs committee, Karl-Heinz Hornhues, indicated their support for a stronger German military profile relatively early in debates. At the same time, however, leaders of the Free Democratic Party were wrestling with questions about whether Germany should deploy troops to Turkey, the connections between German firms and the Iraqi war machine, and the constitutionality of Operation Provide Comfort. Genscher and Kinkel were able to maintain a modicum of party consensus in support of checkbook diplomacy and troop deployments. It should be noted, however, that criticism inside the FDP that they had "sold out" to the Conservatives encouraged Genscher to resign from his post in 1992, and led to the ousting of Kinkel as party leader in 1995.

Conservative party support was again instrumental in the German response to the humanitarian crisis in Somalia. Conservative party leaders believed that Germany should join with key Western allies to respond to the crisis by participating in Operation Restore Hope in a carefully bounded way. Furthermore, they believed that the Somalia operation could be conducted legally within the existing interpretation of the Basic Law. Meanwhile, the Free Democrats remained divided on the matter after reflecting on the Gulf War experience. Genscher and Kinkel nonetheless held firm in negotiations with Conservatives on the question, and forced a concession to enter into negotiations on amending the Basic Law in January 1993. That deal and subsequent negotiations quieted party disagreements inside the FDP and set the stage for the Constitutional Court ruling of 1994.

The evolution of party support for German foreign policy responses to the dilemmas of the civil war in the Balkans is a very interesting story in itself. At the outset, Conservative parties favored an assertive German diplomatic role in brokering peace. CSU leaders had been particularly vocal in support of government recognition of Croatia and Slovenia, reflecting religious and ethnic ties in southern Germany, and both the

CDU and CSU generally favored rapid German foreign policy normalization throughout the decade. In a number of instances, leaders like Wolfgang Schäuble, Karl-Heinz Hornhues, and Karl Lamers were actually ahead of the government in terms of willingness to accept certain military contingencies, and they regularly backed up stands taken by Chancellor Kohl and Defense Minister Rühe in parliamentary debates.

The Free Democratic Party played a different role in the evolution of German foreign policy responses to the civil war in the Balkans. Genscher helped lead the campaign to recognize Croatia and Slovenia, but his resignation in early 1992 limited FDP influence over foreign policy restructuring. A relative newcomer, Foreign Minister Klaus Kinkel largely followed the lead of the Conservatives. A notable exception to this relationship—and one that underscores the extent to which the FDP felt marginalized on Balkan policy in the wake of Genscher's resignation—occurred when the FDP actually joined with opposition parties to challenge the Conservative decision to allow German aircrews to work on AWACS planes deployed over Bosnia. This led to the rather remarkable political tightrope walk by Klaus Kinkel between his formal defense of government policy before the Constitutional Court, and the foreign policy position staked out by his own party organization. The Court eventually ruled in favor of the government—thanks in part to Kinkel's testimony—and the FDP seemed thereafter resigned to less influence on Balkan policy. From 1993 onward, the FDP seemed to turn inward and became quite focused on the standing of the party in domestic elections. The Union Party counted on, and received, FDP support for normalization throughout this period.

Following the dramatic federal election victory of the Social Democrats and Greens in September 1998, both party organizations gained control of German foreign policy. Gerhard Schröder exhibited a unique ability in his party to unify support from both the left and moderate wings of the organization, and was able to articulate a fairly unified position for the party in support of NATO coercive diplomacy during the Kosovo crisis. While there were defections from the party during this time, including the resignation of Finance Minister Oskar Lafontaine, most members remained in favor of German participation in Operation Allied Force. This was not the case for the Green Party, however. Green maneuvering during the Kosovo crisis became a subject of media attention and a real worry for cabinet leaders attempting to chart the proper course for the German response to Kosovo. Joschka Fischer was able to maintain relative party unity in the early months of 1999, even obtaining an endorsement for limited German participation in its first offensive military action since World War II. Party support soon unraveled, and the Green Party conference in Bielefeld in May 1999 showed just how close the organization had come to defection from the government position on Kosovo.

The evidence examined here suggests that inter-party coalition politics helped to shape the evolution of German foreign policy. Conservative support for greater foreign policy activism was regularly tempered by FDP concerns about the scope and pace of normalization. Hans-Dietrich Genscher and Klaus Kinkel played particularly important roles as party leaders, attempting to define Liberal stances on major foreign policy matters. When questions of party independence became muddled, their leadership positions were challenged. Kinkel's loss of the party chairmanship in 1995 to Wolfgang Gerhardt was a sign of the FDP commitment to stand independent from Conservative party positions. The role of junior party activism was even more stark during the Kosovo crisis, when Green Party opposition to any NATO plans for a ground invasion in the Balkans defined the absolute limits of government stability. Ultimately, coalition politics had a marked impact on foreign policy restructuring. It set the stage for a very interesting change in government in the federal elections of 1998, and it defined the scope of German foreign policy normalization to the end of the decade.

Public Opinion and Foreign Policy Restructuring

Public opinion was the third important set of conditions believed to influence the scope and nature of foreign policy restructuring. This study suggests, however, that public opinion had only a residual effect on the scope and timing of German foreign policy change. The evidence shows that public attitudes were quite dynamic and malleable in response to strategic dilemmas of the 1990s.

Public opinion on German foreign policy restructuring changed considerably in response to the three stages of the Gulf crisis, for example. The Iraqi invasion of Kuwait occurred at a time when most Germans were focused on domestic political transitions associated with unification. Accordingly, opinion polls showed that most citizens were opposed to direct German involvement in the allied military response, and they provided diffuse support for checkbook diplomacy. Germans continued to oppose a move toward deployment of German troops in the Gulf theater through the winter months of 1990–1991, and this period uncovered lingering pacifistic sentiments among the populace. Indeed, hundreds of thousands of Germans participated in vocal protests against military action in the Gulf through January 1991. However, the revelation that German firms had contributed to the development of chemical and biological munitions and missiles in Iraq that directly threatened Israel changed German public attitudes overnight. In February 1991, the same Germans that had been marching against the use of force against Iraq suddenly were marching in favor of swift and decisive allied military action, and opinion polls in February and March 1991 reflected this change. Popular support for some German role in response to the Gulf crisis enabled the government to confidently deploy troops to participate in the Kurdish relief effort in April 1991.

Public attitudes toward the civil war in the former Yugoslavia reflected the general trends exhibited during the crises in the Persian Gulf and Somalia. Germans supported diplomatic responses to the crisis, including the recognition of the independence of Croatia and Slovenia, but they were wary of troop deployments in potential combat zones. Without a clear UN mandate for a blue-helmet peacekeeping operation, public opinion polls showed a majority of Germans opposed the deployment of naval vessels and aircraft for the Western European Union monitoring mission in the Adriatic. Nevertheless, the government moved ahead on the Adriatic deployment and secured a simple majority of support for the mission in the *Bundestag*. Later, Germans opposed the participation of German air crews on AWACS planes that were monitoring the no-fly zone over the Balkans, but the government was able to push this initiative through as well.

Public attitudes during the Kosovo crisis seemed to have a limited impact on German foreign policy decision making. In fact, experts noted a general absence of public discourse on Kosovo in the months leading up to the initial decision to commit aircraft and support personnel for Operation Allied Force. One editorial noted a "general public emptiness" on the matter at the time in Germany, suggesting popular support for a normalized foreign policy profile. This was not the case in other European countries, however, where public attitudes varied from support for NATO (67% in Britain, for example) to strong opposition to allied intervention (97% in Greece). Public opinion in Germany did slide as the war continued in April and May of 1999, and government leaders were aware of changing public attitudes as they formulated their response to NATO plans for a ground war in Kosovo. Opponents of government policy were encouraged by the growing salience of the issue, and they frequently cited opinion polls in their challenge to continued support for Operation Allied Force. Nevertheless, it should be noted that waning public support for the air war (and even a few organized protests) never led to a true, mass mobilization against German involvement. In summary, public opinion seems to have lagged behind elite attitudes on German foreign policy restructuring in the 1990s, rather than shaping the parameters of acceptable behavior (Figure 7.2).

Summary

How important were the intervening conditions described in the conceptual framework? Overall, the importance of the variables for shaping

Figure 7.2
Summary of the Role of Domestic Constraints

Strategic Dilemma/German Response	Position on Question of Foreign Policy Change		
	Elites	Parties	Public
The Persian Gulf Crisis, 1990–1991			
Iraqi Invasion of Kuwait/ Checkbook Diplomacy	Support	Support	Support
Operation Desert Storm/ Logistical Support	Mixed	Mixed	Mixed
Iraqi Attack on Kurds/ Troops and Refugee Crisis Relief	Support	Support	Mixed
Humanitarian Crisis in Somalia, 1992–1994			
Civil War and Famine/ Troops in Operation Restore Hope	Support	Oppose	Mixed
Mission Creep and Attacks/ Troop Withdrawal	Mixed	Support	Support
The Civil War in the Former Yugoslavia, 1991–1995			
Croatia and Slovenia Secede/ Diplomatic Recognition	Support	Support	Support
WEU Enforcement of Embargo/ Adriatic Monitoring	Support	Oppose	Oppose
AWACS Deployment over Bosnia/ German Aircrews Participate	Support	Oppose	Oppose
NATO Request for Aircraft/ ECR-Tornado Deployment	Support	Support	Mixed
Serbian Advances and UN Crisis/ Support the Rapid Reaction Force	Support	Support	Support
The Dayton Peace Accord and IFOR/ Ground Troop Deployment	Support	Support	Support
The Kosovo Crisis, 1989–1999			
Operation Allied Force/ Aircraft and Support Personnel	Support	Support	Support
Prepare for Ground War	Mixed	Oppose	Oppose

foreign policy restructuring seemed to increase with proximity to the political center. The evidence suggests that elite attitudes had by far the most direct bearing on foreign policy decisions regarding restructuring, and the foreign policy discourse of elites generally set the parameters for foreign policy choices.[11] Hagan's argument that two tasks are central to elites' decisions in any foreign policy redirection—coalition building and retaining political power—was confirmed by this study. Given these imperatives, leaders often sought legitimation of all major foreign policy restructuring initiatives.[12] Meanwhile, political parties played a somewhat more complicated role in German foreign policy restructuring in the post-Cold War era. FDP opposition to some normalization measures did constrain government latitude in 1992 and 1993, but in all cases the junior party ultimately adopted the position of the Conservatives. After 1995, more party representatives from across the political spectrum seemed to shift their support to the political center—a trend that continued until the 1998 federal elections. The Green Party joined the SPD in support of German involvement in Operation Allied Force, but concerns about a ground war in Kosovo did seem to influence government action in May 1999.

Finally, public opinion represented the most dynamic level of domestic conditions relative to foreign policy restructuring—and the least significant. Generally speaking, government leaders worked to establish public support for their actions, consistent with the scholarly perspectives of Pye and Verba, Holsti, and Shapiro. However, Risse-Kappen's contention that public opinion can directly affect the choices of top decision makers "by changing policy goals or how those goals are prioritized, by narrowing the range of options and/or means to implement goals, or by winning symbolic concessions in the sense of changed rhetoric rather than policy reforms," does not seem borne out by these case studies. Rather, elites consistently viewed public opinion as a condition that might be manipulated through concentrated political action, and they often endeavored to widen the zone of acceptable German foreign policy behavior in that context.

Overall, the evidence presented in this study has confirmed the relevance of the external–internal linkages approach for providing a more comprehensive understanding of German behavior in the 1990s. Robert Putnam's study of two-level games and foreign policy development suggested that "on nearly all important issues, central decision makers disagree about what the national interest and the international context demand," making bargaining essential for policy change.[13] To paraphrase his work, one can conclude that the ultimate success or failure of foreign policy restructuring is dependent upon the latitude presented by the domestic climate.[14] When domestic coalitions were difficult to construct (as in the case of the Gulf crisis, Somalia, and the ground troops contingency for Kosovo) the rate of foreign policy change was slowed. When conditions were optimal for a bandwagon of support for restructuring (as in response to ethnic cleansing in Bosnia and Kosovo) change occurred much more rapidly. This acceleration–deceleration model of change helps to explain the fits and starts nature of restructuring for countries like Germany in the 1990s.

This study reinforces the importance of coalition building for government foreign policy change. Both Hagan and Moravcsik identified this theme as significant for understanding state behavior, and this study has confirmed the key role of coalition formation for foreign policy restructuring. As Hagan suggested, German leaders worked hard to build domestic coalitions in support of their preferred foreign policy behavior, and he correctly predicted that this dynamic often becomes a central preoccupation for leaders in democratic systems who attend to the "political imperative of retaining power."[15] This study also bears out Moravcsik's contention that government leaders cannot simply calculate the expected costs and benefits of restructuring, but rather must be open to creative coalition-building for change.[16] German leaders regularly sought to build effective coalitions for foreign policy change, and they allocated government resources within limits set by the coalition, not the international system. In summary, the findings of this book convincingly drive home the conclusion that the study of external–internal linkages is essential to develop more comprehensive models of international politics.

The Domestic Secrets of German Foreign Policy Normalization

A structured, focused comparison of cases has helped to identify two intervening conditions in the German foreign policy restructuring process that were not originally represented in the conceptual framework. According to case evidence, the evolution of thought on foreign policy responsibilities in the post-Cold War era on the political left, and the actual nature of the strategic dilemmas facing the Federal Republic both had a special effect on the scope and pace of foreign policy change.

As noted in chapter 1, political parties were expected to play important roles in restructuring, mainly through coalition maneuvering. However, this study has underscored the important role of opposition parties in reshaping the German foreign profile over time. Scholars agree that party organizations can be quite relevant in parliamentary democracies that are based on proportional representation, where there is an emphasis on power sharing and a special role for the parliament as the arbiter of government power. However, most scholars also suggest that opposition party influence is quite limited in a polyarchy based on majority rule, because they serve more as a voice for policy alternatives than as a real political force.

This study has shown that external foreign policy restructuring was often dependent upon internal opposition platform shifts. That is, that German foreign policy change was fundamentally affected by a broad normalization inside and outside the government. In 1990 and 1991, for example, leaders of the SPD and Green parties rejected the possibility that Germany could deploy troops to participate in Operations Desert Shield and Desert Storm. Instead, they maintained the position that newly unified Germany should play a role as a civilian power in the post-Cold War international security environment. Opposition parties generally denounced government efforts to become engaged in foreign military actions, but the question of deployment of troops to Turkey and material assistance to Israel (including Patriot missile batteries) caused a rift in the SPD regarding German responsibility to respond to specific types of crises. In fact, the linkage uncovered between German firms and Iraqi chemical and biological weapons production drove a wedge in the political left. Some prominent politicians, authors, philosophers, and entertainers broke with those opposing any German role in the crisis because they believed that they now had a special responsibility to prevent genocide and humanitarian tragedies. Soon, thousands of German citizens were marching in the streets in support of a special defense of Israel.

The attitudes of opposition party leaders toward the Somalia deployment were somewhat conflicted. On one hand, the SPD and Greens maintained that the mission was unconstitutional and threatened to stretch legal interpretations of troop deployment requirements. Many leaders openly criticized government plans and warned that German troops would be caught in the crossfire of the civil war in Somalia. These opponents went so far as to challenge the government plan to deploy troops to Somalia in the Constitutional Court in 1993, slowing troop deployment to the region. While the Court ruled in favor of the government in mid-1993, opposition warnings proved insightful, given the attacks on UN peacekeepers in the summer and fall of 1993. The Social Democrats and Greens were the first to call for the removal of German troops in the wake of the attacks, and they actually set the tone for a government retrenchment in the months that followed.

On the other hand, many Social Democrats and Greens were growing increasingly uncomfortable with opposing government plans that essentially meant voting against humanitarian operations. Televised images of starvation and unrest in Somalia moved many to reconsider the question of how and when German troops should be deployed abroad. In the January 1993 inter-party negotiations discussing amending the Basic Law to allow for such deployments in the future, opposition party leaders actually accepted that certain missions should be allowed in the future. SPD officials disagreed with Conservatives about the extent of government latitude on such questions, and the talks quickly collapsed. Nonetheless, their willingness to consider broader international responsibility and even contingencies for the use of force represented an important step toward normalization.

Some of the most interesting debates about the proper German responses to the strategic dilemmas in the Balkans occurred at special party conference meetings for the Social Democrats and the Green Party. Opposition parties grappled with these external strategic dilemmas, and these concerns actually led to splits in the party organizations. In the case of the SPD, one saw both a growing rift between the more moderate and liberal wings of the party from 1990 to 1994, and a move toward the Conservatives, or the "New Middle," one year later. In 1994, *Fraktion* leader and party chairman Rudolf Scharping had articulated the moderate stance that there were no longer any fundamental differences between the government and the SPD on foreign policy matters. Scharping led moderates in the party to support the Tornado deployments, the RRF, and IFOR. This support for the government had its price, however. In November 1995, Scharping lost his position as leader of the SPD to Oskar Lafontaine and the liberal wing of the party. Ironically, Lafontaine garnered a majority of the votes for the chairmanship in part through a surprisingly strong speech on foreign policy at a party Congress, in which he presented a plan for German separation from the Bosnia conflict as a "social democratic virtue."[17] By 1995, even under Lafontaine's leadership, the SPD had experienced a shift toward the political center on foreign policy issues. In late 1995, four-fifths of all SPD parliamentarians voted in favor of government plans to deploy German troops to the Balkans for the NATO Implementation Force. By 1999, the party championed the position of the new government to become actively involved in coercive diplomacy in the Kosovo crisis.

Meanwhile, the Green Party also engaged in some intriguing debates about how Germany should respond to the strategic dilemmas created by events in the Balkans. The Greens had always expressed support for diplomatic efforts to resolve conflicts around the world, and early government initiatives did not trouble the organization. However, most became concerned by what they saw as a rapid progression from diplomatic solutions to military responses. The party was a vocal opponent of the Adriatic deployment and the AWACS decision, and they challenged the government's latitude regularly on the floor of the *Bundestag* and in Federal Constitutional Court. Even as Greens spoke out against these actions, however, party members became engaged in internal debates regarding whether or not to support certain types of military action in response to humanitarian challenges. After a series of party conference meetings in the fall of 1995, half of the Green parliamentarians voted in favor of German troop deployment for the IFOR mission. Thus, even the opposition offered its support to the normalization of German foreign policy through the IFOR deployment.

The Kosovo crisis of 1999 actually made the Green Party the pivotal forum for elite efforts to build consensus in support of government action. Green Party conferences at Erfurt and Bielefeld in 1999 serve as markers of party change. In early March at the Erfurt conference, Fischer defended Germany's plan to support NATO policy and sought party endorsement for participation in Operation Allied Force if needed.[18] While party delegates debated the initiative, they ultimately voted in favor of a resolution of support for the government.[19] The special Green Party conference held in Bielefeld on May 13 was a defining moment in the short history of post-Cold War German foreign policy normalization. Delegates at the meeting debated a *Fundi* resolution calling for an immediate and unconditional halt to NATO air strikes and a compromise resolution urging a temporary cease-fire. Foreign Minister Fischer gave the most important speech of his political life at the conference and held the government coalition (and, arguably, the NATO alliance) together by garnering a majority vote for the compromise resolution (Figure 7.3).

How could the political left consider support for German military action? This intriguing puzzle is answered in the scale of the humanitarian tragedies in the Middle East, Somalia, Bosnia, and Kosovo. In all four cases, groups were being systematically targeted by oppressive power groups, and Germans felt a moral imperative for action. Of course, the Kurdish refugee crisis was not a simple matter for Germany, with its uneven record of support for Kurdish self-determination and shaky relations with Turkey, but it could be seen as an act of genocide against a minority identity group. Genocide and ethnic cleansing were certainly occurring in Bosnia, as Serb groups systematically surrounded, captured, and killed Muslim fighters and civilians. Kosovo seemed a clear-cut case of genocide in light of the Bosnia experience.

Thus, the scale of external shocks to Germany prompted a reexamination of all sides of the proper response. Neither economic power nor diplomacy were sufficient to prevent these tragedies, and even pacifists were forced to consider the use of military force as the final option to end the conflict. Some experts have even suggested that ethnic cleansing in Bosnia eroded the moral legitimacy of pacifism on the German political left. One of the best examples of the cognitive dissonance forced on the left by these events is evidenced by the evolution of thought in the Green Party on the use of force. Debates about German foreign policy restructuring led to a resurfacing of past divisions in the party between moderate delegates and pacifists/liberals. In a 1994 book, *Realos*, Green leader Joschka Fischer wrote of the change in thinking of the political left on the normalization of German foreign policy. Fischer described the party's support for German integration into the EU and for participation in the NATO alliance. Furthermore, he called for a new degree of German foreign policy realism, while maintaining a profile as a civilian power and abstaining from the use of military force abroad.[20] In the summer of 1995, Fischer distributed a position paper to colleagues inside the party

Figure 7.3
The Convergence of Domestic Attitudes

Strategic Dilemma/German Response	Summary of Party Positions on Foreign Policy Change			
	CDU/CSU	FDP	SPD	Greens
The Persian Gulf Crisis, 1990–1991				
Iraqi Invasion of Kuwait/ Checkbook Diplomacy	Support	Support	Support	Oppose
Operation Desert Storm/ Logistical Support	Support	Support	Mixed	Mixed
Iraqi Attack on Kurds/ Support for Refugee Crisis Relief	Support	Support	Support	Mixed
Humanitarian Crisis in Somalia, 1992–1994				
Civil War and Famine/ Operation Restore Hope	Support	Conditional	Oppose	Oppose
Mission Creep and Attacks on Peacekeepers/ Troop Withdrawal	Support	Support	Support	Support
The Civil War in the Former Yugoslavia, 1991–1995				
Croatia and Slovenia Secede/ Diplomatic Recognition	Support	Support	Mixed	Mixed
WEU Enforcement of Embargo/ Adriatic Monitoring	Support	Support	Oppose	Oppose
AWACS Deployment over Bosnia/ German Aircrews Participate	Support	Oppose	Oppose	Oppose
NATO Request for Aircraft/ ECR-Tornado Deployment	Support	Mixed	Oppose	Oppose
Serbian Advances and UN Crisis/ Rapid Reaction Force	Support	Support	Support	Mixed
The Dayton Peace Accord and IFOR/ Ground Troop Deployment	Support	Support	Support	Support
The Kosovo Crisis, 1989-1999				
Operation Allied Force/	Support	Support	Support	Support
Aircraft and Support Personnel Prepare for Ground War	Oppose	Oppose	Mixed	Oppose

that acknowledged the need for German military action in response to pressing international imperatives such as the prevention of genocide. The foreign minister's speech to the delegates at the controversial Biele-feld party conference of May 1999 could be interpreted as his final farewell to the *Fundis*. Historical imperatives such as "never again war" and "never again Auschwitz" became a major influence for all political groups in Germany in the post-Cold War era.

It also became clear by the end of the 1990s that the German left was compelled to cooperate with allies by an ever-deeper commitment to European integration. Thus, Germans felt compelled to act in response to humanitarian tragedies based on a moral imperative combined with prac-tical considerations about multilateral cooperation. Lurking behind alliance disagreements about strategy were persistent fears in Germany about standing isolated on major foreign policy matters. Defense Minister Scharping articulated this concern in the early days of Operation Allied Force, for example. He said that if Germany had withdrawn its support for NATO operations, it would have overlooked its "responsibilities in NATO" and would be forever tied "like an anchor" to its history.[21] He said that in the post-Cold War era, "no state can guarantee security, peace, and stabil-ity for itself alone." Crises in the Balkans, he argued, taught Germany, Europe, and the NATO alliance that they must "adapt to the challenges evolving from a dynamic international security environment."[22] The Kosovo crisis was one such instance where Green party leaders realized that their defection from the government could ultimately shatter the NATO alliance and delay progress toward European integration. These represented heavy, two-level imperatives for cooperation.

NEW TRENDS: DOMESTIC POLITICS, ECONOMIC INTEGRATION, AND THE WAR ON TERRORISM

The Federal Republic of Germany celebrated its fiftieth anniversary in 1999 as a nation proud of its stable democracy and achievements in eco-nomic, political, social, and humanitarian arenas. However, recent events also have reminded Germans that their foreign policy profile may con-tinue to evolve in response to strategic dilemmas and opportunities.

Several factors are likely to define the parameters of future restructur-ing. First, German foreign policy will be shaped by the domestic political climate. The dramatic election victory of the Social Democratic Party (with 40.9% of the popular vote and 298 seats in the *Bundestag*) set Ger-man domestic and foreign policy on a "new middle" course in September 1998. Out of government since 1982, the Social Democrats were eager to take on the mantle of leadership, and the election placed Gerhard Schröder in a very important role as leader of German foreign policy development for the twenty-first century.[23] The Greens had never before been part of governance at the federal level, and they viewed the election outcome as a unique opportunity to shape domestic and foreign policy.

Kosovo was an example of cooperation between the Social Democrats and Greens on a major foreign policy challenge, but the cabinet has since found it difficult to maintain coalition consensus on significant domestic matters. Relations between the SPD and Greens actually deteriorated throughout the remainder of 1999, with differences between the parties surfacing on issues such as economic reform programs, tax cuts, pension programs, and the future of Germany's nuclear energy program. Green Party *Fundis* called on the party to distance itself from the SPD because they represented pro-business centrism, threatening to undermine government support for initiatives from the *Kanzleramt*. Meanwhile, Joschka Fischer worked to consolidate power in the Green Party by streamlining authority at the federal level. Political differences also were reflected in changing popular sentiment toward the government. In September 1999, the SPD lost a great deal of voter support in regional elections in Brandenburg, the Saarland, Thuringia, and Saxony.[24]

Domestic political conditions will continue to influence Germany's international profile. Schröder and the new leadership were well aware that voters favored serious domestic economic reform programs, but sought continuity in foreign policy (an interesting, latent statement of acceptance of the restructuring of the 1990s).[25] The government has labored for the past three years to address internal problems including unemployment woes, immigration policy, and social welfare reform. As in the past, the chancellor has attempted to manage pressures for economic reform proposals from the political left and right. Ironically, the Social Democrat–Green coalition benefited from an implosion on the political right in 2000 when the Conservatives became embroiled in corruption charges against former Chancellor Helmut Kohl (which also extended down through the ranks of the CDU and CSU party organizations). In December 1999, media reports suggested that Kohl had accepted millions in secret donations to ensure his election victories. ARD television reported that former French President Francois Mitterand had arranged payment of some $15 million to the CDU, and that the money was transferred as part of alleged bribes totaling $44 million paid by France's Elf-Aquitaine for its 1992 purchase of the former East German Leuna refinery. As of this writing, government investigations of fundraising practices and improper influence peddling are still underway in Berlin.

German foreign policy also will be shaped increasingly by economic challenges in the twenty-first century. Germany's commitment to EU integration appears politically, socially, and economically different from the constitutional challenges presented by crises such as the Gulf War and Kosovo. European integration has become a preoccupation for German leaders committed to multilateral development of foreign economic policy, but it truly has blurred the lines between external and internal conditions. In the early 1990s, Chancellor Kohl characterized his government's European orientation as one of the foundations of German political culture, and to some degree, Germans have developed a European identity that transcends some boundaries of national interest.[26]

Germany's foreign economic policy has been firmly anchored in a multilateral context through integration, and as a result elites and interest groups seem to have gained a stronger role in guiding the subtleties of integration. For example, German government officials were actively engaged in formulating plans for deepening integration in the 1980s and 1990s. Elites often drove the integration process through seemingly endless summits and intergovernmental conferences. Kohl and Genscher's leadership on the Single European Act in the mid-1980s was instrumental in bringing about a major foreign policy restructuring for European Community member states, and their efforts to secure legitimacy for the agreement back in Germany were crucial. Equally interesting was the reluctance of Conservative leaders to consider a full monetary policy and currency union through the late 1980s, as Kohl and Finance Minister Waigel measured public uncertainty and Bundesbank reluctance to take that major next step.

The external shock of the collapse of the Cold War and the possibility of unification served to focus the minds of government officials on economic integration. German leaders realized in 1989 and 1990 that they might use a commitment to monetary union as a tradeoff for European (specifically, French) endorsement of German unification. Consistent with the adage that converts demonstrate the greatest conviction, Kohl, Genscher, Kinkel, and Waigel emerged as the most vocal proponents for the Maastricht Treaty on European Union (TEU) on the continent. Their high-profile leadership led to the adoption of strict convergence criteria at Maastricht and encouraged ratification of the TEU throughout Europe. Kohl himself appeared on television commercials in France encouraging voters to ratify the TEU, and he led the charge in Germany for adoption of this major foreign economic policy restructuring initiative. The chancellor's leadership on the TEU was clearly one of his greatest accomplishments. Ironically, it may also have contributed to the erosion of public support for Kohl as chancellor and led to his eventual political downfall.

While German officials supported the creation of the TEU, it is clear that interest group pressures changed their approach to the matter beginning in the fall of 1991. German leaders brokered a very hard bargain in a thirty-hour marathon negotiation session at the Maastricht summit, whereby they secured strict convergence criteria for monetary union that would protect German interests. From the Maastricht summit onward, German officials played two-faced roles as leaders of the ratification initiative throughout Europe while at the same time catering to domestic concerns. In negotiations concerning the ratification of the TEU in Germany, government leaders made key concessions to the Bundesbank and regional interests, including Länder governments that essentially created an "opt out" clause in the agreement. Ironically, Germany was the last continental power to ratify the treaty, and since 1992, the government has made controlled concessions to Europe while suggesting that fellow governments consider different ways to implement currency and monetary policy union programs.[27]

The new government coalition agreement of 1998 promised to continue and develop the "baselines" of previous German foreign policy, a pledge which Fischer and Schröder subsequently reiterated.[28] One of the most challenging issues in European integration for the new Social Democrat–Green coalition is the fate of the *Euro*. Since its establishment as a common currency for financial transactions on the continent, the *Euro* steadily lost value in international exchange markets. By September 2000, it had declined in value by 25%, prompting serious concerns among European governments about the future of the program. Facing the deadline for initiation of official cash exchange on January 1, 2002, German leaders joined with the EU in endorsement of European Central Bank initiatives to stabilize the *Euro*. While there have been disagreements inside the coalition government about these programs, Schröder and others have endorsed Central Bank increases in interest rates and other stabilization programs. In many ways, the common currency initiative became a near-term litmus test for EU integration.

Public opinion has not directly influenced foreign economic policy restructuring during European integration. In the case of the 1985 Single European Act, for example, surveys of elite attitudes at the time showed 90% support for integration in Europe. The record suggests that public attitudes were not monitored carefully by government officials, nor did they seem to shape policy development. While opinions were a latent factor in the establishment of Länder positions on the SEA, they were not a direct influence. This trend of elite-driven initiatives carried over to the Treaty on European Union, but here public attitudes did seem to play an indirect role in the development of German foreign economic policy by the mid-1990s. At the time of the Maastricht summit, public opinion polls were quite mixed. Germans tended to support broad objectives of integration including greater monetary policy coordination, but their level of support decreased in relation to specific objectives, such as a common currency. Public opinion favored general trends in integration through 1991, but from 1992 onward, polls showed a steady decline in support for specific integration initiatives. Polls found a marked decrease in the number of Germans who believed that economic integration was a good thing, and a significant increase in the percentage of respondents who believed that integration would be harmful to the national economy.

A steady push toward European integration has been a hallmark of all German leaders since unification, in spite of the dramatic decline in the value of the *Euro*, interest group pressure to constrain participation in some sectors, the challenges of coordinating a Common Foreign and Security Policy, limitations in collective defense capabilities, and public skepticism. Overall, Germany has continued to support broader and deeper integration, and all governments have played a vocal role in debates about expansion of the membership of the EU in the post-Cold War era. German foreign economic policy will likely take center stage in the twenty-first century, but it will continue to be guided by coalition-building and cautious elite maneuvering.

Finally, this study suggests that new and surprising strategic dilemmas are likely to emerge for Germany in the twenty-first century. For example, armed struggles between ethnic Albanian groups and government forces in the Former Yugoslav Republic of Macedonia broke out not long after peace was established in Kosovo. In August 2001, the *Bundestag* approved the deployment of 500 German soldiers to Macedonia as part of NATO's Operation Essential Harvest. They were to participate in a task force of more than 4,000 soldiers from thirteen NATO nations, with a mandate to collect and destroy weapons turned in by Albanian groups as part of a negotiated settlement to the conflict.[29]

Terrorist attacks on the United States in 2001 generated a significant response from the German government. Both Schröder and Fischer visited Washington in the aftermath of the attacks to express their solidarity and deliver specific pledges of support. In a surprising twist on past domestic political struggles concerning AWACS deployments, German soldiers were asked to staff NATO planes deployed over the United States to direct combat air patrols over metropolitan areas. Dozens of *Bundeswehr* soldiers were deployed to this U.S.-based operation in October 2001.[30] The German government also froze bank accounts believed to be linked to terrorist networks (worth an estimated $4 million). As chair of the Afghan Support Group (ASG, the coordinating panel of fifteen major states and dozens of nongovernmental organizations providing assistance to the region), Germany increased its emergency food aid and refugee assistance by nearly $25 million.[31] Finally, on November 6, 2001, Schröder pledged 3,900 *Bundeswehr* soldiers to support the war against the Taliban in Afghanistan, calling this an "historic decision" by the German government.[32] This move was endorsed by the cabinet, and defense ministry officials designated specific units for potential deployment (as they awaited further instructions from the U.S. and British governments). As of this writing, the ground war in Afghanistan seems to be drawing to a close, and allied coalition partners are developing plans for a more comprehensive war on terrorism.

CONCLUSION

The future of German foreign policy is clear. Germany has assumed the mantle of great power status but maintains its commitment to multilateral cooperation and a latent culture of restraint. All of the cases examined for this project demonstrate the importance of domestic constraints on the scope and nature of German foreign policy change. Indeed, these conditions have played a powerful role in determining how, when, and where Germany has become engaged in world politics. None of the case studies suggests that these dynamics have become obsolete in the post-Cold War era. German foreign policy for the twenty-first century may be designed by new governing coalitions, but its foundations lie in the two-level normalization of the decade since unification.

NOTES

1. "Ansprache des Bundesministers der Verteidigung Volker Rühe, anläßlich der Begrüßung und Außerdienststellung des deutschen Understützungsverbandes Somalia am 23 März in Köln-Bonn," Bundesministerium der Verteidigung, Material für die Presse, Bonn 23 March 1994.

2. Joschka Fischer, transcript of press conference with Madeline Albright at the U.S. Department of State, televised on C-SPAN, 3 November 1998.

3. Gerhard Schroeder, transcript of speech to the Bundestag, "Bundestag Supports Military Strikes in Afghanistan," German Information Center, October 12, 2001, www.germany-info.org/newcontent/np/politics_a2.html.

4. See Bengt Sundelius, "Changing Course: When Neutral Sweden Chose to Join the European Community," in Walter Carlsnaes and Steve Smith, eds., *European Foreign Policy: The EC and Changing Perspectives in Europe* (London: Sage, 1994), pp. 177–201.

5. James N. Rosenau, *The Study of Political Adaptation: Essays on the Analysis of World Politics* (New York: Nichols Publishing, 1981), p. 42.

6. Charles F. Hermann, "Changing Course: When Governments Choose to Redirect Foreign Policy," *International Studies Quarterly*, vol. 34, no. 1, 1990, p. 14.

7. Rosenau, *The Study of Political Adaption*, 1981, p. 50; for a more recent perspective on the importance of systemic factors for foreign policy, see Fareed Zakaria, "Realism and Domestic Politics: A Review Essay," *International Security*, vol. 17, no. 2, Summer 1992, p. 198.

8. Wolfram F. Hanrieder, "Actor Objectives and International Systems," *Journal of Politics*, vol. 27, no. 1, February 1965, p. 109.

9. Wolfram F. Hanrieder, "Compatability and Consensus: A Proposal for the Conceptual Linkage of External and Internal Dimensions of Foreign Policy," *American Political Science Review*, vol. 61, no. 4, December 1967, p. 977.

10. Juliet Kaarbo, "Influencing Peace: Junior Partners in Israeli Coalition Cabinets," *Cooperation and Conflict*, vol. 31, no. 3, 1996, pp. 243–284.

11. See Ole Waever, "Resisting the Temptation of Post Foreign Policy Analysis," in Walter Carlsnaes and Steve Smith, eds., *European Foreign Policy: The EC and Changing Perspectives in Europe* (London: Sage, 1994).

12. Joe D. Hagan, *Political Opposition and Foreign Policy in Comparative Perspective* (Boulder, CO: Lynne Rienner Publishers, 1993).

13. Robert D. Putnam, "Diplomacy and Domestic Politics: The Logic of Two-Level Games," *International Organization*, vol. 42, no. 2, 1988, p. 432.

14. Ibid., p. 437.

15. Hagan, *Political Opposition*, p. 49.

16. Andrew Moravcsik, "Introduction: Integrating International and Domestic Explanations of World Politics," Chapter 1 in Peter B. Evans, Harold K. Jacobson, and Robert D. Putnam, eds., *Double-edged Diplomacy: International Bargaining and Domestic Politics* (Berkeley, CA: University of California Press, 1993), p. 14.

17. See Elke Leonard, *Aus der Opposition an die Macht: Wie Rudolf Scharping Kanzler werden will* (Cologne: Bund Verlag, 1995).

18. "German Foreign Minister Rejects Criticism of NATO's Foreign Policy," British Broadcasting Corporation, 7 March 1999.

19. Michael Schwelien, "Dann fließt viel Blut," *Die Zeit*, 11 February 1999, p. 2.

20. See Joschka Fischer, *Risiko Deutschland: Krise und Zukunft der deutschen Politik* (Cologne: Kiepenheuer and Witsch, 1994).

21. "Alle hatten Skrupel," *Der Spiegel*, vol. 13, 29 March 1999, p. 218.

22. "German Minister of Defense, Rudolf Scharping, at the Eisenhower Lecture NATO Defense College in Rome," German Information Center, 11 January 2000, p. 2.

23. Supporters claimed that the new chancellor would bring a great deal of expertise and leadership skills to the job from past work inside the SPD organization and as Minister President of Niedersachsen. Detractors charged that Schröder's record of state leadership was poor and that he had done little to focus on the needs of social and economic development. Most everyone agreed on one thing in the wake of the election victory: Schröder was a quick study and adapted well to new circumstances. He would bring these qualities to office as he defined the proper domestic and foreign policy profile for the Federal Republic in the twenty-first century; confidential interview, Deutsche Gesellschaft für Auswärtige Politik, Bonn, 14 September 1998.

24. Haig Simonian, "Schröder under pressure as Greens rock coalition," *Financial Times*, 21 September 1999, p. 1.

25. Confidential Interview, Auswärtiges Amt, Bonn, 6 October 1998.

26. John S. Duffield, *World Power Forsaken: Political Culture, International Institutions, and German Security Policy After Unification* (Stanford, CA: Stanford University Press, 1998), p. 40.

27. This reference excludes Denmark, which had established an alternative plan for the ratification of the treaty after a failed referendum in the spring of 1992. The United Kingdom had also taken a slower path to ratification. Both countries eventually supported the Maastricht Treaty, albeit with conditions, in the spring of 1993.

28. "Aufbruch und Erneuerung—Deutschlands Weg ins 21. Jahrhundert" (Koalitionsvereinbarung zwischen der Sozialdemokratischen Partei Deutlands und Bündnis 90/Die Grünen, Bonn 20 Oktober 1998), p. 41; see also "Fischer verspricht Kontinuität," *Süddeutsche Zeitung*, 11 November 1998.

29. "German Parliament Approves Deployment of Troops to Macedonia—Up to 500 Soldiers Will Join the Operation," German Embassy Press Release, Nr. 65/01, 29 August 2001, www.germany-info.org/newcontent/np/PRRL65.htm.

30. "Press Release on German Soldiers' Participation in NATO AWACS Patrols in the United States," German Information Center, 8 October 2001, www.germany-info.org/newcontent/np/pr_10_08_01.htm.

31. "Bundestag Supports Military Strikes in Afghanistan," press release, German Information Center, 12 October 2001, www.germany-info.org/newcontent/np/politics_a2.html.

32. Steven Erlanger, "Germany Ready to Send Force of 3,900—Not Clear If They Would Be Combat Soldiers," *New York Times*, 7 November 2001, p. B4; see also "German Troops to Join 'Terror War,'" CNN Worldnews, 6 November 2001, http://cnn.worldnews.com.

Selected Bibliography

ARCHIVES

Deutsche Gesellschaft für Auswärtige Politik, Bonn
Europäische Institut, Bonn
Friedrich Ebert Stiftung, Bonn
Friedrich Naumann Stiftung, Bonn
Konrad Adenauer Stiftung, Sankt Augustin
Presse- und Informationsamt der Bundesregierung, Bonn/Berlin

MAJOR NEWSPAPER AND NEWS MAGAZINE SOURCES

Christian Science Monitor
Economist
Financial Times
Frankfurter Allgemeine Zeitung
Frankfurter Rundschau
General Anzeiger
International Herald Tribune
Kölner Stadt-Anzeiger
New York Times
Der Spiegel
Die Stern
Stuttgarter Zeitung
Süddeutsche Zeitung

U.S. News and World Report
United Nations Chronicle
Wall Street Journal
Washington Post
Die Welt
Die Zeit

NEWS AGENCY DISPATCHES—WIRE SERVICES

Agence Europe
Associated Press
Deutsche-Press Agentur
Foreign Broadcast Information Service Daily Reports
Reuters

SPECIALIST JOURNALS

American Political Science Review
Armed Forces and Society
Aussenpolitik
Bulletin der Europäischen Gemeinschaften
Comparative Politics
Defense News
Diplomacy and Statecraft
Europa Archiv
Europa Archiv: Dokumente und Berichte
Foreign Affairs
Foreign Policy
German Politics
German Politics and Society
International Affairs
International Organization
International Security
Internationale Politik
Jahrbuch der Europäischen Integration
Journal of Common Market Studies
NATO Review
New Perspectives Quarterly
OECD Main Economic Indicators
Official Journal of the European Communities
Orbis
Survival
World Politics
The World Today
Zeitschrift für Parlamentsfragen

CONFIDENTIAL INTERVIEW LOCATIONS

Auswärtiges Amt, Bonn
Bundestag Legislative Offices, Bonn
Bundesministerium der Verteidigung, Bonn
Deutsche Gesellschaft für Auswärtige Politik, Bonn
Europäische Institut, Bonn
European Commission, Brussels
Friedrich Ebert Stiftung, Bonn
Hessische Institut für Friedens-und Konfliktforschung, Frankfurt
Kanzleramt, Bonn
Konrad Adenauer Stiftung, Sankt Augustin
Mershon Center, The Ohio State University, Columbus, OH
North Atlantic Treaty Organization, Headquarters, Brussels
Presse-und Informationsamt der Bundesregierung, Bonn
Stiftung Wissenschaft und Politik, Ebenhausen

UNPUBLISHED MATERIALS

Berger, Thomas U. 1991. "America's Reluctant Allies: The Genesis of the Political Military Cultures of Japan and West Germany." Ph.D. dissertation. Cambridge, MA: Massachusetts Institute of Technology.
Brown, Eric C., John P. Frendries, and Dennis W. Gleiber. 1982. "The Process of Cabinet Dissolution: An Exponential Model of Duration and Stability in Western Democracies." Paper presented to the Annual Meeting of the American Political Science Association.
Clemens, Clayton Marc. 1986. "The CDU-CSU and West German Ostpolitik, 1969–1982." Ph.D. dissertation. Medford, MA: Fletcher School of Law and Diplomacy, Tufts University.
Crawford, Beverly. 1993. "German Foreign Policy After the Cold War: The Decision to Recognize Croatia." Center for German and European Studies. Working Paper 2.21.
George, Alexander. 1982. "Case Studies and Theory Development." Paper presented to the Second Annual Symposium on Information Processing in Organizations, Carnegie-Mellon University.
Knopf, Jeffrey W. 1991. "Domestic Politics, Citizen Activism, and U.S. Nuclear Arms Control Policy." Ph.D. dissertation. Stanford, CA: Stanford University.
Wolinsky, Yael. 1997. "Two-level Game Analysis of International Environmental Politics." Paper presented at the Annual Meeting of the International Studies Association.

DOCUMENTS

Bundesminister der Verteidigung. 1994. *WeiBbuch 1994: Zur Sicherheit der Bundesrepublik Deutschland und zur Entwicklung der Bundeswehr.* Bonn: Presse-und Informationsamt der Bundesregierung.
Bundesministerium der Verteidigung. October 1994. *Navy Staff Document* 3 (2).

Bundesministerium der Verteidigung. 23 March 1994. *Hintergrundinformationen und Leistungsdaten zum Einsatz des Deutschen Unterstützungsverbandes in Somalia.* Bonn: Presse- und Informationsamt der Bundesregierung.

Bundesministerium der Verteidigung. 1994. *Konzeptionelle Leitlinie zur Weiterentwicklung der Bundeswehr.* Bonn: Presse- und Informationsamt der Bundesregierung.

Bündnis 90/Die Grünen. 11 November 1995. *Peace-Keeping als Bestandteil von Konfliktschlichtung im Rahmen einer kooperativen europäischen Sicherheitsordnung.* Bundestagsfraktion Bündnis 90/Die Grünen, Referat Öffentlichkeitsarbeit: Bundeshaus Hochhaus Tulpenfeld.

Bündnis 90/Die Grünen. 1995. *Unsere Kontroverse um Dayton.* Bundestagsfraktion Publication. Lang und Schlüssig 13 (27).

Bündnis 90/Die Grünen. 1995. "Beschluß der 6. Ordentlichen Bundesversammlung Bremen." In *Unsere Kontroverse um Dayton,* Bundestagfraktion Publication. Lang und Schlüssig 13 (27): 1–6.

Christian Demokratische Union/Christian Sozialistische Union Pressedienst. 22 March 1993. "Hornhues: AWACS-Beteiligung Testfall für deutsche Verläßlichkeit in UNO und NATO," no. 6029.

Christian Demokratische Union/Christian Sozialistische Union Pressedienst. 1992. "Zum Appell von UNO-Generalsekretär Boutros Ghali, deutsche Soldaten für die UN-Eingrifftruppe zu stellen." Erklärung von der Stellvertretetende Vorsitzende der CDU/CSU Bundestagsfraktion.

Christian Demokratische Union/Christian Sozialistische Union Pressedienst. 16 December 1992. "Hornues: Kein neues Nein Deutschlans zur Beteiligung an UNO-Militärmissionen," no. 5145.

Christian Demokratische Union. 1991. "Die weltpolitische Verantwortung des geeinten Deutschlands." 36: 9.

Clinton, William Jefferson. 1999. "Statement By the President to the Nation." http://www2.whitehouse.gov/WH/Newhtml/19990324-2872.html. March 24.

Commission of the European Communities. 1973. "Proposals for a Community Regional Policy." *Official Journal of the European Communities,* OJ C86 and OJ C106.

Commission of the European Communities. 1970. "Economic and Monetary Union in the Community: The Werner Report." *Bulletin of the European Communities,* Supplement 11/70.

"EC to Recognize Breakaway Yugoslav Republics," *Facts on File—World News Digest,* 19 December 1991. p. 957 F1.

Europa Archiv: Zeitschrift für Internationale Politik. 1986. Beitrage und Berichte. Bonn: Deutsche Gesellschaft für Auswärtige Politik.

European Community Committee for the Study of Economic and Monetary Union. 1989. *Report on Economic and Monetary Union in the European Community, the "Delors Report."* Luxembourg: Office for Official Publications of the European Community.

European Commission. 1996. *Eurobarometer* 44. Luxembourg: European Communities.

European Commission. 1995. "Conclusions of the Presidency, Madrid, December 15–16, 1995. *Bulletin of the European Union,* no. 12. Luxembourg: European Communities.

European Commission. 1994. *Eurobarometer: 1974–1994*. Luxembourg: European Communities.

Forschungsgruppe Wahlen—Mannheim. 1991. *Politbarometer in Deutschland.* Reports Nos. 731 and 732.

German Embassy. 21 July 1999. "Speech by Foreign Minister Joschka Fischer on the Conclusion of the German Presidency of the European Union to the European Parliament."

Genscher, Hans-Dietrich. 21 May 1991. "Liberale Außenpolitik für das vereinte Deutschland." *Leiteantrag für den Bundeshauptausshuss der FDP.* Hamburg.

International Monetary Fund. *International Financial Statistics.* Washington, DC: International Monetary Fund Publishing, Selected Issues.

Kinkel, Klaus. April 1995. "Ansprache von Bundesaußenminister Klaus Kinkel anläßlich der Feier des 125jährigen Jubiläums des Auswärtigen Amtes am 16 Januar 1995 in Bonn." *Dokumente zur deutschen Außenpolitik. Internationale Politik*, pp. 80–84.

Naumann, Klaus. 15 July 1994. "Address at a Roundtable of the Konrad Adenauer Foundation." Washington, DC.

Office of Management and Budget. 11 November 1991. *United States Costs in the Persian Gulf Conflict and Foreign Contributions to Offset such Costs.* 9th Report to Congress required by Section 401 of Public Law 102–25.

"Operation Wüstensturm; zweiter Golfkrieg—Allierten gegen Irak: Friedensbemühungen." January 1991. *Archiv der Gegenwart* 2: 35266–35267.

Pressemitteilung: Presse- und Informationsamt der Bundesregierung. 2 April 1993. "Erklärung der Bundesregierung in der Sitzung des Bundeskabinetts am 2 April 1993," no. 116/9.

Presse- und Informationsamt der Bundesregierung. 1990–1999. *Bulletin.* Select Articles:

"Bemühungen der Bundesregierung zur friedlichen Lösung der Golfkrise." 10 January 1991. *Bulletin* 2.

"Beschluß der Bundesregierung zur Unterstützung von UNOSOM II in Somalia." 23 April 1993. *Bulletin* 32: 280.

"Beschlüsse der EG-Außenminister—Erklärung zu Jugoslawien." 16 December 1991. *Bulletin* 144: 1173–1175.

"Discussion between Chancellor Helmut Kohl and the President of Croatia." 10 December 1991. *Bulletin* 40: 1144.

"Erklärung von Rom über Frieden und Zusammenarbeit." 13 November 1991. *Bulletin* 128: 1033–1037.

"Erklärung zur Lage im ehemaligen Jugoslawien." 12 June 1995. *Bulletin* 48: 429.

"Entscheidung des NATO-Rates vom 22. April 1994 in Brüssel zu Gorazde." 1994. *Bulletin* 39.

Genscher, Hans-Dietrich. 23 February 1991. "Erklärung der Bundesregierung zur jüngsten Entwicklung in der Golfregion." *Bulletin* 20.

Kinkel, Klaus. 1995. "Erklärung der Bundesregierung zur Friedensvereinbarung für Bosnien." *Bulletin* 100: 973.

Kinkel, Klaus. 3 March 1993. "Die Rolle Deutschlands in der Weltpolitik." *Bulletin* 18: 141.

Kohl, Helmut. 23 November 1994. "Regierungserklarung des Bundeskanzlers vor dem Deutschen Bundestag." *Bulletin* 108: 990–991.

Kohl, Helmut. 6 February 1993. "Die Sicherheitsinteressen Deutschlands."
     Bulletin 13: 101.
Kohl, Helmut. 25 June 1991. "Fünf Jahre EUREKA." *Bulletin* 73.
Kohl, Helmut. 21 March 1991. "Herausforderungen und Chancen der
     Außen- und Innenpolitik." *Bulletin* 26: 210–211.
"Kommunique der Ministertagung des Nordatlantikrats." 12 June 1995.
     Bulletin 48: 425–429.
"Pressekonferenz: Urteil des Bundesverfassungsgericht zum Bundes-
     wehreinsatz in Somalia." *Bulletin* (23 June 1993) 64: 386–389.
"Regierungserklärung, abgegeben von Außenminister Kinkel." 23 July
     1992. *Bulletin* 83: 805–808.
"Zu Einsätzen der Bundeswehr im Rahmen der Uno. " July 1994. *Bulletin*
     91: 412–413.
Presse- und Informationsamt der Bundesregeirung Referat Außen, Sicherheits-
     und Europapolitik. 28 November 1995. *Beschluß der Bundesregierung zur
     deutschen Beteiligung zur Absicering des Friedensvertrages für Bosnien-Herzegowin
     und Beschlußvorschlag für den Deutschen Bundestag.*
Resolution on Foreign, Peace, and Security Policy Passed at the Bremen Party Congress. 31
     May 1991. Presseservice der SPD.
Stenographischer Bericht des Deutscchen Bundestag, Deutscher Bundestag. Selected Vol-
     umes, 1979–1997.
Stercken, Hans. 20 November 1990. "Jugoslawien und die Europaeische Gemein-
     schaft: Nationalismus und Separatismus bringen keine Loesung."*Deutschland-
     Union-Dienst*, p. 2.
Stichworte zur Sicherheitspolitik. Select Articles:
     "Allgemeines Rahmen-übereinkommen für den Frieden in Bosnien-
          Herzegowina, paraphiert am 21. November 1995 in Dayton, Ohio
          (Auszuge)." 1996.
     "Beschluß des Bundeshauptausschusses der FDP vom 25.05.91 in Ham-
          burg (Auszug)." June 1991.
     "Bundeskabinett beschließt Stritkräfteaufenthaltsgesetz." 21 December 1994.
     "Bundesminister des Auswärtigen Dr. Klaus Kinkel, Deutlandfunk." 16
          December 1992.
     Kohl, Helmut. February 1991."Bundeswehr im Mittelmeer."
     "Pressekonferenz zum Kabinettbeschluß vom BM des Auswärtigen Dr.
          Kinkel, BM der Verteidigung Rühe und des Generalinspekteurs der
          Bundeswehr Naumann." 1995.
     "Weitere Einsätze der NATO Luftstreitkräfte im Bosnien-Konflikt." Decem-
          ber 1994.
Stiftung Wissenschaft und Politik: Forschungsinstitute fur Internationale Politik
     und Sicherheit. May 1991. *Die Reform der NATO-Strategie unter Bedingungen
     Strategischer Entflechtung in Europa.* Ebenhausen.
Subcommittee on Europe and the Middle East. 1980. "The Modernization of
     NATO's Long-Range Theater Nuclear Forces." Report prepared for the U.S.
     House Committee on Foreign Affairs. Washington, DC: U.S. Government
     Printing Office.
U.S. Department of State. 1987. *Documents on Germany, 1944–1985.* Public Docu-
     ment no. 9446.

Vorsitzender der SPD-Bundestagsfraktion. 1995. Document from *Vorlage für die Sitzung der Fraktion am 28.11.1995*. Bonn: Bundeshaus.

WGBH. *Frontline: War in Europe, 2000*. http://www.pbs.org/wgbh/pages/frontline /shows/kosovo/interviews/daalder.html.

MAJOR BOOKS AND ARTICLES

Aberbach, Joel D., Robert D. Putnam, and Bert A. Rockman, eds. 1981. *Bureaucrats and Politicians in Western Democracies*. Cambridge, MA: Harvard University Press.

Adler, Emanuel. 1992. "Europe's New Security Order: A Pluralistic Security Community." In *The Future of European Security*. Beverly Crawford, ed. Berkeley, CA: University of California Press.

Albrecht, Ulrich. 1993. "Konfliktfelder in einer neuen Weltordnung." In *Grüne Außenpolitik: Aspekte einer Debatte*. Hans-Peter Hubert, ed. Gottingen, Germany: Die Werkstatt.

Alderman, R. K., and J. A. Cross. 1987. "The Timing of Cabinet Re-Shuffles." *Parliamentary Affairs* 40(1): 1–19.

Allen, Polly A. 1989. "The ECU and Monetary Management in Europe." In *The ECU and European Monetary Integration*. Paul de Grauwe, and Theo Peters, eds. London: Macmillan.

"Allgemeines Rahmenübereinkommen für den Frieden in Bosnien-Herzegowina, paraphiert am 21. November 1995 in Dayton, Ohio (Auszüge)." 1996. *Internationale Politik*.

Allison, Graham T. 1969. *The Essence of Decision: Explaining the Cuban Missile Crisis*. Boston, MA: Little, Brown.

Allison, Graham T., and Morton A. Halperin. 1971. "Bureaucratic Politics: A Paradigm and Some Policy Implications." In *Theory and Policy in International Relations*. Raymond Tanter, and Richard H. Ullman, eds. Princeton, NJ: Princeton University Press.

Almond, Gabriel A. 1993. "The Study of Political Culture," in Dirk Berg-Schlosser and Ralf Rytlewski, eds. *Political Culture in Germany*. New York: St. Martin's Press.

Almond, Gabriel, and Sidney Verba, eds. 1980. *The Civic Culture Revisited*. Boston, MA: Little, Brown.

Almond, Gabriel A. 1950. *The American People and Foreign Policy*. New York: Praeger Publishers.

Anderson, Jeffrey, and John B. Goodman. "Mars or Minerva: A United Germany in a Post-Cold War Europe." In *After the Cold War: International Institutions and State Strategies in Europe, 1989–1991*. Robert O. Keohane, and Stanley Hoffman, eds. Cambridge, MA: Harvard University Press.

Art, Robert J. 1975. "Bureaucratic Politics and American Foreign Policy: A Critique." *Policy Science* 4.

Ash, Timothy Garton. 1994. "Germany's Choice." *Foreign Affairs* 73: 65–81.

Ash, Timothy Garton. 1993. *In Europe's Name: Germany and the Divided Continent*. New York: Random House.

Asmus, Ronald. 1994. *German Strategy and Opinion after the Wall, 1990–1993*. Santa Monica, CA: RAND.

Asmus, Ronald D. 1993. "The Future of German Strategic Thinking." In *Germany in a New Era*. Gary L. Geipel, ed. Indianapolis, IN: The Hudson Institute.

Asmus, Ronald. 1993. *Germany's Geopolitical Maturation*. Santa Monica, CA: RAND.

Asmus, Ronald. 1992. *Germany in Transition: National Self-Confidence and International Reticence*. N-3522-AF. Santa Monica, CA: RAND.

Asmus, Ronald D. 1991. *Germany After the Gulf War*. N-3391-AF. Santa Monica, CA: RAND.

Axelrod, Robert, and Robert O. Keohane. 1985. "Achieving Cooperation Under Anarchy: Strategy and Institutions." *World Politics* 38(1): 226–254.

Axelrod, Robert. 1984. *The Evolution of Cooperation*. New York: Basic Books.

Axt, Heinz-Jürgen. 1993. "Hat Genscher Jugoslawien entzweit? Mythen und Fakten zur Außenpolitik des vereinten Deutschlands." *Europa-Archiv* 12: 351–361.

Baker, Kendall L., Russel J. Dalton, and Kai Hildebrandt. 1981. *Germany Transformed: Political Culture and the New Politics*. Cambridge, MA: Harvard University Press.

Baldwin, David A. 1985. *Economic Statecraft*. Princeton, NJ: Princeton University Press.

Banchoff, Thomas. 1999. *The German Problem Transformed: Institutions, Politics, and Foreign Policy, 1945–1995*. Ann Arbor, MI: The University of Michigan Press.

Bardehle, Peter. 1989. "'Blue Helmets' from Germany? Opportunities and Limits of UN Peacekeeping." *Aussenpolitik* 40: 381–389.

Baring, Arnulf. 1995. "Wie neu ist unsere Lage? Deutschland als Regionalmacht." *Internationale Politik* 2: 12–21.

Barnes, Samuel, and Max Kaase. 1979. *Political Action: Mass Participation in Five Western Democracies*. London: Sage.

Bastian, Till. 1993. *Frieden schaffen mit deutschen Waffen: Krieg als Mittel der Politik? Plädoyer für ein ziviles Deutschland*. Köln: PapyRossa Verlag.

Beck, Ulrich. 1995. "Weltrisikogesellschaft: Zur politischen Dynamik globaler Gefahren." *Internationale Politik* 50: 13–20.

Bennett, Christopher. 1995. *Yugoslavia's Bloody Collapse: Causes, Course and Consequences*. London: Hurst.

Bennett, S. E. 1972. "Attitude Structures and Foreign Policy Opinions." *Social Science Quarterly* 55: 732–742.

Berger, Suzanne D., ed. 1985. *Organizing Interests in Western Europe: Pluralism, Corporatism, and the Transformation of Politics*. Cambridge: Cambridge University Press.

Berger, Thomas U. 1998. *Cultures of Antimilitarism: National Security in Germany and Japan*. Baltimore, MD: Johns Hopkins University Press.

Berger, Thomas U. 1997. "The Past in the Present: Historical Memory and German National Security Policy." *German Politics* 6(1): 37–59.

Berger, Thomas U. 1996. "Norms, Identity, and National Security in Germany and Japan." In *The Culture of International Security. Norms and Identity in World Politics*. Peter J. Katzenstein, ed. New York: Columbia University Press.

Berger, Thomas U. 1993. "From Sword to Chrysanthemum: Japan's Culture of Anti-militarism." *International Security* 17(4): 119–150.

Bergfleth, Gerd. 1995. "Erde und Heimat: Über das Ende der Ära des Unheils." In *Dic scibstbewußte Nation*. Heimo Schwilk, and Ulrich Schacht, eds. Berlin: Ullstein.

Bertram, Christopher. 1994. "The Power and the Past: Germany's New International Loneliness." In *Germany's New Position in Europe: Problems and Perspectives*. Arnulf Baring, ed. Providence, RI: Berg Publishers.

Bicksler, Barbara, and Gregory Treverton. 1992. "Germany and the New Europe." *Society Abroad* 19: 48–56.

Biedenkopf, Kurt. 1994. *Einheit und Erneurung: Deutschland nach dem Umbruch in Europa*. Stuttgart: Deutsche Verlags-Anstalt.

Bismarck, Otto von. 1929. *Gedanken und Erinnerungen*. Three volumes, originally published 1898 (Vol. 1 and 2) and 1919 (Vol. 3). Stuttgart: J. G. Cotta'sche Buchhandlung Nachfolger.

Blechman, Barry, and Cathleen Fisher, eds. 1988. *The Silent Partner: West Germany and Arms Control*. Cambridge, MA: Ballinger.

Bluth, Christoph. 1992. "Germany: Towards a New Security Format." *The World Today* 48(11): 196–198.

Bogdanor, Vernon, ed. 1983. *Coalition Government in Western Europe*. New York: Heinemann Educational Books.

Börner, Karl-Heinz. 1996. "The Future of German Operations Outside NATO." *Parameters* 26(1): 62–72.

Boutwell, Jeffrey. 1990. *The German Nuclear Dilemma*. Ithaca, NY: Cornell University Press.

Boutwell, Jeffrey. 1983. "Politics and the Peace Movement in West Germany." *International Security* 7(4): 72–92.

Braunthal, Gerard. 1996. *Parties and Politics in Modern Germany*. Boulder, CO: Westview Press.

Brecher, Michael, Belma Steinberg, and Janice Stein. 1972. *The Foreign Policy System of Israel: Setting, Images, Process*. New Haven, CT: Yale University Press.

Brecher, Michael, Belma Steinberg, and Janice Stein. 1969. "A Framework for Research on Foreign Policy Behavior." *Journal of Conflict Resolution* 13(1): 75–101.

Brenner, Michael, Wolfgang F. Schlör, and Phil Williams. 1994. *German and American Foreign and Security Policies: Strategic Convergence or Divergence?* Interne Studie, no. 98. Sankt Augustin, Germany: Konrad Adenauer Stiftung.

Breyer, Hiltrud. 1993. "Von der ökologischen Außenpolitik zur ökologischen Weltinnenpolitik." In *Grüne Außenpolitik: Aspekte einer Debatte*. Hans-Peter Hubert, ed. Gottingen, Germany: Die Werkstatt.

Brill, Heinz. 1993. "Deutschland im geostrategischen Kraftfeld der Super- und Großmächte (1945–1990)." In *Westbindung: Chancen und Risiken für Deutschland*. Rainer Zitelmann, Karlheinz Weißmann, and Michael Grossheim, eds. Frankfurt: Propyläen.

Brunner, Stefan. 1993. *Deutsche Soldaten im Ausland. Fortsetzung der Außenpolitik mit militärischen Mitteln*. Munchen: C. H. Beck.

Bühl, Walter L. 1995. "Gesellschaftliche Grundlagen der Deutschen Außenpolitik." In *Deutschlands neue Außenpolitik, Band 1: Grundlagen*. Karl Kaiser, and Hanns W. Maull, eds. München: R. Oldenbourg Verlag.

Bulmer, Simon, and William Paterson. 1987. *The Federal Republic of Germany and the European Community*. London: Allen & Unwin.

Bulmer, Simon, and William E. Paterson. 1996. "Germany in the European Union: Gentle Giant or Emergent Leader?" *International Affairs* 72(1): 9–32.

Bulmer, Simon. 1984. "The Federal Republic of Germany." In *Direct Elections to the European Parliament 1984*. J. Lodge, ed. New York: St. Martin's Press.

Byman, Daniel L., and Matthew C. Waxman. 2000. "Kosovo and the Great Air Power Debate." *International Security* 24(4): 5–38.

Caldwell, Dan. 1991. *The Dynamics of Domestic Politics and Arms Control: The SALT II Treaty Ratification Debate*. Columbia, SC: University of South Carolina Press.

Calingaert, Michael. 1996. *European Integration Revisited: Progress, Prospects, and U.S. Interests*. Boulder, CO: Westview Press.

Calingaert, Michael. 1988. *The 1992 Challenge from Europe: Development of the European Community's Internal Market*. Washington, DC: National Planning Association.

Callahan, Patrick, Linda Brady, and Margaret Hermann, eds. 1982. *Describing Foreign Policy Behavior*. Beverly Hills, CA: Sage Publications.

Calleo, David. 1978. *The German Problem Reconsidered*. Cambridge: Cambridge University Press.

Cameron, David R. 1996. "National Interest, the Dilemmas of European Integration, and Malaise." In *Chirac's Challenge: Liberalization, Europeanization, and Malaise in France*. John T. S. Keeler, and Martin A. Schain, eds. New York: St. Martin's Press.

Campbell, David. 1992. *Writing Security: United States Foreign Policy and the Politics of Identity*. Minneapolis, MN: University of Minesota Press.

Caporaso, James A. 1997. "Across the Great Divide: Integrating Comparative and International Politics." *International Studies Quarterly* 41(4): 563–592.

Caporaso, James A. 1996. "The European Union and Forms of State: Westphalian, Regulatory or Post-Modern?" *Journal of Common Market Studies* 34: 46–47.

Caporaso, James A., and John T. S. Keeler. 1995. "The European Union and Regional Integration Theory." In *The State of the European Community: Building a European Polity*. Carolyn Rhodes and Sonia Mazey, eds. Boulder, CO: Lynne Rienner.

Carlsnaes, Walter. 1993. "On Analyzing the Dynamics of Foreign Policy Change. A Critique and Reconceptualism." *Cooperation and Conflict* 28(1): 5–30.

Carr, E. H. 1954. *The Twenty Years Crisis, 1919–1939: An Introduction to the Study of International Politics*. London: Macmillan.

Central Intelligence Agency. 1995. *CIA World Factbook 1995*. Washington, DC: Government Printing Office.

Cerny, Karl H. 1978. *Germany at the Polls: The Bundestag Election of 1976*. Durham, NC: Duke University Press.

Clark, General Wesley. 1999. "When Force Is Necessary: NATO's Military Response to the Kosovo Crisis." *NATO Review* 2(2): 14–18.

Clemens, Clay, and William E. Patterson, eds. 1998. "The Kohl Chancellorship. " Special Issue of *German Politics* 7(1).

Clemens, Clayton M. 1994. "The Chancellor as Manager: Helmut Kohl, the CDU, and the Governance in Germany." *West European Politics* 17(1): 28–51.

Clemens, Clay. 1989. "Beyond INF: West Germany's Center-Right Party and Arms Control in the 1990s." *International Affairs* 65(1): 55–74.

Clemens, Clay. 1989. *Reluctant Realists: The Christian Democrats and West German Ostpolitik*. Durham, NC: Duke University Press.

Coffey, J. I., and Friedhelm Solms. 1995. *Germany, the European Union, and the Future of Europe*. Princeton, NJ: Princeton University Press.

Cooper, Alice Holmes. 1997. "When Just Causes Conflict with Accepted Means: The German Peace Movement and Military Intervention in Bosnia." *German Politics and Society* 15(3): 99–118.

Crawford, Beverly, ed. 1995. *The Future of EU Security.* Berkeley, CA: University of California Press.

Crawford, Beverly. 1988. "Western Control of East-West Trade Finance: The Role of U.S. Power and the International Regime." In *Controlling East-West Trade and Technology Transfer: Power, Politics and Policies.* Gary K. Bertsch, ed. Durham, NC: Duke University Press.

Daalder, Ivo. 2000. *Winning Ugly: NATO's War Against Yugoslavia.* Washington, DC: Brookings Institution Press.

Dahl, Robert A., ed. 1973. *Regimes and Oppositions.* New Haven, CT: Yale University Press.

DeHaven, Mark J. 1991. "Internal and External Determinants of Foreign Policy: West Germany and Great Britain During the Two-Track Missile Controversy." *International Studies Quarterly* 35: 87–108.

Delors, Jacques. 1989. *Committee for the Study of Economic and Monetary Union: Report on Economic and Monetary Union in the European Community.* Luxembourg: Office for Official Publications of the EC.

Denitch, Bogdan. 1994. *Ethnic Nationalism: The Tragic Death of Yugoslavia.* Minneapolis, MN: Univeristy of Minnesota Press.

Deubner, Christian. 1995. *Deutsche Europapolitik: Von Maastricht nach Kerneuropa?* Baden-Baden: Nomos Verlag.

Deutsch, Karl W. 1957. *Political Community and the North Atlantic Area: International Organization in the Light of Historical Experience.* Princeton, NJ: Princeton University Press.

Deutsch, Karl W., and Lewis J. Edinger. 1959. *Germany Rejoins the Powers: Mass Opinion, Interest Groups, and Elites in Contemporary German Foreign Policy.* Stanford, CA: Stanford University Press.

Diehl, Ole. 1993. "UN-Einsätze der Bundeswehr: Außenpolitische Handlungszwänge und innenpolitischer Konsensbedarf." *Europa-Archiv* 8: 219–227.

Diskin, Abraham, and Itzhak Galnoor. 1990. "Political Distances Between Knesset Members and Coalition Behavior: The Peace Agreements with Egypt." *Political Studies* 38(4): 710–717.

Dodd, Lawrence C. 1976. *Coalitions in Parliamentary Government.* Princeton, NJ: Princeton University Press.

"Dokumente zum Konflikt im ehemaligen Jugoslawien." 1993. *Europa-Archiv* 7: D143–D161.

"Dokumente zum Konflikt im früheren Jugoslawien II: Der Vance-Owen Plan und der Sicherheitsrat bis Juni 1993." 1993. *Europa-Archiv* 18: D357–D368.

Duffield, John S. 1999. "Political Culture and State Behavior: Why Germany Confounds Neorealism." *International Organization* 53(4): 765–803.

Duffield, John S. 1998. *World Power Forsaken: Political Culture, International Institutions, and German Security Policy After Unification.* Stanford, CA: Stanford University Press.

Duffield, John S. 1994. "German Security Policy after Unification: Sources of Continuity and Restraint." *Contemporary Security Policy* 15(3): 170–198.

Dyson, Kenneth. 1998. "Chancellor Kohl as Strategic Leader: The Case of Economic and Monetary Union." In "The Kohl Chancellorship." Clay Clemens, and William E. Patterson, eds. Special Issue of *German Politics* 7(1): 37–63.

Dyson, Kenneth H. F. 1977. *Party, State, and Bureaucracy in Western Germany.* Beverly Hills, CA: Sage Publications.

Eckstein, Harry. 1988. "A Culturalist Theory of Political Change." *American Political Science Review* 62(3): 789–804.

Eckstein, Harry. 1975. "Case Study and Theory in Political Science." In *Handbook of Political Science.* Fred Greenstein, and Nelson W. Polsby, eds. Reading, MA: Addison-Wesley.

Edinger, Lewis J. 1986. *West German Politics.* Basingstoke, NY: Columbia University Press.

Ehlermann, Claus-Dieter. 1990. "The Institutional Development of the EC Under the Single European Act." *Aussenpolitik* 22(5): 134–157.

Eichenberg, Richard C. "Dual Track and Double Trouble: The Two-Level Politics of INF." In *Double Edged Diplomacy.* Peter B. Evans, Harold K. Jacobson, and Robert D. Putnam, eds. Berkeley, CA: University of California Press.

Eichenberg, Richard C. 1989. *Public Opinion and National Security in Western Europe.* New York: Macmillan Publishers.

Eichenberg, Richard, ed. 1986. *Drifting Together or Apart?* Cambridge, MA: Center for International Affairs, Harvard University.

Elkins, David J., and Richard E. B. Simeon. 1979. "A Cause in Search of Its Effect, of What Does Political Culture Explain." *Comparative Politics* 11(2): 127–146.

"Erklärung der Westeuropäischen Union zur Lage in Sarajewo, berabshiedet am 7 Februar 1994 in Brüssel." *Europa-Archiv* 7.

"Erklärung des Bundesministers des Auswärtigen, Klaus Kinkel, vor dem Deutschen Bundestag am 14. April 1994 in Bonn zur Lage im ehemaligen Jugoslawien." *Europa-Archiv* 21: D621–D631.

Eusebio, Mujal-Leon. 1987. "The West German Social Democratic Party and the Politics of Internationalism in Central America." *Journal of Interamerican Studies and World Affairs* 29.

Evangelista, Matthew. 1997. *Taming the Bear: Transnational Relations and the Demise of the Soviet Threat.* Ithaca, NY: Cornell University.

Evangelista, Matthew. 1995. "The Paradox of State Strength: Transnational Relations, Domestic Structures, and Security Policy in Russia and the Soviet Union." *International Organization* 49: 1–38.

Evangelista, Matthew. 1991. "Sources of Moderation in Soviet Security Policy." In *Behavior, Society, and Nuclear War.* Philip E. Tetlock, Jo L. Husbands, Robert Jervis, Paul C. Stern, and Charles Tilly, eds. New York: Oxford University Press.

Evangelista, Matthew. 1990. "Cooperation Theory and Disarmament Negotiations in the 1950s." *World Politics* 42: 503–528.

Evangelista, Matthew. 1989. "Issue Area and Foreign Policy Revisited." *International Organization* 43(1): 147–171.

Evangelista, Matthew. 1988. *Innovation and the Arms Race.* Ithaca, NY: Cornell University Press.

Evans, Peter B., Harold K. Jacobson, and Robert D. Putnam, eds. 1993. *Double-Edged Diplomacy: International Bargaining and Domestic Politics*. Berkeley, CA: University of California Press.

Fearon, James D. 1997. "Signaling Foreign Policy Interests: Tying Hands Versus Sinking Costs." In *The Journal of Conflict Resolution*. Special Issue. Robert Pahre, and Paul A. Papayoanou, eds. 41(7): 68–90.

Feldman, Lily G. 1994. "Germany and the EC: Realism and Responsibility." *Annals of the American Academy of Political Science* 531: 25–43.

Feldman, Lily G. 1984. *The Special Relationship between Israel and West Germany*. London: Unwin Hyman.

Fischer, Joseph (Joschka). 1994. *Risiko Deutschland: Krise und Zukuft der deutschen Politik*. Cologne, Germany: Kiepenheuer and Witsch.

Finnemore, Martha. 1996. *National Interests in International Society*. Ithaca, NY: Cornell University Press.

Foyle, Douglas C. 1999. *Counting the Public In: Presidents, Public Opinion, and Foreign Policy*. New York: Columbia University Press.

Foyle, Douglas C. 1997. "Public Opinion and Foreign Policy: Elite Beliefs as a Mediating Variable." *International Studies Quarterly* 41(2): 141–170.

Frankland, Gene E. 1988. "The Role of the Greens in West German Parliamentary Politics, 1980–1987." *The Review of Politics* 50: 99–120.

Fratiani, Michele, and Theo Peeters, eds. 1994. *One Money for Europe*. Boulder, CO: Westview Press.

Fratianni, Michele, and Jürgen von Hagen. 1992. *The European Monetary System and European Monetary Union*. Boulder, CO: Westview Press.

Fromkin, David. 1999. *Kosovo Crossing: American Ideas Meet Reality on the Balkan Battlefields*. New York: Free Press.

Fukui, Haruhito. 1970. *Party in Power*. Berkeley, CA: University of California Press.

Gallarotti, Giulio. 1991. "The Limits of International Organization: Systematic Failure in the Management of International Relations." *International Organization* 45: 183–220.

Gamson, William A. 1990. *The Strategy of Social Protest*. Belmont, CA: Wadsworth Press.

Gatzke, Hans W. 1980. *Germany and the United States: A Special Relationship?* Cambridge, MA: Harvard University Press.

Gaubatz, Kurt T. 1991. "Election Cycles and War." *Journal of Conflict Resolution* 35(2).

Genscher, Hans-Dietrich. 1982. "Toward an Overall Western Strategy." *Foreign Affairs* 61(1): 17–26.

Genscher, Hans-Dietrich. 1995. *Erinnerungen*. Berlin: Siedler Verlag.

George, Alexander L., and Andrew Bennett. Forthcoming. *Case Studies and Theory Development*. Cambridge, MA: MIT Press.

George, Alexander. 1997. "Knowledge for Statecraft: The Challenge for Political Science and History." *International Security* 22(1): 47.

George, Alexander. 1988. "Strategies for Facilitating Cooperation." In *U.S.-Soviet Security Cooperation: Achievements, Failures, Lessons*. Alexander L. George, Philip J. Farley, and Alexander Dallin, eds. New York: Oxford University Press.

George, Alexander. 1980. "Domestic Constraints on Regime Change in U.S. Foreign Policy: The Need for Policy Legitimacy." In *Change in the International*

System. Ole R. Holsti, Randolph M. Siverson, and Alexander L. George, eds. Boulder, CO: Westview Press.

George, Alexander L. 1980. *Presidential Decisionmaking in Foreign Policy: The Effective Use of Information and Advice*. Boulder, CO: Westview Press.

George, Alexander. 1979. "Case Studies and Theory Development: The Method of Structured, Focused Comparison." In *Diplomacy: New Approaches in History, Theory, and Policy*. Paul G. Lauren, ed. New York: Free Press.

George, Stephen. 1991. *Politics and Policy in the European Community*. London: Pinter Publishers.

Giavazzi, Francesco, and Micossi Pagano. June 1988. "The Advantage of Tying One's Hand: EMS Discipline and Central Bank Credibility." *European Economic Review* 32: 1055–1075.

Giavazzi, Francesco, Stefano Micossi, and Marcus Miller, eds. 1988. *The European Monetary System*. Cambridge: Cambridge University Press.

Gilpin, Robert. 1983. *War and Change in World Politics*. New York: Cambridge University Press.

Ginsberg, Benjamin. 1986. *The Captive Public: How Mass Opinion Promotes State Power*. New York: Basic Books.

Glenny, Misha. 1992. *The Fall of Yugoslavia: The Third Balkan War*. New York: Penguin Books.

Goldberger, Bruce N. 1993. "Why Europe Should Not Fear the Germans." *German Politics* 2(2): 288–310.

Gompert, David. 1994. "How to Defeat Serbia." *Foreign Affairs* 73(4): 30–42.

Gordon, Philip H. 1995. *France, Germany, and the Atlantic Alliance*. Boulder, CO: Westview Press.

Gordon, Philip H. 1994. "Berlin's Difficulties: The Normalization of German Foreign Policy." *Orbis* 38: 225–243.

Gourevitch, Peter. 1986. *Politics in Hard Times*. Ithaca, NY: Cornell University Press.

Gourevitch, Peter. 1978. "The Second Image Reversed: The International Sources of Domestic Politics." *International Organization* 32(4): 881–911.

Graham, Thomas W. 1994. "Public Opinion and U.S. Foreign Policy Decision Making." In David A. Deese, ed. *The New Politics of American Foreign Policy*. New York: St. Martin's Press.

Graham, Thomas. 1989. *American Public Opinion on NATO, Extended Deterrence, and the Use of Nuclear Weapons*. Cambridge, MA: Center for Science and International Affairs, Harvard University.

Grant, Rebecca. 1999. "Air Power Made It Work." *Air Force Magazine*.

Grundgesetz für die Bundesrepublik Deutschland. 1990. Bonn, Germany: Bundeszentrale für politische Bildung.

Gow, James. 1997. *The Triumph of the Lack of Will: International Diplomacy and the Yugoslav War*. New York: Columbia University Press.

Gowa, Joanne. 1989. "Bipolarity, Multipolarity, and Free Trade." *American Political Science Review* 83: 1245–1256.

Gowa, Joanne. 1986. "Anarchy, Egoism, and Third Images: The Evolution of Cooperation and International Relations." *International Organization* 40: 167–186.

Grieco, Joseph M. 1990. *Cooperation Among Nations: Europe, America, and Non-Tariff Barriers to Trade*. Ithaca, NY: Cornell University Press.

Grieco, Joseph M. 1988. "Anarchy and the Limits of Cooperation: A Realist Critique of the Newest Liberal Institutionalism." *International Organization* 42: 485–507.

Haas, Ernst B. 1964. *Beyond the Nation-State: Functionalism and International Organization.* Stanford, CA: Stanford University Press.

Haas, Ernst B. 1958. *The Uniting of Europe: Political, Economic, Social and Economic Forces, 1950–1957.* Stanford, CA: Stanford University Press.

Hacke, Christian. 1993. "Die Entscheidung für politische Westbindung nach 1945." In *Westbindung: Chancen und Risiken für Deutschland.* Rainer Zitelmann, Karlheinz Weißmann, and Michael Großheim, eds. Frankfurt, Germany: Verlag Ullstein.

Hacke, Christian. 1988. *Weltmacht Wider Willen: Die Außenpolitik der Bundesrepublik Deutschland.* Stuttgart, Germany: Ernst Klett-Cotta Verlag.

Haftendorn, Helga. 1994. "Gulliver in der Mitte Europas: Internationale Verflechtung und nationale Handlungsmöglichkeiten." In *Deutschlands neue Außenpolitik. Band 1: Grundlagen.* Karl Kaiser and Hanns W. Maull, eds. München: R. Oldenbourg Verlag.

Haftendorn, Helga. 1988. "Transatlantische Dissonanzen: Der Bericht uber Selective Abschreckung und die Strategiediskussion in den USA." *Europa Archiv* 8: 213–222.

Haftendorn, Helga. 1986. *Sicherheit und Stabilität: Aussenbezihungen der Bundesrepublisk zwischen Ölkrise und NATO Doppelbeschluss.* München: Deutscher Taschenbuch Verlag.

Haftendorn, Helga. 1983. *Sicherheit und Entspannung: Zur Aussenpolitik der Bundesrepublick Deutschland, 1955–1982.* Baden-Baden, Germany: Nomos Verlaggesellschaft.

Haftendorn, Helga. 1980. *Sicherheit und Stabilität: Aussenbeziehungen der Bundestrepublik zwischen Ölkrise und NATO Doppelbeschluss.* Berlin, Germany: Deutscher Tagenbuch Verlag.

Haftendorn, Helga. 1980. "West Germany and the Management of Security Relations." In *The Foreign Policy of West Germany.* Ekkehart Krippendorff, and Volker Rittberger, eds. Baden-Baden, Germany: Nomos Verlaggesellschaft.

Haftendorn, Helga, Wolf-Dieter Karl, Joachim Krause, and Lothar Wilker, eds. 1978. *Verwaltete Aussenpolitik: Sicherheits- und entspannungspolitische Entscheidungsprozesse in Bonn.* Cologne: Nottbeck Verlag.

Haftendorn, Helga. 1974. *Abrustungs- und Entspannungspolitik zwischen Sicherheitsbefriedigung und Friedenssicherung: Zur Aussenpolitik der BRD 1955–1973.* Düsseldorf, Germany: Bertelsmann Universitätsverlag.

Hagan, Joe D. 1993. *Political Oppositions and Foreign Policy in Comparative Perspective.* Boulder, CO: Lynne Rienner.

Hagan, Joe D. 1989. "Domestic Political Regime Changes and Foreign Policy Restructuring in Western Europe: A Conceptual Framework and Initial Empirical Analysis." *Cooperation and Conflict* 24: 141–162.

Hagan, Joe D. 1987. "Regimes, Political Oppositions, and the Comparative Analysis of Foreign Policy." In *New Directions in the Study of Foreign Policy.* Charles F. Hermann, Charles Kegley, and James Rosenau, eds. Boston, MA: Allen and Unwin.

Hagen, William. 1999. "Kosovo: The History Behind It All." *Foreign Affairs* 74(4): 4.

Halperin, Morton H. 1974. *Bureaucratic Politics and Foreign Policy.* Washington, DC: The Brookings Institution.

Hamilton, Daniel. 1991. "A More European Germany, A More German Europe." *Journal of International Affairs* 45: 127–149.

Hampton, Mary N. 1996. "Institutions and Learning: Explaining Incremental German Foreign Policy Innovation." *European Security* 5(4): 543–563.

Hanmer, Stephen. 1980. "NATO's Long-Range Theater Nuclear Forces: Modernization in Parallel with Arms Control." *NATO Review* 28: 357–374.

Hanrieder, Wolfram. 1989. *Germany, America and Europe: Forty Years of German Foreign Policy.* New Haven, CT: Yale University Press.

Hanrieder, Wolfram, ed. 1980. *West German Foreign Policy 1949–1979.* Boulder, CO: Westview Press.

Hanrieder, Wolfram. 1967. "Compatibility and Consensus: A Proposal for the Conceptual Linkage of External and Internal Dimensions of Foreign Policy." *American Political Science Review* 61(4): 971–982.

Hanrieder, Wolfram. 1965. "Actor Objectives and International Systems." *Journal of Politics* 27(1): 109–132.

Hellmann, Gunther. 1996. "Goodbye Bismarck? The Foreign Policy of Contemporary Germany." *Mershon International Studies Review* 40: 1–39.

Hellmann, Gunther. (1995) "'Einbindungspolitik': German Foreign Policy and the Art of Declaring 'Total Peace'." In *Die Zukunft der Außenpolitik. Deutsche Interessen in den internationalen Beziehungen.* Jörg Calließ, and Bernhard Moltmann, eds. Rehburg-Loccum: Evangelische Akademie Loccum.

Herf, Jeffrey. 1991. *War By Other Means: Soviet Power, West German Resistance, and the Battle of the Euromissiles.* New York: Macmillan Publishers.

Herf, Jeffrey. 1986. "War, Peace, and the Intellectuals: The West German Peace Movement." *International Security* 31: 172–200.

Hermann, Charles F. 1990. "Changing Course: When Governments Choose to Redirect Foreign Policy." *International Studies Quarterly* 34: 3–22.

Hermann, Charles F., Charles W. Kegley Jr., and James N. Rosenau, eds. 1987. *New Directions in the Study of Foreign Policy.* Boston, MA: Unwin Hyman.

Hermann, Charles F., Margaret G. Hermann, and Joe D. Hagan. 1987. "How Decision Units Make Foreign Policy: Development of a Model." In *New Directions in the Study of Foreign Policy.* Charles F. Hermann, Charles W. Kegley, and James N. Rosenau, eds. Boston, MA: Allen and Unwin.

Hermann, Charles F. 1983. "Foreign Policy." In *Encyclopedia of Policy Studies.* Stuart Nagel, ed. New York: Dekker Publishing.

Hermann, Charles F. 1969. *Crises in Foreign Policy.* Indianapolis, IN: Bobbs-Merrill Company.

Hofferbert, R. J., and H. D. Klingemann. 1983. "The Policy Impact of Party Programmes and Government Declarations in the Federal Republic of Germany." *European Journal of Political Research* 18: 277–304.

Hoffman, Stanley. 1990. "Abschied von der Vergangenheit: Politik und Sicherheit im Europa der neunziger Jahre." *Europa Archiv* 45: 595–606.

Hoffmann, Arthur, and Kerry Longhurst. 1999. "German Strategic Culture in Action." *Contemporary Security Policy* 20(2): 31–49.

Holland, Martin. 1995. *EU Common Foreign Policy: EPC to CFSP.* New York: St. Martin's Press.

Holsti, K. J. 1982. *Why Nations Realign: Foreign Policy Restructuring in the Postwar World*. London: Allen and Unwin.

Holsti, Ole R. 1987. "Public Opinion and Containment." In *Containing the Soviet Union: A Critique of U.S. Policy*. Terry L. Deibel, and John Lewis Gaddis, eds. Washington, DC: Pergamon-Brassey's.

Holsti, Ole R. 1992. "Public Opinion and Foreign Policy: Challenges to the Almond-Lippmann Consensus." *International Studies Quarterly* 36: 439–466.

Holsti, Ole R., and James N. Rosenau. 1988. "The Domestic and Foreign Policy Beliefs of American Leaders." *Journal of Conflict Resolution* 32: 248–294.

Horsley, William. 1992. "United Germany's Seven Cardinal Sins: A Critique of German Foreign Policy." *Millenium: Journal of International Studies* 21(2).

Howe, Johnathan T. 1995. "The United States and the United Nations in Somalia: The Limits of Involvement." *The Washington Quarterly* 18(3): 49–62.

Hrbek, Rudolf, and Thomas Läufer. 1986. "Die Einheitliche Europäische Akte: Das Luxemburger Reformpaket: Eine Neue Etappe Integrationsprozeß." *Europa-Archiv* 6: 173–185.

Hubel, Helmut. 1991. *Der zweite Golfkrieg in der internationalen Politik*. Bonn: Forschungsinstitut der Deutschen Gesellschaft für Auswärtige Politik.

Hudson, Valerie M., and David Skidmore, eds. 1993. *The Limits of State Autonomy: Societal Groups and Foreign Policy Formulation*. Boulder, CO: Westview Press.

Hudson, Valerie M., and Eric Singer. 1992. *Political Psychology and Foreign Policy*. Boulder, CO: Westview Press.

Huelshoff, Michael G., Andrei S. Markovits, and Simon Reich, eds. 1993. *From Bundesrepublik to Deutschland: German Politics after Unification*. Ann Arbor, MI: University of Michigan Press.

Iida, Keisuke. 1993. "When and How Do Domestic Constraints Matter?" *Journal of Conflict Resolution* 37: 403–426.

Ikenberry, John G., Davic Lumsdaine, and Lisa Anderson. 1996. "Polity Forum: The Intertwining of Domestic Politics and International Relations." *Polity* 29: 293–310.

Inacker, Michael. 1995. "Macht und Moralitat: Über eine neue deutsche Sicherheitspolitik." In *Die selbstbewußteNation*, 3rd edition. Heimo Schwilk, and Ulrich Schacht, eds. Berlin: Ullstein.

"Interview des deutschen Außenministers, Klaus Kinkel, mit dem 'Rheinischen Merkur' vom 24 February 1994 zur Lage in Bosnien-Herzegowina." 1994. *Europa-Archiv* 7: D234–D237.

James, Patrick, and John R. Oneal. 1995. "The Influence of Domestic and International Politics on the President's Use of Force." *Journal of Conflict Management* 35: 307–332.

Janda, Kenneth. 1980. *Political Parties*. New York: The Free Press.

Janning, Josef. 1996. "A German Europe—A European Germany? On the debate over Germany's Foreign Policy." *International Affairs* 72(1): 33–42.

Jentleson, Bruce W. 1984. "From Consensus to Conflict: The Domestic Political Economy of East-West Energy Trade Policy." *International Organization* 38(4): 625–660.

Jervis, Robert. 1978. "Cooperation Under the Security Dilemma." *World Politics* 30: 167–214.

Jervis, Robert. 1976. *Perception and Misperception in International Politics*. Princeton, NJ: Princeton University Press.

Joffe, Josef. 1987. *The Limited Partnership: Europe, the United States, and the Burdens of Alliance*. Cambridge, MA: Ballinger.

Johnston, Alastair Iain. 1995. "Thinking about Strategic Culture." *International Security* 19(4): 32–64.

Kaarbo, Juliet. 1996. "Influencing Peace: Junior Partners in Israeli Coalition Cabinets." *Cooperation and Conflict* 31(3): 243–284.

Kaarbo, Juliet. 1996. "Power and Influence in Foreign Policy Decision Making: The Role of Junior Coalition Partners in German and Israeli Foreign Policy." *International Studies Quarterly* 40(2): 501–530.

Kaiser, Karl, and Wolf-Dieter Eberwein, eds. 1998. *Deutschlands neue Außenpolitik, Band 4: Instutionen und Ressourcen*. München: Oldenbourg.

Kaiser, Karl, and Joachim Krause, eds. 1996. *Deutschlands neue Außenpolitik, Band 3: Interessen und Strategien*. München: Oldenbourg.

Kaiser, Karl. 1995. "Deutsche Außenpolitik in der Ära des Globalismus." *Internationale Politik* 50: 27–36.

Kaiser, Karl. 1995a. "Die standige Mitgliedschaft im Sicherheitsrat: Ein berechtigtes Ziel der neuen deutschen Außenpolitik." *Europa-Archiv* 48: 541–552.

Kaiser, Karl. 1994. "Das vereinigte Deutschland in der internationalen Politik." In *Deutschlands neue Außenpolitik, Band 1: Grundlagen*. Karl Kaiser, and Hanns W. Maull, eds. München: Oldenbourg.

Kaiser, Karl, and Hanns W. Maull. 1995. "Einleitung: Die Suche nach Kontinuitäten in einer Welt des Wandels." In *Deutschlands neue Außenpolitik. Band 1: Grundlagen*. Karl Kaiser, and Hanns W. Maull, eds. München: R. Oldenbourg Verlag.

Kaiser, Karl. 1993. Europäischer Pfeiler und atlantische Kooperation: Eine alte Frage neu gestellt." In *Die Zukunft der Europäischen Integration: Folgerungcn für die deutschc Politik*. Karl Kaiser, and Hanns W. Maull, eds. Bonn: Europa Union Verlag.

Kaiser, Karl. 1982. "Nuclear Weapons and the Preservation of Peace: A German Response." *Foreign Affairs* 60(5): 1157–1170.

Kaiser, Karl, and Markus Kreis, eds. 1977. *Sicherheitspolitik or neuen Aufgaben*. Frankfurt, Germany: Metzner Publishers.

Kaiser, Karl, and Klaus Becher. 1992. *Deutschland und der Irak-Konflikt: Internationale Sicherheitsverantwortung Deutschlands und Europeas nach der deutschen Vereinigung*, Arbeitspapiere zur Internationalen Politik 68. Bonn, Germany: Forschungsinstitut der Deutschen Gesellschaft für Auswärtige Politik.

Kaltenthaler, Karl. 1998. *Germany and the Politics of Europe's Money*. Durham, NC: Duke University Press.

"Kambodscha—der unvollendete Frieden." 1994. *Europa-Archiv* 1: 21–26.

Kamp, Karl-Heinz. 1990. "Germany as a Part of the Alliance in the 1990s." *Enjeux Atlantiques* 2.

Kamp, Karl-Heinz. 1993. "The German Bundeswehr in Out-of-Area Operations: To Engage or Not to Engage?" *The World Today* 4: 165–168.

Karl, Wolf-Dieter, Joachim Krause, and Lother Wilker, eds. 1980. *Verwaltete AuBenpolitik: Sicherheits- und Entspannungspolitische Entscheidungsprozesse in Bonn*. Bonn, Germany: Nomos Verlagsgesellschaft.

Katzenstein, Peter J., ed. 1998. *Tamed Power Germany in Europe*. Ithaca, NY: Cornell University Press.

Katzenstein, Peter J. 1993. "Taming of Power: German Unification, 1989–1990." In *Past as Prelude: History in the Making of a New World Order*. Meredith Woo-Cummings, and Michael Lorriaux, eds. Boulder, CO: Westview Press.

Katzenstein, Peter J., ed. 1996. *The Culture of National Security: Norms and Identity in World Politics*. New York: Columbia University Press.

Katzenstein, Peter J., ed. 1989. *Industry and Politics in West Germany*. Ithaca, NY: Cornell University Press.

Katzenstein, Peter J. 1988. "The Third West German Republic: Continuity in Change." *Journal of International Affairs* 41(2): 325–344.

Katzenstein, Peter J. 1987. *Policy and Politics in West Germany: The Growth of a Semi-sovereign State*. Philadelphia, PA: Temple University Press.

Katzenstein, Peter J., ed. 1978. *Between Power and Plenty: Foreign Economic Policies of Advanced Industrial States*. Madison, WI: University of Wisconsin Press.

Katzenstein, Peter J., and Nobuo Okawara. 1993. *Japan's National Security: Structures, Norms, and Policy Responses in a Changing World*. Ithaca, NY: Cornell University East Asia Program.

Kehr, Eckart. 1965. *Der Primat der Innenpolitik*. Veroffentlichungen der Historischen Kommission. Berlin, Germany: Walter de Gruyter Verlag.

Keohane, Robert O., and Stanley Hoffman, eds. 1991. *The New European Community: Decision-Making and Institutional Change*. Boulder, CO: Westview Press.

Keohane, Robert O. 1989. "Reciprocity in International Relations." In *International Institutions and State Power*. Robert O. Keohane, ed. Boulder, CO: Westview Press.

Keohane, Robert O. 1988. "International Institutions: Two Approaches." *International Studies Quarterly* 32(4): 379–396.

Keohane, Robert O. 1986. "Theory of World Politics: Structural Realism and Beyond." In *Neo-Realism and Its Critics*. Robert O. Keohane, ed. New York: Columbia University Press.

Keohane, Robert O. 1984. *After Hegemony: Cooperation and Discord in the World Political Economy*. Princeton, NJ: Princeton University Press.

Keohane, Robert O., and Joseph Nye. 1977. *Power and Interdependence*. Boston, MA: Little, Brown.

Kinkel, Klaus. 1995. "Rede von Außenminister Kinkel anläßlich des Festaktes '125 Jahre Auswärtiges Amt' am 16. January 1995." *Bulletin* 6: 42–45.

Kinkel, Klaus. 1995. Die NATO-Erweiterung—ein Beitrag zur gesamteuropäischen Sicherheit. *Internationale Politik* 50: 22–25.

Kinkel, Klaus. 1994. "Peacekeeping Missions: Germany Can Now Play Its Part." *NATO Review* 5: 3.

Kinkel, Klaus. 1993. "Speech to the Grüner and Jahr Dialogue in Hamburg, October 21, 1992." *Statements and Speeches*, 15(16): New York: German Information Center.

Kirchner, Emil J. 1990. "Genscher and What Lies Behind Genscherism." *West European Politics* 2: 139–159.

Kirchner, Emil, and K. Schwaiger. 1981. *The Role of Interest Groups in the European Community*. Aldershot, NH: Gower Press.

Kitfield, James. 1999. "A War of Limits." *Foreign Affairs* 6 (78): 21–54.

Kitschelt, Herbert P. 1988. "Organization and Strategy of Belgian and West German Ecology Parties: A New Dynamic of Party Politics in Western Europe?" *Comparative Politics* 20.

Kloten, Norbert. 1995. "Die Bundesrepublik als Weltwirtschaftsmacht." In *Deutschlands neue Außenpolitik, Band 1: Grundlagen*. Karl Kaiser and Hanns W. Maull, eds. München: R. Oldenbourg Verlag.

Knopf, Jeffrey W. 1998. *Domestic Society and International Cooperation: The Impact of Protest on U.S. Arms Control Policy*. Cambridge: Cambridge Univesity Press.

Knopf, Jeffrey W. 1997. "The Nuclear Freeze Movement's Effect on Policy." In *Coalitions and Political Movements: The Lessons of the Nuclear Freeze*. Thomas R. Rochon and David S. Meyer, eds. Boulder, CO: Lynne Reiner Publishers.

Knopf, Jeffrey W. 1993. "Beyond Two-Level Games: Domestic–International Interaction in the Intermediate-Range Nuclear Forces Negotiations." *International Organizations* 47: 599–628.

Kohl, Helmut. 1973. *Zwischen Ideologie und Pragmatismus*. Bonn: Bonn Aktuell.

"Kommunique des KSZE-Krisenmechanismus über eine Mission nach Jugoslawien, Prag, 3 July 1991." 1991. *Europa-Archiv* 21: D534–D536.

Krasner, Stephen D. 1978. *Defending the National Interest: Raw Materials Investments and U.S. Foreign Policy*. Princeton, NJ: Princeton University Press.

Krasner, Stephen D. 1972. "Are Bureaucracies Important?" *Foreign Policy* 7: 159–179.

Kratochwil, Friedrich, and John Gerard Ruggie. 1986. "International Organization: A State of the Art on an Art of the State." *International Organization* 40: 753–775.

Kreile, Michael. 1995. "Will Germany Assume a Leadership Role in the European Union?" *American Foreign Policy Interests* 17: 11–21.

Krell, Gert. 1976. *Rüstungsdynamik und Rüstungskontrolle: Die gesellschaftlichen Auseinandersetzungen um SALT in den USA 1969–1975*. Frankfurt am Main, Germany: Haag und Herchen.

Kruse, D. C. 1980. *Monetary Integration in Western Europe: EMU, EMS and Beyond*. London: Butterworths.

Kühnhardt, Ludger. 1996. *Beyond Divisions and After: Essays on Democracy, the Germans, and Europe*. New York: P. Lang Publishers.

Kühnhardt, Ludger. 1995. "Weltgrundlagen der Deutschen Aussenpolitik." In *Deutschlands neue Außenpolitik, Band 1: Grundlagen*. Karl Kaiser and Hanns W. Maull, eds. München: R. Oldenbourg Verlag.

Lankowski, Carl F., ed. 1993. *Germany and the European Community: Beyond Hegemony and Containment?* New York: St. Martin's Press.

Lantis, Jeffrey S. 1997. *Domestic Constraints and the Breakdown of International Agreements*. Westport, CT: Praeger Publishers.

Lantis, Jeffrey S., and Matthew F. Queen. 1998. "Negotiating Neutrality: The Double-Edged Diplomacy of Austrian Accession to the European Union." *Cooperation and Conflict* 33: 2.

Lantis, Jeffrey S. 1996. "Rising to the Challenge: German Security Policy in the Post-Cold War Era." *German Politics and Society* 14: 2.

Lantis, Jeffrey S. 1992. "A United Germany in the United Nations: Promise for the Future?" *German Politics and Society* 26(2): 75–89.

Legro, Jeffrey W., and Andrew Moravcsik. 1999. "Is Anybody Still a Realist?" *International Security* 24(2): 5–55.

Laursen, Finn, and Sophie Vanhoonacker, eds. 1994. *Ratification of Maastricht*. Boston, MA: M. Nijhoff.

Layne, Christopher. 1994. "Kant or Cant: The Myth of Democratic Peace." *International Security* 19(2).

Layne, Christopher. 1993. "The Unipolar Illusion: Why New Great Powers Will Rise." *International Security* 17(2): 5–51.

Leaman, Jeremy. 1988. *Political Economy of West Germany, 1945–1985.* New York: St. Martin's Press.

Lehman, Howard P., and Jennifer L. McCoy. 1992. "The Dynamics of the Two-Level Bargaining Game: The 1988 Brazilian Debt Game." *World Politics* 44.

Leonard, Elke. 1995. *Aus der Opposition an die Macht: Wie Rudolf Scharping Kanzler werden will.* Cologne: Bund Verlag.

Lepper, Mary Milling. 1971. *Foreign Policy Formulation: A Case Study of the Nuclear Test Ban Treaty of 1963.* Columbus, OH: Charles E. Merrill.

Levy, Jack S. 1989. "The Divisionary Theory of War: A Critique." In *Handbook of War Studies.* Manus I. Midlarsky, ed. Boston, MA: Unwin Hymann.

Levy, Jack S. 1988. "Domestic Politics and War." *Journal of Interdisciplinary History* 18: 653–673.

Libal, Michael. 1997. *Limits of Persuasion: Germany and the Yugoslav Crisis.* Westport, CT: Praeger Publishers.

Lijphart, Arend, ed. 1992. *Parliamentary Versus Presidential Government.* New York: Columbia University Press.

Lijphart, Arend. 1975. "The Comparable-Case Study in Comparative Research." *Comparative Political Studies* 8(2): 159–177.

Lijphart, Arend. 1971. "Comparative Politics and the Comparative Method." *American Political Science Review* 65.

Lohmann, Susanne. 1997. "Linkage Politics." *Journal of Conflict Resolution* 41(7): 38–67.

Ludlow, Peter. 1991. "The European Commission." In *The New European Community: Decision-Making and Institutional Change.* Robert O. Keohane, and Stanley Hoffman, eds. Boulder, CO: Westview Press.

Ludlow, Peter. 1989. *Beyond 1992, Europe and its Western Partners.* Brussels, Belgium: Brussels Center for European Policy Studies.

Ludlow, Peter. 1982. *The Making of the European Monetary System.* London: Butterworth Publishers.

Lützeler, Paul Michael. 1986. *Western Europe in Transition: West Germany's Role in the European Community.* Baden-Baden, Germany: Nomos Verlaggesellschaft.

Lyons, Terrence. 1995. *Somalia: State Collapse, Multilateral Intervention, and Strategies for Political Reconstruction.* Washington, DC: The Brookings Institution.

Magas, Branka. 1993. *The Destruction of Yugoslavia: Tracking the Breakup 1980–92.* New York: Verso Publishing.

Makinda, Samuel. 1993. "Somalia: From Humanitarian Intervention to Military Offensive." *The World Today* 49(10): 184–186.

Malcolm, Noel. 1994. *Bosnia: A Short History.* New York: New York University Press.

Mandelbaum, Michael. 1999. "A Perfect Failure: NATO's War Against Yugoslavia." *Foreign Affairs* 78(5): 2.

Manigart, Philippe, and Eric Marlier. 1993. "European Public Opinion on the Future of Its Security." *Armed Forces and Society* 19(3): 335–352.

Maoz, Zeev, and N. Abdolali. 1989. "Regime Types and International Conflict." *Journal of Conflict Resolution* 33: 3–35.

Markovits, Andrei S., ed. 1982. *The Political Economy of West Germany*. New York: Praeger Publishers.

Marra, Robin F., Charles W. Ostrom, and Dennis M. Simon. 1989. "Foreign Policy and Presidential Popularity: Creating Windows of Opportunity in the Perpetual Election." *Journal of Conflict Resolution* 34: 588–623.

Mastanduno, Michael, David A. Lake, and G. John Ikenberry. 1989. "Toward a Realist Theory of State Action." *International Studies Quarterly* 33: 457–474.

Maull, Hanns W. 1993. "Großmacht Deutschland? Anmerkungen und Thesen." In *Die Zukunft der europäischen Integration: Folgerungen für die deutsche Politik*. Karl Kaiser, and Hanns W. Maull, eds. Bonn: Europa Union Verlag.

Maull, Hanns W. 1993. "Germany's New Foreign Policy." In *German Foreign Policy and the German "National Interest": German and American Perspectives*, Seminar Paper #5. Hanns W. Maull, and Philip H. Gordon, eds. Washington, DC: American Institute for Contemporary German Studies.

Maull, Hanns W. 1990. "Germany and Japan: The New Civilian Powers." *Foreign Affairs* 69: 91–106.

Mayer, Frederick W. 1992. "Managing Domestic Differences in International Negotiations: The Strategic Use of Internal Side Payments." *International Organization* 46.

Mazzucelli, Colette. 1997. *France and Germany at Maastricht*. New York: Garland Publishers.

McAdams, A. James. 1997. "Germany after Unification: Normal at Last?" *World Politics* 49: 282–308.

McGinnis, Michael D., and John T. Williams. 1993. "Policy Uncertainty in Two-Level Games: Examples of Correlated Equilibria." *International Studies Quarterly* 37.

Mearsheimer, John. 1995. "The False Promise of International Institutions." *International Security* 19: 5–49.

Mearsheimer, John. 1990. "Back to the Future: Instability in Europe after the Cold War." *International Security* 15: 5–56.

Meiers, Franz-Josef. 1996. "NATO's Peacekeeping Dilemma," Arbeitspapere zur Internationalen Politik. *Forschungsinstitut der Deutschen Gesellschaft für Auswärtige Politik* 94.

Mesquita, Bueno de, and Randolph M. Siverson. 1997. "Nasty or Nice? Political Systems, Endogenous Norms, and the Treatment of Adversaries." In *The Journal of Conflict Resolution* 41(7): 175–199.

Mesquita, Bueno de, and Randolph M. Siverson. 1995. "War and the Fate of Political Leaders: A Comparative Study of Regime Types and Political Accountability." *American Political Science Review* 89: 841–855.

Mey, Holger H. 1993. "Germany, NATO, and the War in the former Yugoslavia." *Comparative Strategy* 12: 239–245.

Milner, Helen V. 1997. *Interests, Institutions, and Information: Domestic Politics and International Relations*. Princeton, NJ: Princeton University Press.

Milner, Helen V., and B. Peter Rosendorff. 1997. "Democratic Politics and International Trade Negotiations: Elections and Divided Government as Constraints on Trade Liberalization." In *Special Issue of The Journal of Conflict Resolution*. Robert Pahre, and Paul A. Papayoanou, eds. 41(7): 117–146.

Milner, Helen V. 1993. "Maintaining International Commitments in Trade Policy." In *Do Institutions Matter? Government Capabilities in the United States and*

Abroad. R. Kent Weaver, and Bert A. Rockman, eds. Washington, DC: Brookings.

Milner, Helen V. 1992. "International Theories of Cooperation Among Nations: Strengths and Weaknesses." *World Politics* 44: 466–496.

Milner, Helen V. 1988. *Resisting Protectionism: Global Industries and the Politics of International Trade.* Princeton, NJ: Princeton University Press.

Mo, Jongryn. 1995. "Domestic Institutions and International Bargaining: The Role of Agent Veto in Two-Level Games." *American Political Science Review* 89: 914–924.

Mo, Jongryn. 1994. "Two-Level Games with Endogenous Domestic Coalitions." *Journal of Conflict Resolution* 38: 402–422.

Moravcsik, Andrew. 1993. "Introduction: Integrating International and Domestic Theories of International Bargaining." In *Double-Edged Diplomacy: International Bargaining and Domestic Politics.* Peter B. Evans, Harold K. Jacobson, and Robert D. Putnam, eds. Berkeley, CA: University of California Press.

Moravcsik, Andrew. 1991. "Negotiating the Single European Act." In *The New European Community: Decision-Making and Institutional Change.* Robert O. Keohane, and Stanley Hoffman, eds. Boulder, CO: Westview Press.

Morgenthau, Hans J. 1978. *Politics Among Nations.* New York: Knopf.

Morrow, James D. 1997. "When Do 'Relative Gains' Impede Trade?" *The Journal of Conflict Resolution* 41(7): 12–37.

Morrow, James D. 1991. "Electoral and Congressional Incentives and Arms Control." *Journal of Conflict Resolution* 35: 245–265.

Mueller, Harald, and Thomas Risse-Kappen. 1987. "Origins of Estrangement: The Peace Movement and the Changed Image of America in West Germany." *International Security* 12: 52–88.

Mueller, John E. 1973. *War, Presidents, and Public Opinion.* New York: John Wiley.

Nerlich, Uwe. 1994. "Deutsche Sicherheitspolitik: Konzeptionelle Grundlagen für multilaterale Rahmenbedingungen." In *Deutschlands neue Außenpolitik. Band 1: Grundlagen.* Karl Kaiser and Hanns W. Maull, eds. München: Oldenbourg.

Nerlich, Uwe. 1992. "Instrumente künftige Sicherheitspolitik." In *Sicherheitspolitik Deutschlands: Konstellationen, Risiken, Instrumente.* Wolfgang Heydrich, Joachim Krause, Uwe Nerlich, Jurgen Nötzold, and Reinhardt Rummel, eds. Baden-Baden: Nomos.

Nincic, Miroslav. 1992. "A Sensible Public: New Perspectives on Popular Opinion and Foreign Policy." *Journal of Conflict Resolution* 36: 772–789.

Noelle-Neumenn, Elisabeth, ed. 1981. *The Germans: Public Opinion Polls, 1967–1980.* Westport, CT: Greenwood Press.

Nuttall, Simon. 1994. "The EC and Yugoslavia—Deus ex Machina or Machina sine Deo?" In *The European Union 1993: Annual Review of Activities.* Neil Nugent, ed. Oxford: Blackwell.

Olson, Mancur, Jr. 1965. *The Logic of Collective Action.* Cambridge, MA: Harvard University Press.

Ornstein, Norman J., and Shirley Elder. 1978. *Interest Groups, Lobbying, and Policy-making.* Washington, DC: Congressional Quarterly Press.

Oye, Kenneth A., ed. 1986. *Cooperation Under Anarchy.* Princeton, NJ: Princeton University Press.

Padgett, Stephen, and Tony Burkett. 1986. *Political Parties and Elections in West Germany: The Search for a New Stability.* New York: St. Martin's Press.

Padoa-Schioppa, Tommaso. 1985. "Policy Coordination and the EMS Experience." In *International Policy Coordination*. W. Butler, and R. Marston, eds. Cambridge: Cambridge University Press.

Page, Benjamin I., and Robert Y. Shapiro. 1992. *The Rational Public: Fifty Years of Trends in American's Policy Preferences*. Chicago, IL: University of Chicago Press.

Page, Benjamin, and Robert Shapiro. 1983. "Effects of Public Opinion on Policy." *American Political Science Review* 77(1): 175–190.

Pahre, Robert. 1997. "Endogenous Domestic Institutions in Two-Level Games and Parliamentary Oversight of the European Union." *The Journal of Conflict Resolution* 41(7): 147–174.

Pahre, R., and P. A. Papayoanou. 1997. "Using Game Theory to Link Domestic and International Politics." *Journal of Conflict Resolution* 41(7).

Papayoanou, Paul A. 1997. "Intra-Alliance Bargaining and U.S. Bosnia Policy." *The Journal of Conflict Resolution* 41(7): 91–116.

Paterson, William E. 1996. "Beyond Bipolarity: German Foreign Policy in a Post–Cold War World." *Developments in German Politics* 2: 144.

Peterson, Susan. 1996. *Crisis Bargaining and the State: The Domestic Politics of International Conflict*. Ann Arbor, MI: University of Michigan Press.

Peterson, Susan. 1995. "How Democracies Differ: Public Opinion, State Structure, and the Lessons of the Fashoda Crisis." *Security Studies* 5(3): 3–37.

Pond, Elizabeth. 1996. "Germany as a Satisfied Power." *Washington Quarterly* 19(1): 25–44.

Pond, Elizabeth. 1993. *Beyond the Wall*. Washington, DC: The Brookings Institution.

Pond, Elizabeth. 1992. "Germany in the New Europe." *Foreign Affairs* 71(2): 127.

Pond, Elizabeth, and David Schoenbaum. 1996. *The 'German Question' and Other German Questions*. New York: St. Martin's Press.

Poquntke, Thomas. 1992. "Unconventional Participation in Party Politics: The Experience of the German Greens." *Political Studies* 40: 310–321.

Posen, Barry R. 2000. "The War for Kosovo: Serbia's Political-Military Strategy." *International Security* 24(4): 39–84.

"Press Statement on Gorazde by NATO Secretary General Willy Claes." 1995. *NATO Review* 7.

"Press Statement on Safe Areas by the Secretary General Following North Atlantic Council Meeting on 1 August 1995." 1995. *NATO Review* 8.

Pridman, Geoffrey. 1987. "Coalition Behavior and Party Systems in Western Europe: A Comparative Approach." *Parliamentary Affairs* 40(3): 374–388.

Pridham, Geoffrey. 1977. *Christian Democracy in Western Germany*. London: Croom Helm Ltd.

Pulzer, Peter. 1994. "Unified Germany: A Normal State?" *German Politics* 3(1): 1–12.

Putnam, Robert D. 1988. "Diplomacy and Domestic Politics: The Logic of Two-Level Games." *International Organization* 42(3): 427–460.

Putnam, Robert D. 1973. *The Beliefs of Politicians: Ideology, Conflict, and Democracy in Britain and Italy*. New Haven, CT: Yale University Press.

Putnam, Robert D. 1971. "Studying Elite Political Culture: The Case of Ideology." *American Political Science Review* 65(3): 651.

Putnam, Robert D., and C. Randall Henning. 1986. "The Bonn Summit of 1978: A Case Study in Coordination." In *Can Nations Agree? Issues in International Economic Cooperation*. Richard C. Cooper, ed. Washington, DC: The Brookings Institution.

Putnam, Robert D., and Nicholas Bayne. 1987. *Hanging Together: The Seven-Power Summits*. London: Sage.

Pye, Lucian W. 1965. "Introduction: Political Culture and Political Development." In *Political Culture and Political Development*. Lucian Pye and Sidney Verba, eds. Princeton, NJ: Princeton University Press.

Pye, Lucian W., and Sidney Verba, eds. 1965. *Political Culture and Political Development*. Princeton, NJ: Princeton University Press.

Quandt, William. 1986. "The Electoral Cycle and the Conduct of Foreign Policy." *Political Science Quarterly* 101(5): 829.

Quirk, Paul J. 1989. "The Cooperative Resolution of Policy Conflict." *American Political Science Review* 83(3): 905–921.

Rabinbach, Anson. 1991. "German Intellectuals and the Gulf War." *Dissent* 3: 459–463.

Rattinger, Hans. 1989. *Public Opinion and National Security in Western Europe: Consensus Lost?* London: Pinter Publishers.

Rattinger, Hans. 1987. "Change Versus Continuity in West German Public Attitudes on National Security and Nuclear Weapons in the Early 1980s." *Public Opinion Quarterly* 51(4): 495–521.

Rattinger, Hans, Joachim Benke, and Christian Holst. 1995. *Aussenpolitik und öffentliche Meinung in der Bundestrepublik: Ein Datenhand Buch zu Umfragenseit 1954*. Frankfurt am Main, Germany: Peter Lang.

Rawson, David. 1993. *The Somali State and Foreign Aid*. Washington, DC: Foreign Service Institute, U.S. Department of State.

Reed, John. 1987. *Germany and NATO*. Washington, DC: National Defense University Press.

Reif, Karl-Heinz. 1993. "Ein Ende des 'Permissive Consensus?' Zum Wandel europapolitishcer Einstellungen in der öffentliche Meinung der EG-Mitgliedstaaten." In *Der Vertrag von Maastricht in der wissenschaftlichen Kontroverse*. Rudolf Hrbek, ed. Baden-Baden, Germany: Nomos.

"Resolution 913 (1994) des Sicherheitrats über die Entwicklung des Krieges in Bosnien-Herzegowina, verabschiedet am 22. April 1994 in New York." 1994. *Europa-Archiv* 21: D629–D630.

"Resolution 781 (1992) des Sicherheitsrats der Vereinten Nationene über ein Verbot militärischer Flüge im Luftraum über Bosnien-Herzegowina, verabshiedet am 9. Oktober 1992 in New York." 1993. *Europa-Archiv* 7.

Risse-Kappan, Thomas. 1996. "Exploring the Nature of the Beast: International Relations Theory and Comparitive Policy Analysis Meet the European Union." *Journal of Common Market Studies* 34: 53–80.

Risse-Kappan, Thomas, ed. 1995. *Bringing Transnational Relations Back In: Non-State Actors, Domestic Structures, and International Institutions*. Cambridge: Cambridge University Press.

Risse-Kappen, Thomas. 1995. *Cooperation Among Democracies: The European Influence on U.S. Foreign Policy*. Princeton, NJ: Princeton University Press.

Risse-Kappen, Thomas. 1994. "Ideas Do No Float Freely: Transitional Coalitions, Domestic Structures, and the End of the Cold War." *International Organization* 48: 185–214.

Risse-Kappen, Thomas. 1994. "Masses and Leaders: Public Opinion, Domestic Structures, and Foreign Policy." In *The New Politics of American Foreign Policy*. David A. Deese, ed. New York: St. Martin's Press.

Risse-Kappen, Thomas. 1991. "Public Opinion, Domestic Structure, and Foreign Policy in Liberal Democracies." *World Politics* 43(2): 479–512.

Risse-Kappen, Thomas. 1988. *Die Krise der Sicherheitspolitik: Neuorientierungen und Entscheidungsprozesse im politischen System der Bundesrepublik Deutschland, 1977–1984.* Mainz-Munich, Germany: Grünewald-Kaiser.

Roberts, Adam. 1999. "NATO's 'Humanitarian War' over Kosovo." *Survival* 41(3): 99–117.

Rosati, Jerel A., Joe D. Hagan, and Martin W. Sampson III. 1994. *Foreign Policy Restructuring.* Columbia, SC: University of South Carolina Press.

Rosati, Jerel A., Joe D. Hagan, and Martin W. Sampson III. 1994. "The Study of Change in Foreign Policy." In *Foreign Policy Restructuring.* Jerel A. Rosati, Joe D. Hagan, and Martin W. Sampson III, eds. Columbia, SC: University of South Carolina Press.

Rosati, Jerel A. 1994. "Cycles in Foreign Policy Restructuring: The Politics of Continuity and Change in U.S. Foreign Policy." In *Foreign Policy Restructuring.* Jerel A. Rosati, Joe D. Hagan, and Martin W. Sampson III, eds. Columbia, SC: University of South Carolina Press.

Rosenau, James N. 1981. *The Study of Political Adaptation: Essays on the Analysis of World Politics.* New York: Nichols Publishing.

Rosenau, James N. 1971. *Domestic Sources of Foreign Policy.* New York: Random House.

Rosenau, James N. 1966. "Pre-Theories and Theories of Foreign Policy." In *Approaches to Comparative and International Politics.* R. Barry Farrell, ed. Evanston, IL: Northwestern University Press.

Rosenau, James N. 1961. *Public Opinion and Foreign Policy.* New York: Random House.

Ross, George. 1995. *Jacques Delors and European Integration.* New York: Oxford University Press.

Rotfeld, Adam Daniel, and Walther Stützle, eds. 1991. *Germany and Europe in Transition.* Oxford: Oxford University Press.

Ruggie, John Gerard. 1994. "Peacekeeping and U.S. Interests." *The Washington Quarterly* 17(4): 181–182.

Rühe, Volker. 1995. "Deutsche Sicherheitspolitik: Die Role der Bundeswehr." *Internationale Politik* 50(4): 26–29.

Rühe, Volker. 1994. *Deutschlands Verantwortung: Perspektiven für das neue Europa.* Frankfurt am Main, Germany: Ullstein.

Rummel, Reinhardt. 1992. *Toward Political Union: Planning a Common Foreign and Security Policy.* Boulder, CO: Westview.

Russett, Bruce M. 1993. *Grasping the Democratic Peace: Principles for a Post-Cold War World.* Princeton, NJ: Princeton University Press.

Russett, Bruce. 1990. *Controlling the Sword: The Democratic Governance of National Security.* Cambridge, MA: Harvard University Press.

Russett, Bruce, and Thomas W. Graham. 1989. "Public Opinion and National Security Policy: Relationships and Impacts." In *Handbook of War Studies.* Manus I. Midlarshky, ed. New York: Macmillan.

Salmon, Trevor C. 1992. "Testing Times for European Political Cooperation: The Gulf and Yugoslavia, 1990–1992." *International Affairs* 68(2): 233–254.

Sandholtz, Wayne. 1993. "Choosing Union: Monetary Politics and Maastricht." *International Organization* 47: 235–269.

Sandholtz, Wayne, and John Zysman. 1989. "1992: Recasting the European Bargain." *World Politics* 42: 95–128.

Scharping, Rudolf. 1994. *Was jetzt zu tun ist.* München, Germany: Verlag Piper.

Schäuble, Wolfgang. 1994. *Und der Zukunft zugewandt.* Berlin, Germany: Siedler.

Schäuble, Wolfgang. 1991. *Der Vertrag: Wie ich über die deutsche Einheit verhandelte.* Stuttgart: Deutsche Verlags-Anstalt.

Schild, Georg. 1996. "Die USA und der Bürgerkrieg in Bosnien." *Aussenpolitik* 1: 22–32.

Schlör, Wolfgang F. 1993. "German Security Policy: An Examination of the Trends in German Security Policy in a New European and Global Context." *Adelphi Paper* 277. London: The International Institute of Strategic Studies.

Schmidt, Helmut. 1995. "Europa und die Deutschen in einer sich ändernden Welt." *Internationale Politik und Gesellschaft* 2: 5–14.

Schmidt, Helmut. 1987. *Menschen und Mächte.* Berlin, Germany: Goldmann Verlag.

Schmidt, Helmut. 1971. *The Balance of Power: Germany's Peace Policy and the Powers.* London: Kimber.

Schmidt, Helmut. 1962. *Defense or Retaliation: A German View.* New York: Praeger Publishers.

Schmidt, Manfred G. 1995. "The Parties-Do-Matter Hypothesis and the Case of the Federal Republic of Germany." *German Politics* 4(3): 1–21.

Schoppa, Leonard J. 1993. "Two-Level Games and Bargaining Outcomes: Why *Gaiatsu* Succeeds in Japan in Some Cases But Not Others." *International Organization* 47(3): 353–386.

Schulzte, Rainer-Olaf. 1990. "Föderalismus als Alternative? Überlegungen zur territorialen reorganization von Herrschaft." *Zeitschrift für Parlamentsfragen* 3.

Schüttmeyer, Suzanne. 1990. "Die Ergebnisse der Landtagswahlen 1946–1990." *Zeitschrift für Parlamentsfragen* 21(3): 464–472.

Schwarz, Hans-Peter. 1995. "Das Deutsche Dilemma." In *Deutschlands Außenpolitik, Band 1: Grundlagen.* Karl Kaiser and Hanns W. Maull, eds. München: R. Oldenbourg Verlag.

Schwarz, Hanz-Peter. 1994. *Die Zentralmacht Europas: Deutschland Rückkehr auf die Weltbühne.* Berlin, Germany: Siedler Verlag.

Schwarz, Hans-Peter. 1994c. "Außenpolitische Agenda für das Fin de siechle." *Merkur* 48: 771–789.

Schweigler, Gerhard. 1984. *West German Foreign Policy, The Domestic Setting.* New York: Praeger Publishers.

Seers, David, and C. Vaitsos, eds. 1980. *Integration and Unequal Development: The Experience of the EEC.* London: Macmillan.

Shapiro, Robert Y., and Benjamin I. Page. 1988. "Foreign Policy and the Rational Public." *Journal of Conflict Resolution* 32: 211–247.

Shonfield, Andrew. 1976. *International Economic Relations of the Western World, 1959–1971.* New York: St. Martin's Press.

Silber, Laura, and Alan Little. 1997. *The Death of Yugoslavia.* London: Penguin.

Simmons, Beth A. 1994. *Who Adjusts? Domestic Sources of Foreign Economic Policy During the Interwar Years.* Princeton, NJ: Princeton University Press.

Skidmore, David. 1994. "Explaining State Responses to International Change: The Structural Sources of Foreign Policy Rigidity and Change." In *Foreign Policy Restructuring.* Jerel A. Rosati, Joe D. Hagan, and Martin W. Sampson III, eds. Columbia, SC: University of South Carolina Press.

Skidmore, David, and Valerie M. Hudson, eds. 1993. *The Limits of State Autonomy: Society Groups and Foreign Policy Formulation.* Boulder, CO: Westview Press.

Skidmore, David. 1993. "The Politics of National Security Policy: Interest Groups, Coalitions, and the SALT II Debate." In *The Limits of State Autonomy*. David Skidmore and Valerie M. Hudson, eds. Boulder, CO: Westview Press.

Smyser, W. R. 1993. *Germany and America: New Identities, Fateful Rift?* Boulder, CO: Westview Press.

Snidal, Duncan. 1986. "The Game Theory of International Politics." In *Cooperation Under Anarchy*. Kenneth A. Oye, ed. Princeton, NJ: Princeton University Press.

Snyder, Glenn H., and Paul Diesing. 1977. *Conflict Among Nations: Bargaining, Decision Making, and System Structure in International Crises*. Princeton, NJ: Princeton University Press.

Snyder, Jack. 1991. *Myths of Empire: Domestic Politics and International Ambition*. Ithaca, NY: Cornell University Press.

Snyder, Jack. 1989. "International Leverage on Soviet Domestic Change." *World Politics* 42(1): 1–30.

Snyder, Richard C., H. W. Bruck, and Burton Sapin. 1954. "Decision-Making as an Approach to the Study of International Politics." *Foreign Policy Analysis Project Series*, no. 3.

Solana, Javier. 1999. "NATO's Success in Kosovo." *Foreign Affairs* 78 (6): 114–120.

Sperling, James. 1994. "German Security Policy in Post-Yalta Europe." In *German Unification: Process and Outlook*. M. Donald Hancock, and Helga Welsh, eds. Boulder, CO: Westview Press.

Sperling, James. 1991. "German Security Policy after the Cold War: The Strategy of a Civilian Power in an Uncivil World." *Arms Control* 12: 77–98.

Stein, Janice Gross, ed. 1989. *Getting to the Table: The Processes of International Prenegotiation*. Baltimore, MD: Johns Hopkins University Press.

Stoessinger, John G. 1998. *Why Nations Go to War*. New York: St. Martin's Press.

Stoltenberg, Gerhard. 1991. "Die wachsende Verantwortung des vereinten Deutschlands." *Europäische Sicherheit (EWK/WWR)*, no. 3, p. 137.

Stürmer, Michael. 1995. "Wohin die Bundeswehr? Über Diplomatie, Strategie und Bündnistreue." *Internationale Politik* 50(2): 30–37.

Stürmer, Michael. 1994. "Deutsche Interessen." In *Deutschlands neue Außenpolitik. Band 1: Grundlagen*. Karl Kaiser, and Hanns W. Maull, eds. München, Germany: Oldenbourg.

Stürmer, Michael. 1992. *Die Grenzen der Macht: Begegnungen der Deutschen mit der Geschichte*. Berlin: Siedler Verlag.

Stuth, Reinhard. 1992. "Germany's New Role in a Changing Europe." *Außenpolitik*, English ed. 43: 1.

Sundelius, Bengt. 1994. "Changing Course: When Neutral Sweden Chose to Join the European Community." In *European Foreign Policy: The EC and Changing Perspectives in Europe*, Walter Carlsnaes, and Steve Smith, eds. London: Sage.

Szabo, Stephen F. 1992. *The Diplomacy of German Unification*. New York: St. Martin's Press.

Szabo, Stephen F. 1990. *The Changing Politics of German Security*. London: Pinter Publishers.

Tanaka, Toyozo. 1987. "Breakup of the Tanaka Faction: End of an Era." *Japan Quarterly* 7: 114–129.

Tarrow, Sidney. 1994. *Power in Movement: Social Movements, Collective Action, and Politics*. Cambridge: Cambridge University Press.

Taylor, Paul. 1991. "The European Community and the State: Assumptions, Theories, and Propositions." *Review of International Studies* 17: 125.

Taylor, Trevor. 1994. "Securing Europe: West European Security and Defence Cooperation: Maastricht and Beyond." *International Affairs* 70(2): 1–1.

Teltschik, Horst. 1990. *329 Tage: Innenansichten der Einigung*. Berlin: Siedler Verlag.

Thakur, Ramesh. 1994. "From Peacekeeping to Peace Enforcement: The UN Operation in Somalia." *The Journal of Modern African Studies* 32(3): 387–410.

Thaysen, Uwe, Roger Davidson, and Robert Gerald Livingston. 1990. *The U.S. Congress and the German Bundestag: Comparisons of Democratic Processes*. Boulder, CO: Westview Press.

Thies, Jochen. 1995. "Germany: Europe's Reluctant Great Power." *The World Today* 51(10): 186–190.

Thies, Jochen, and Wolfgang Wagner, eds. 1989. *Auf dem Wege zum Binnenmarkt: Eurpaische Integration und deutscher Föderalismus*. Bonn: Verlag für Internationale Politik.

"Transcript of Resolution 48/88 der Generalversammlung der Vereinten Nationen zum Krieg in Bosnien-Herzegowina, am 20 December 1993 in New York." 1998. *Europa-Archiv* 7: D222–D223.

Trumbore, Peter F. 1997. "A Seat at the Bargaining Table: Public Opinion as a Domestic Constraint in Two-Level International Negotiations." Paper presented at the Annual Meeting of the International Studies Association, Toronto, Canada.

Tsebelis, George. 1990. *Nested Games: Rational Choice in Comparative Politics*. Berkeley, CA: University of California Press.

Tsoukalis, Loukas. 1991. *The New European Economy: The Politics and Economics of Integration*. Oxford: Oxford University Press.

Tsoukalis, Loukas. 1977. *The Politics and Economics of European Monetary Integration*. London: Allen & Unwin.

"Urteil des Bundesverfassungsgerichts über Verfassungsbeschwerden gegen internationale Einsätze der Bundeswehr, verkündet in Karlsruhe am 12. Juli 1994." 1994. *Europa-Archiv* 15: D427–D431.

Van Ypersele, Jacques, and Jean-Claude Koeune. 1984. *The European Monetary System*. Brussels, Belgium: Commission of the EC, European Perspectives Series.

Verba, Sidney. 1965. "Conclusion: Comparative Political Culture." In *Political Culture and Political Development*. Lucian Pye, and Sidney Verba, eds. Princeton, NJ: Princeton University Press.

Vogel, Bernhard, Dieter Nohlen, and Rainer Olaf-Schultze. 1971. *Wahlen in Deutschland: Theorie-Geschichte-Dokumente*. Berlin, Germany: Walter DeGruyter.

Vogel, Hans-Jochen. 1991. "Mäßiger Start in schwieriger Zeit." *Das Parlament* February 8–15: 4–5.

Volgy, Thomas J., and John E. Schwarz. 1994. "Foreign Policy Restructuring and the Myriad Webs of Restraint." In *Foreign Policy Restructuring*, Jerel A. Rosati, Joe D. Hagan, and Martin W. Sampson III, eds. Columbia, SC: University of South Carolina Press.

Waever, Ole. 1994. "Resisting the Temptation of Post Foreign Policy Analysis." In *European Foreign Policy: The EC and Changing Perspectives in Europe*. Walter Carlsnaes, and Steve Smith, eds. London: Sage.

Waever, Ole. 1990. "Thinking and Rethinking Foreign Policy." *Cooperative and Conflict* 25: 153–170.

Wagner, Wolfgang. 1994. "Abenteuer in Somalia." *Europa-Archiv* 6: 151–159.

Walker, David B. 1991. "Germany Searches for a New Role in World Affairs." *Current History* 34: 368–373.

Wallace, Helen. 1985. "Negotiations and Coalition Formation in the European Community." *Government and Opposition* 20(4): 452–472.

Wallace, William, ed. 1991. *The Dynamics of European Integration*. London: Pinter Publishers.

Walt, Stephen. 1987. *The Origins of Alliances*. Ithaca, NY: Cornell University Press.

Waltz, Kenneth N. 1993. "The Emerging Structure of International Politics." *International Security* 18(2): 66–67.

Waltz, Kenneth. 1986. "Reflections on *Theory of International Politics:* A Response to My Critics." In *Neorealism and Its Critics*. Robert O. Keohane, ed. New York: Columbia University Press.

Waltz, Kenneth. 1979. *The Theory of International Politics*. Reading, MA: Addison-Wesley.

Waltz, Kenneth. 1967. *Foreign Policy and Democratic Politics: The American and British Experience*. Boston: Little, Brown.

Wehler, Hans-Ulrich. 1970. "Bismarck's Imperialism, 1862–1890." *Past and Present* 48: 119–155.

Weidenfeld, Werner. 1986. "Basic Questions of European Integration Seen From a German Point of View." In *Western Europe in Transition: West Germany's Role in the European Community*. Paul Michael Lützeler, ed. Baden-Baden: Nomos Verlaggesellschaft.

Wessels, Wolfgang. 1986. "Die Einheitliche Eurpäische Akte-Zementierung des Status Quo oder Einstieg in die Europäische Union?" *Integration* 2: 65–79.

Wilker, Lothar. 1990. "Foreign Policy in the Bundestag." In *The U.S. Congress and the German Bundestag*. Uwe Thaysen, Roger Davidson, and Robert Gerald Livingston, eds. Boulder, CO: Westview Press.

Wittkopf, Eugene. 1990. *Faces of Internationalism: Public Opinion and American Foreign Policy*. Durham, NC: Duke University Press.

Wolf, Klause Dieter. "Das neue Deutschland—eine 'Weltmacht?'" *Leviathan* 19: 247–260.

Wolf, Klause Dieter. 1995. "Eine neue Rolle Deutschlands? Optionen deutscher Außenpolitik nach der Vereinigung." *Der Bürger im Staat* 45: 59–63.

Woodward, Susan L. 1995. *Balkan Tragedy: Chaos and Dissolution After the Cold War*. Washington, DC: Brookings Institution Press.

Young, Thomas D. 1994. *Trends in German Defense Policy: The Defense Policy Guidelines and the Centralization of Operational Control*. Carlisle, PA: Strategic Studies Institute of the U.S. Army War College.

Zakaria, Fareed. 1992. "Realism and Domestic Politics: A Review Essay." *International Security* 17(1): 198.

Zelikow, Philip, and Condoleeza Rice. 1995. *Germany Unified and Europe Transformed: A Study in Statecraft*. Cambridge, MA: Harvard University Press.

Zimmerman, Warren. 1995. "The Last Ambassador: A Memoir of the Collapse of Yugoslavia." *Foreign Affairs* 74(2): 2–20.

Zimmerman, William. 1973. "Issue Area and Foreign Policy Process." *American Political Science Review* 67: 1204–1212.

Index

ABOUT THE AUTHOR

Jeffrey S. Lantis is Chair of the International Relations Program and Associate Professor of Political Science at The College of Wooster. He is author of *Domestic Constraints and the Breakdown of International Agreements* (Praeger, 1997) and co-editor of *Foreign Policy in Comparative Perspective: Domestic and International Influences on State Behavior* (2001).